Sylvia Fraser is one of Canada's most respected journalists and writers, especially noted for her exploration of human consciousness and the mysteries of existence. She is the bestselling and award-winning author of ten books, including *The Rope in the Water: A Pilgrimage to India*; the internationally acclaimed *My Father's House: A Memoir of Incest and Healing*; and *The Quest for the Fourth Monkey: A Thinking Person's Guide to the Psychic and Spiritual Revolution*. She lives in Toronto.

D0792437

Books of Merit

The Rope in the Water

The Rope

Sylvia Fraser

in the Water

A
Pilgrimage
to India

Thomas Allen Publishers
Toronto

National Library of Canada Cataloguing in Publication

Fraser, Sylvia
    The rope in the water: a pilgrimage to India / Sylvia Fraser

Includes bibliographical references.
ISBN 0-919028-43-8 (bound). – ISBN 0-88762-126-0 (pbk.)

1. Fraser, Sylvia—Journeys—India. 2. India—Description and travel.
3. Pilgrims and pilgrimages—India. 4. India—Religious life and customs.
1. Title.

DS414.2.F73 2001   915.404'52   C00-933235-9

Cover and text design: Gordon Robertson
Editor: Patrick Crean
Cover photographs: David Laurence and Michael Darter / Photonica

Published by Thomas Allen Publishers,
a division of Thomas Allen & Son Limited,
145 Front Street East, Suite 209,
Toronto, Ontario M5A 1E3 Canada

www.thomas-allen.com

ONTARIO ARTS COUNCIL
CONSEIL DES ARTS DE L'ONTARIO

The publisher gratefully acknowledges the support of
the Ontario Arts Council for its publishing program

We acknowledge the Government of Ontario through the
Ontario Media Development Corporation's Ontario Book Initiative

The author gratefully acknowledges the support of
the Canada Council and the Ontario Arts Council.

Printed and bound in Canada

Acknowledgement

I wish to thank all those who helped in the production and publication of this book: Jim Allen for his faith in, and enthusiasm for, Canadian publishing; Patrick Crean for his depth of understanding and keen editorial eye; Lily Poritz Miller, who read an early draft of this manuscript and made substantive editing suggestions; my agent Bruce Westwood along with Hilary Stanley, Samantha Haywood, and Nicole Winstanley of Westwood Creative Artists; book designer Gordon Robertson, the ever-resourceful Katja Pantzar, line-editor Alison Reid and photographer Joy von Tiedemann.

A special thanks to Anna Porter, who helped assure my landing in India would be a soft one, as well as to Pramod and Kiran Kapoor, Nalini and Tim Stewart, and their extended families, for their warm and gracious hospitality.

contents

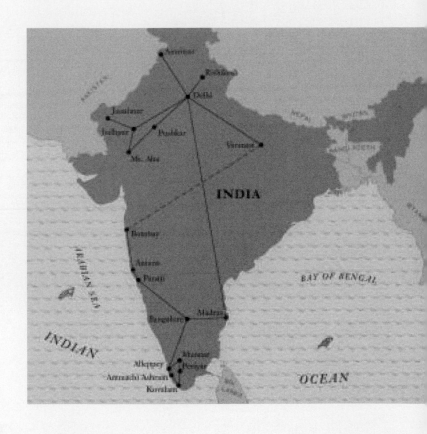

introduction

At Kovalam Beach on India's southwestern shore, I plunge into the Arabian Sea, the same soft temperature as the air. While revelling in my first ocean swim in two years, I hear a frenzy of whistles. Looking shoreward, I see lifeguards gesturing. Since I'm much farther out than I imagined, I begin a determined swim toward them. Five minutes later, I check my position. I'm no closer. I embark on another even more concerted effort. When I inspect for the second time, I'm farther away. The lifeguards continue to blast and gesture, but I'm powerless against the riptide irresistibly sweeping me out to sea. Though my situation appears hopeless, I'm about to undergo the most remarkable and mysterious event of my life. . . .

My purpose in travelling to India was to spiritually transform myself.

Though I was born into a staunchly Protestant family, my attraction to matters transcendental didn't surface until college, when I chose to study philosophy while my friends more sensibly trained to become teachers, doctors, lawyers and stockbrokers. However, despite a rich smorgasbord of mystical and spiritual ideas offered by philosophers from Pythagoras to William James, I firmly opted for those who favoured the pragmatic, the rational and the intellectual. During the sixties, while another generation was mystically flying high on psychedelics, I was laying the foundations for a journalistic career and a marriage, and it wasn't until the seventies Human Potential Movement that I once again became fascinated with ideas. Spurred on by what I thought to be merely a journalist's curiosity, I researched therapies from primal to Jungian while carefully preserving my preferred stance as the detached observer.

All that changed in December 1983, when I spontaneously recalled my father's sexual abuse of me. This was a story that I told in *My Father's House: A Memoir of Incest and of Healing*, published in 1987, when incest was still considered a rare and freaky perversion seldom mentioned even in therapeutic circles. Overnight my pride of intellect was shattered: if I could block out of consciousness such a vital chunk of my own life, what else was missing in my pragmatic version of the Universe? Inspiring such questions was the intriguing fact that with my consciousness newly opened, I began to undergo experiences usually labelled paranormal—dreams of prophecy, webs of weird coincidences, episodes involving telepathy— powerful, sometimes unnerving and always deeply meaningful. Again, this was a story I told in 1992 in *The Book of Strange* (republished as *The Quest for the Fourth Monkey: A Thinker's Guide to the Psychic and Spiritual Revolution*), in which I researched sciences from neurology to quantum physics in an attempt to balance my mysterious right-brain experiences with updated left-brain knowledge.

Instead of being an ending, this proved yet another beginning, for having faced down my personal dragons and caught a glimpse of a greater Universe, I began to yearn for something larger than myself, something deeper, something more. When I reviewed my life, I saw that my long-range choices still seemed appropriate and that I liked most everything I was doing. What was missing was the fuel: without the goad of survival or ambition, I no longer felt engaged enough with myself to animate my actions, and while I was surrounded by good friends and goodwill, I believed no one other person could, or should, be the focus of my energy. The moral alternative—selfless service to humanity—required an altruistic leap I was not yet prepared to make. I began to sense that, ironically, the strong ego-fortress that I had needed to survive childhood had become my prison, and since the narcissistic society that bred me was wounded and defended in much the same way as I, it couldn't provide a solution. What I needed was spiritual renewal. I would go on a quest.

Quest is one of the most enduring themes of Western culture: a person travels to an unknown land to solve a mystery or to perform a rescue or to recover something that is lost. In the medieval myth of Parsifal, the task of that youthful well-intentioned knight, whose name means "innocent fool," is to rescue the Fisher King, who suffers the despair of a wound that will not heal. In modern metaphor, the Fisher King can be likened to the world-weary ego in middle age with the longed for cure being a spiritual one: by returning to the state of vulnerability represented by the innocent fool, the king rediscovers the joy of an unfettered heart.

I decided to seek my illumination in India.

Even as a child I was fascinated with this country that hangs like a beating red heart in a sea of blue trailed by a single drop of blood. Though I wasn't expecting to discover a bottle containing a wise genie conveniently washed up on shore, as a solitary traveller free of the props, masks, habits and distractions of my ordinary life, I did expect to find a mirror in which each turn of the kaleidoscope offered new challenges requiring new responses. Reduced to an innocent fool by the strangeness of another culture, I intended to approach India less as a geographical location than as a fabulous dream in which everything that happens does so for the purpose of teaching me something of value. This approach reflects Eastern philosophy (you see what you are) and karmic law (you create your own future). Amid India's spiritual riches, I longed to discover the thing hardest to find at home: a more compassionate, more engaged and more enlightened version of myself. As Eastern mystics promise, *Change yourself and you change everything*.

meditation

"Like a wave, the mind at rest
discovers that it's an ocean"

MY FIRST GLIMPSE of the mighty Ganges is disappointing: a dry riverbed threaded with a skein of dull grey water. So is the sacred town of Rishikesh located on its banks in the foothills of the Himalayas: a hot crush of dusty shops and dilapidated houses. So is my hotel: everything is painted the same dismal brown, making me feel like one of those blind sub-oceanic creatures forced to exist without light. Self-doubt rises as my spirits plummet. Three months seems both impossibly short and unendurably long to wander alone in another culture without a plan.

I hike along a potholed road that lurches down to the river. Veering right in pursuit of a ribbon of shade, I become lost in a jumbled cul-de-sac with all the charm of a used-car lot. A high-walled complex bears the sign "SWAMI DAYANANDA ASHRAM." The gate is open. Before me stretch undulating lawns shaded by graceful groves and low-slung white buildings linked by curved paths. I enter, then stop, in calm suspension, as if stillness itself could create a density in the air. Several figures in white stroll toward me—actually, they float, their limbs moving in slow motion, shawls and saris rippling. As they pass in

silent greeting, even their smiles hang in the air for a few
seconds before reaching me. Over a grassy lip I see the
Ganges—not the stingy trickle I spotted earlier but a full-
breasted, foaming torrent, as if Mother Ganges has gener-
ously ripped open her rocky bodice to nourish the parched
land. A pristine white temple beckons me down marble
steps to a boulder-strewn shore where a chanting ascetic,
stripped to his orange G-string, alternately kisses the water
and pours it over his matted hair and spare body. Close
by, a pregnant woman in blue sari drenched to the knees
washes a hamper of brightly coloured clothes. Though
Ganga Mata is worshipped as a living goddess, apparently
like most mothers she is still expected to do the laundry!

I too wade into the cascading water birthed in icy
mountain caves, now on the first lap of its 2,500-kilometre
rush to the ocean, feeling it wrap around my ankles and then
my shins with a texture both light and heavy, like leaden
green silk, before churning into bubbles so invigorating
that they penetrate to bone and marrow. As I gaze at the
misty green shore, my spirits climb like the white butterfly
that flirts with my shoulder scarf before sweeping upward.
It pauses against the sky as if impaled. Time stops, and for
this one perfect moment I'm exactly where I want to be.

I return the way I came, looking for the other *ashrams* for
spiritual study that entitle this town of 82,000, five hours

by train north of Delhi, to call itself the Yoga Capital of the World. Growing sodden and disoriented in the afternoon heat, I cross one bridge, then encounter another. The first was a workaday strip of asphalt for cars and carts. This second is a soaring and delicate footbridge spun out of steel with a floor so sensitive that it dances at every footfall. With a thousand of those striking it during a single heartbeat, it feels like an electrical eel, a living thing with a will of its own, as I stride across it. Half a kilometre away, a fantasy city takes shape. Exuberant with colour from the palest pastels to garish orange emboldened with yellow, it has spires and stupas and pavilions that leap from the Ganges up the side of darkening hills. Where am I? And where in the midst of this splendid peacock's tail is my ugly brown hotel?

Since I've crossed two bridges, I assume I'm on the side of the Ganges where I began, but isn't the sun setting in the wrong direction?

I seem to be in a place without public transportation or taxis; I encounter no other tourists, and none of the locals has heard of my hotel. Following a flock of saris up a white staircase, I enter a courtyard filled with life-size Hindu gods engaged in dramas of heroism, suffering, love, conquest and death—an Indian Olympus, animated and impassioned. Though intrigued, I'm also conscious of the sun disappearing behind rooftops like a coin into a meter with less than thirty minutes to run. Since I'm this disoriented in daylight, how will I cope after dark without even street lamps? No matter where I turn, I keep ending back in this sculpture garden like a blindfolded child spun at a birthday party, then confronted by masked faces. I start down another promising lane, only to find it blocked by a black bull with nasty eyes and menacing horns. Two male tourists materialize from a doorway, their visors and cameras catching the last rays of sun like helmets and breastplates. In calm voices, weighted with German accents, they reassure me that, yes, I'm still in Rishikesh. Instead of crossing and recrossing the Ganges, I traversed a dried-up tributary and then the Ganges itself.

As I retrace my steps over what I now know to be Shivanand Bridge, I watch the sun god complete his nightly act of alchemy: turning a leaden river into copper and then into gold. The pot of gold for me at the end of this rainbow is a yellow taxi that whisks me back to my hotel.

Next morning, with the help of another taxi and a porter, I transfer from my brown hotel to the Green Hotel, located across Shivanand Bridge in an area called Swarg Ashram. Apparently I was in the commercial section of Rishikesh, the equivalent of mistaking Hoboken for New York. Now instead of living at the bottom of a brackish brown well, I inhabit a high-ceilinged, second-storey room with windows opening onto a courtyard. My furnishings are spare and my walls pea green, but with plenty of sun and air any shortcomings can be written off as part of an adventure.

Daylight has enhanced rather than diminished my fairy-tale city. What appeared from the bridge as a soft, lemony blur transmogrifies into a Hindu temple with cupcake domes trimmed with green and pink garlands. A humped and coiled orange-and-yellow dragon becomes the Sri Ved Niketan Ashram with its entrance lined in gaudy Hindu gods in orange cages. A white marble arch turns out to be the pedestal for a four-horse chariot driven by Lord Krishna, one of Hinduism's best-loved god incarnations. A waterfront bazaar yields heaps of iridescent saris, glass bangles, *bindis* (the decorations Indian women paste on their foreheads) and kohl (the black mixture of soot and vegetable oil that they use to enhance their eyes). Broad staircases lead male pilgrims wearing white *dhotis*, or sarongs drawn up through their legs, down to the Ganges to bathe. Cows eat yesterday's garbage, which they convert into patties to be dried as fuel; puddles of dogs sleep all day so they can bay all night; monkeys scold from out-of-reach branches.

A two-kilometre stroll north takes me past stony rapids tucked between the forested folds of the Himalayan foothills. Caves under my feet rumble with the chants and cymbals of *sadhus* who have renounced the material world for staff, water pot and begging bowl. Some perch motionless on stones that are like bleached skulls, their hair in dreadlocks, their kelp-coloured skin smeared with ashes. Others walk the path in white and ochre robes or

lungi, intoning "*Shivo'am*" ("I am Shiva") or "*Hare Krishna.*"
Though Hinduism has millions of gods and demons,
three are paramount: Brahma the creator, Vishnu the
preserver, Shiva the destroyer. While Brahma is the One
God manifested in all others, it's Shiva and Vishnu,
along with Vishnu's earthly incarnations said to include
Krishna, Rama, Buddha and Jesus, who inspire *puja*, or
worship. As I encounter sadhus on the path, I discreetly
check to see whether their foreheads are dabbed with vertical lines of sandalwood paste (followers of Vishnu) or
horizontal lines (followers of Shiva) as if identifying exotic birds. Abruptly, through the branches of banyans
and other old growth, I glimpse what seems to be a mi-
rage: from both shores of the Ganges arises a congrega-
tion of wood towers even madder than the ones I've just
left. They are orange and yellow ashrams with twelve- and
thirteen-storey pagoda spires vying for aerial mastery like
bank towers in a North American city. All that I need for
my inner journey seems to be here in Rishikesh, whose
name means Home of Seekers: how will I gain entry?

I've already discovered that the Dayananda Ashram,
which I visited my first day, is a retreat for the serious
study of sacred Indian texts with no accommodation for
short-term guests. However, poking from the forest like
an impudent, red-tipped white finger is the ashram of the

late Maharishi Mahesh Yogi, renowned during the sixties and seventies as the guru of the Beatles and Mia Farrow. At a time when few Westerners understood the profundity of Eastern wisdom, the Maharishi toured North America teaching Transcendental Meditation. I personally remember paying $25 to one of his disciples, camped in a room over Dressmakers' Supply in Toronto, to receive my own *mantra*, or sacred sound, never to be revealed to anyone. Gazing intently into my eyes, the disciple presented me with a banana as he whispered, "Om." Since this is the universal mantra shared by all, I used to tell this as an anecdote with its punchline centring on my $25 banana. At that time, even the Maharishi's Western converts advertised TM as a tool for relaxation, although its true aim is to establish blissful union with the Divine. As the Maharishi—dubbed "the giggling guru" because of his gurgling chuckle—later commiserated, "I went to the West to wake them up but all they wanted was to be put to sleep!"

My impetus for TM initiation had been professional: I was assigned by the now-defunct Toronto *Star Weekly* to join the media hordes pursuing the Beatles to Rishikesh—a trip they wisely cancelled to sneak in at a later date. Now, three decades later, I arrive at the Maharishi's ashram at the top of a steep and winding forest road. It seems abandoned. Climbing the spiral staircase around the pagoda, I encounter altars on several floors, along with one monk dispensing blessings and sacred souvenirs. Since he doesn't speak English, I place an offering before departing, belatedly paying my respects to the Maharishi to whom history has given the last chuckle: his disciple, the best-selling author Dr. Deepak Chopra is now awakening millions of Westerners to ancient mind-body healing techniques, for which he credits the Maharishi.

During my next two days in Rishikesh I explore other ashrams, taking yoga classes where drop-ins are allowed.

As I sit cross-legged on the floor of a high-ceilinged room with two dozen other students, hands folded in prayer, a stocky swami in orange pants and tunic with thinning grey hair slicked into a ponytail leads us in a Sanskrit chant also designed to turn our bodies into a conduit to the Divine. Then, for the next hour, we perform exercises demonstrated by a senior student. Some, like the camel, in which we arch back from a kneeling position to touch our heels, are difficult to assume, let alone to hold for the required three minutes. Others, like the butterfly, in which we flap our arms, seem deceptively easy until shoulder muscles shriek. Each exercise utilizes the breath in a precise way: long, deep inhalations and exhalations timed to each movement, or the held breath, or the short rapid "breath of fire" performed by pumping the navel. Whereas Western exercises target muscles that will turn flabby with neglect, yoga works on the spine, the breathing system, the glands and other organs to permanently improve their function.

As we sweat through the regimen, Swamiji patrols the hall, shiny forehead bulging like a fist over piercing, coffee-bean eyes, staff at the ready. With well-aimed whacks he straightens spines and unlocks legs—a shock to Western seekers who've been socialized into thinking of yoga as a gentle art. His gaze fixes on a young man with a bionic chest, sucked-in gut and high shoulders. "Breed! Breed! Breed!" he shouts, striking the young man's navel. Lifting his own tunic, he pumps his diaphragm so rapidly that it disappears like the whirring blades of a fan. "East man breed in belly, West man breed in chest. Man trapped in chest is not free to feel. Such a man is an army man fit only to follow orders."

Just as important as the exercises are the minutes between them, when we relax on our backs experiencing their effects—the coursing of energy through tingling limbs, the deepened breathing that increases oxygen to the brain to produce feelings of well-being and even euphoria.

"Release the snake!" encourages Swamiji. "Feel snake bite navel and heart, then open crown for bliss."

He's referring to *kundalini* energy, which, according to a five-thousand-year-old Indian tradition is the life force that fuels us physically, emotionally, intellectually and spiritually. When activated, it rises up from the base of the spine, where it lies coiled metaphorically like a snake, through seven main energy centres known as *chakras:* root, sex, navel, heart, throat, brow, crown. In this holistic model, disease begins with a block in the energy system that later manifests as symptoms on the physical plane.

For example, a block at the root centre manifests as kidney problems, while one at the navel centre leads to digestive disorders. To treat the body with drugs and surgery merely alleviates the symptoms. Genuine healing requires nurturing the energy system through deep breathing, exercise, diet, meditation and the vibrations from chanting or music. However, good health is but a by-product of yoga. Its primary goal is to entice kundalini up the spine to the crown chakra for spiritual Enlightenment.

I squat in an airless and crowded marble room with twenty others awaiting another guru. Like a bird, Eastern teaching has two wings: one is yoga and the other is meditation, the art of silence. The mind averages twenty-five to thirty thoughts in a single minute, but the best I've been able to do after years of intermittent practice is to tone down that chatter, not turn it off. Learning to meditate is one of the reasons I've come to India because I know the payoff to be well worth the effort. Under laboratory conditions, yogis have proven their ability to sustain theta brainwaves associated with creative, artistic and even supernormal ability for several hours instead of just minutes; they can control metabolic rates and other body processes thought to be involuntary, endure extremes of hot and cold and override pain till it becomes "merely an opinion." However, the highest goal of meditation, as with yoga, is Enlightenment through union with the Divine: the mind, like an agitated cesspool, gradually stills and purifies until it become a mirror reflecting All That Is.

After half an hour, two devotees carry in an orange nest containing a large white egg. Rising from the nest, the egg turns into the bald head of an ancient swami whose face cracks into a sweet smile. Though I know he is a highly revered guru whose presence alone bestows blessings, what preoccupies me during the following hour of meditation is the hardness of the marble floor, the anonymous knee pressed into my back, the sweat worms trickling down my armpits and the dry cough tickling my throat.

I escape with relief toward Shivanand Bridge and into a heavenly evening rippling with soft breezes. Halfway across, I pause to gaze down at the obsidian river dancing with stars. Despite the beauty of the night, I feel disheartened: if I can't make it through one hour of meditation, how can I hope to commit to the two weeks to a month of intense study required by most ashrams? Suddenly, a pair of motorcyclists roar toward me from both ends of the bridge, turning this narrow span into a drag-race challenge. As I flatten myself against the rail, I realize that I am—like their helmeted drivers—too fuelled with North American expectations and impatience to settle down. Only this morning a fruit-seller stopped me as I paced the main road of Swarg Ashram to ask, "What do you want, madame? You have passed here four times and you don't seem to be going anywhere."

I decide to take myself in hand. Since I'm wakened anyway at five each morning by Hare Krishna chanting from
a nearby temple, I make up my mind to meditate then for
half an hour, again at noon and once more before going to
bed, while trying to maintain a consistent state of tranquil-
ity during the rest of the day. Squatting cross-legged on my
bed, I ponder which method to use: shall I count breaths or
focus my closed eyes between my brows? Shall I visualize
a violet flame or a thousand-petaled lotus? Shall I choose
a physical object such as a stone and perceive it in all its
essence without words? Shall I count beads? Shall I pray?

"What you need is a guru," insists a firm voice.

An Indian in burnt orange lungi with peppery hair
and beard squats between me and my mirror, his skin
the colour and smoothness of a pecan shell. From his
wiry limbs forming the base of an isosceles triangle to his
aquiline face, he seems composed entirely of straight
lines: his pencil nose intersects high flat cheekbones and
thin lips; his even brows parallel a squint of yellow-flecked
cat's eyes. I check the sandal-paste lines on his forehead:
both vertical and horizontal, creating the grid for an X's
and O's game. *Good.* A sadhu with a sense of humour.

"Who are you?"

"Your guru." He gestures with fingers as long as chop-
sticks. "Since India is your dream, you can have anything
you can imagine. Carl Jung had a spirit guide with horns

and wings named Philemon whom he saw as clearly as he saw everyone else. Socrates was often observed in spirited debate with an entity only he could see. Ask me what you need to know."

Okay. "How shall I meditate?"

"When something is difficult, enter by the easiest door."

"That would be through breath control. Whenever my motor is running too fast, slowing my breath calms me."

"Fine. Close your eyes, press your palms together, then slowly raise them above your head while inhaling to the count of eight. With arms and spine as straight as a pine tree, hold your breath for another eight counts, then exhale while lowering your folded hands, once again counting to eight. Repeat this until you feel anxiety melt away like snow on a warm day. Remember, meditation isn't just contemplation or relaxation. It's a scientific tool of transcendence. On the wings of meditation, you pass through the state of ordinary consciousness to a place beyond time, beyond pain, despair, disease and death." His voice slows along with my breathing. "Now make a nest of your hands in your lap and continue to breathe deeply to the count of eight. If your mind wanders, gently bring it back to its small task as if it were a bird that you're offering a palmful of seeds. Training the mind is like training the body. You can't expect to enter the Olympics without years of practice, so why expect to close your eyes and turn into a guru?"

As my breathing deepens, he intones, "Now let your consciousness sink slowly like a stone through water till it comes to rest on white sand. Think of that place as the centre of your being, the place you call home where all longing ceases. . . . Like a wave, the mind at rest discovers it is an ocean."

I stroll along the Ganges experiencing Rishikesh as it stretches like a drowsy dog in the first rays of morning, with my senses freshly washed, aware of the stirring of wind on my cheeks and of the cracks in the pavement under my sandals. My ears vibrate to the tinkling of bicycle bells, the rumbling of carts, the chopping of axes, the chanting of pilgrims and the pulse of children's laughter. My nostrils quiver with the delicate scent of sandalwood, the richness of frying fat and the heaviness of fresh cow dung. My eyes marvel at the dance of blues and greens and browns across the Ganges and the blinding iridescence of a fuchsia sari.

After savouring a cup of sweet, spicy Indian *chai* at a roadside restaurant, I descend the *ghats*, or stairs, to the water, where I discover as many ways to bathe as there are pilgrims. While the few women immerse fully clothed, trailing their saris like Ophelia her watery weeds, the men strip to G-strings or boxer shorts. Some creep in, some plunge, some drench themselves with pails of water. Some go joyfully, some solemnly, some weep. Some recite the 108 names of Mother Ganges:

Born from the lotus-like foot of Vishnu . . .
Flowing to the ocean . . .
A light in the darkness of ignorance . . .
Leaping over the mountains in sport . . .
Imperishable . . .
Eternally pure . . .
Having beautiful limbs . . .
Full of fish . . .
Destroyer of sin . . .
Making a noise like a conch shell and drum . . .
Taking pride in the broken egg of Brahma . . .

The man of pride arrives in a three-piece suit accompanied by three servants. While one tends his suitcase, hat and umbrella, the second helps him off with his clothes and the third folds them. The man of pride has more in his monogrammed luggage than I brought to India for three months, and his trousers bear the label "Specially Crafted for. . ." He prays loudly and conspicuously on each step before diving, then surfaces with eyes on the bleachers. Of course he must demonstrate through vigorous splashing that he experiences more joy than ordinary folk, and when he slips in the swift current and has to be fished out on the hook of his umbrella, he harshly scolds the servant who saved him.

From the ghats I amble south with my guru's bare feet marking the stones alongside mine, feeling the sun hot on my bare arms, the stickiness of the putty-coloured sand

under my toes and the smoothness of the white stones filling my arches. I pick up one, washed and bleached like a
bone, suddenly remembering last night's dream . . . *myself
along a shore like this, picking up a stone like this, putting it like
a seashell to my ear, hearing it sing and knowing I must release
the bird trapped inside.*

As I draw back my arm to throw the stone into the
Ganges, my guru stops me. "Keep it. You may want it."

I sit with my guru on a bench watching a stream of pilgrims, labourers, clerks and peripatetic cows cross Shivanand Bridge. This is only the second day of my regimen,
and already I'm growing restless with the feeling that I
should be doing something useful like taking a tour or
conducting an interview.

"You're supposed to be dreaming India, not docu-
menting it," my guru reminds me. "You're afraid of the
very plotlessness you came here to find. You want to weave
a safety net of words across the silence." Tucking his orange lungi around his long legs, he continues: "Every moment contains Infinity if you dive deeply enough into it.
Think of the energy that's released when your scientists
split a single atom of matter. For a holy man, one moment
of thought contains just as much power."

I offer him an orange, which he cups in his hands as if
in benediction. "How else do you suppose Eastern sages

discovered, without technology, that matter isn't solid but just a concentration of energy? How do you suppose they knew, several thousands of years before Western astrophysicists, that time and space aren't 'real' but just a sensory illusion?"

"I suppose you want me to say they did it through meditation."

"Exactly." My guru cracks open his orange as if it were an egg. "To discover the structure of a house you can physically crawl over it with a measuring tape or you can study the blueprint. Do you think Einstein received his inspiration by measuring things in a lab? His theories came to him in dreams or after he'd fiddled his brain into a theta state. Like Eastern sages, he looked inward. He accessed the blueprint."

My guru isolates a seed on his palm. "How would you describe this?"

Following his train of thought, I reply, "As the blueprint for an orange tree."

"Yes, and if you knew everything about this one seed you'd know everything about an orange tree, and if you knew everything about an orange tree, you'd know the whole universe." Popping the seed into his mouth, he chews it thoroughly. "Hindu seers describe the universe metaphorically as a web of threads strung with pearls, with each pearl reflecting every other." He distributes the orange sections to a family of monkeys. "Do you know Superstring Theory?"

"Just that it's Western science's latest attempt to explain Everything."

"Your physicists now agree with our sages that our five senses process only about one-billionth of the information that we're bombarded with every moment in the form of energy waves and particles. They also say that our universe is pervaded with billions of unseen Superstrings originating in a reality with more dimensions than our four, and possessing different frequencies that give rise to matter, energy, time and space." He draws a worn leather book from his lungi. "These *Vedas*, composed orally before writing was known, tell that same story of creation by playing on those Superstrings like a giant lyre." Opening the hand-stitched pages, he reads:

"There is an endless net of threads throughout the Universe.

"The horizontal threads are in space; the vertical threads in time;

"At every crossing of threads there is an individual, and every individual is a pearl.

"The great light of Absolute Being illuminates and penetrates every pearl.

"And also, every pearl reflects not only the light from every other pearl in the net

"But also every reflection of every reflection throughout the Universe."

My guru closes his book: "That is the poetry of science and the science of poetry."

Everywhere I go in Rishikesh—across the bridge, along the main street, to a restaurant—I'm overwhelmed by beggars and sadhus wanting rupees, but when I turn to my guru for instruction, he merely shrugs. "They think you're a rich woman."

"Given the exchange rate, I suppose I am, but there's only one of me and sometimes I pass the same beggars a dozen times a day. On the bridge alone there may be over a hundred lined up with their bowls."

"It's a beggar's job to disturb you, to give you an opportunity to work off bad karma through generosity."

"The sadhus as well?"

"Of course. Many immerse themselves in the scriptures in perpetual devotion or undertake gruelling pilgrimages or isolate themselves for years in caves. They practise these torturing austerities on behalf of humankind."

"But most of the sadhus I see in Rishikesh are hard to tell from ordinary beggars, and they're not impoverished. The temples dole out food twice a day and give them a place to sleep if they need it."

With a flash of his yellow-brown eyes, my guru sternly overrides my protest: "On the summit of Mount

Arunachala there's a yogi who hasn't eaten in over six years and who covers his eyes with a cloth so they don't burn visitors. Members of the Naga Babas control their sex drive by stretching their penises till they can be tucked between their buttocks. A sadhu at Varanasi spent a couple of decades standing on one leg in the Ganges with the nails of his raised left hand growing right through the palm. A nine-year-old boy at Varanasi has stood since age three aided only by a swing, where he slumps to sleep."

"But how do I know such sacrifices are of any value, or even that they actually happened?"

"How do you know the two of us are walking down this road?" asks my guru with a sly grin.

I gesture toward a dozen sadhus squatting on the corner ahead. "I'll know that *I* am when they start to swarm me. Quick. I need some practical advice."

"India is *your* dream. You're responsible for everyone who turns up in it."

The sadhus have begun clanking their bowls. "When I give them the same amount as Indians do, so I'll have enough change to go around, they hoot in derision. If I give them more, they expect the same every time. I don't want to play the bountiful tourist, lavishing coins on the peasants—that doesn't show any respect for them or for me."

"You're right to honour the local economy," concedes my guru. "Tourists who don't, arouse envy, cause inflation and breed corruption."

I fumble through the pockets of my purse without success. "My problem right now—the biggest problem most of the time—is finding any change at all. No vendors in India ever want to cash a 100 rupee note and 10 rupee ones are in such tight supply that If I don't hoard a few I have no change for chai and fruit. "

With another shrug, my guru exclaims, "Welcome to *Karma Bhoomi!*"

"What's that?"

"The Land of Experience!" He pretends to hook his staff around my neck. "Like the man of pride, you're on the hook to all of them and they know it."

It is my last evening in Rishikesh. I descend the temple steps under a white arch bearing the chariot of Krishna into the slanting rays of the sun. On a grand marble promenade, squatting men and women sing and chant to the strains of a harmonium, while a warm breeze sweeps the pavilion, whipping banners into a colourful froth.

It is the sweet time.

For half an hour I clap and sway with the rest. Then, after the crowd disperses, I descend a second flight to the Ganges, under a sky like a black net bulging with luminous fish and anchored by the new moon. Wading to my waist in this river, worshipped by hundreds of millions of

Indians over thousands of years, I grasp a chain allowing me to sink to my neck in the swift current.

> *Carrying away fear. . .*
> *Melodious . . .*
> *Flowing through the mountain country . . .*
> *Moon-crested . . .*

As the river bites my flesh, I feel embraced by India after a week of hesitating on her doorstep.

> *Auspicious . . .*
> *A light amid the darkness of ignorance . . .*
> *Bestowing happiness . . .*
> *Flowing like a staircase to heaven . . .*

Emerging from the Ganges, I wring out my skirt near the statue of a blue-skinned, flute-playing Krishna. I hear a real flute, its silvery notes as unobtrusive and welcome as a lark's. Following this enchantment to its source, I discover a blind boy in yellow robes swaying gently to the music, his sealed eyes fixed on an inner vision. After holding a 100 rupee note in my palms to bless it, I give it to his mother. For a few seconds the air around me lightens with the brightness of her gap-toothed smile, and I'm astonished at how happy I feel, having just experienced the first law of karma: that giving with a grateful heart most benefits the giver.

o m
shanti

"Peace is never more
than one thought away"

I AM SEATED at a window on the Shatabdi Express from Rishikesh to Delhi when they enter: three men dressed in white tunics and pants of such radiance that they recall the Rinso soapflake commercials of my childhood, except as I will discover, they deal with cleansing of a higher sort. After settling beside me like three white hens on a roost, the one to my right holds up a white pen banded with Hindu gods. Smiling, he asks, "Do you want this?"

Though he seems to be tempting me like a stranger with a lollipop, it would be churlish to refuse. "Thank you." A slot down the pen's side reveals homilies that rotate when I press a button. "HONESTY IS DIVINITY," "NO EFFORT NO LUCK" and this puzzler: "BE SIMPLE BE SAMPLE." The one highlighted when I receive it is "BE GOOD DO GOOD."

"We are a trio and you are one," continues my benefactor. "Would you change places with our companion across the aisle so we can visit three across?"

Now, I lined up for an hour to reserve my window seat, the trip is five hours long, and this will be my only chance to see this countryside. "I'll be happy to switch to another window seat but not onto the aisle."

He asks around. Polite refusals.

Feeling guilty but unrepentant, I glue myself to the window to watch India—in Panavision and Technicolor— slide past: fields of sky-high cattails and drifts of snowy egrets; bell-shaped straw huts entwined with golden flowers; artistically arranged patty cakes of cow dung drying for fuel; one lone elephant rummaging through a garbage dump. Though the aisle seems no bar to communications, my white-clad trio eventually shuffle seats so that I am beside the one foreigner among them. An elegant man with finely chiselled features under a stylish coxcomb of white hair, Robin Ramsay is an Australian actor and director who easily charms me with his wit and goodwill. Apparently, he and his Indian companions belong to the Brahma Kumaris, an international spiritual organization with headquarters at Mount Abu in the state of Rajasthan, where Ramsay will be attending a meditation conference.

"That's basically why I'm in India too," I tell him. "Spiritual quest."

"Then you should come to Mount Abu."

Though sceptical of that possibility, I write down names, addresses and phone numbers with my new white pen.

"Just phone and they'll put you on the list. Everything's free."

I'm incredulous. "Room and board?"

"Everything. The Brahma Kumaris are supported by voluntary donation."

I study my pen, "BE SIMPLE BE SAMPLE," as if it might be a Zen koan. *What's the catch?*

The hill station of Mount Abu, in Rajasthan, more than six hundred kilometres southwest of Delhi, is accessible only by toll road. So far today I've travelled seven hours by bus through oxen-plowed fields and rugged green hills to what will prove to be a one-hour upward spiral into the setting sun. Pressing palm to horn and foot to gas, my driver swings his aging vehicle up single-lane switchbacks that remind me of the slot machine called Pike's Peak found in ice-cream parlours of my youth. By rotating the wrist you manoeuvred a marble up a zigzag path past yawning holes to safety at the top. My marble never made it. Now all that shores my confidence is the conviction that my pilgrimage to Mount Abu is fated: in the week since I left Rishikesh, flagstone after flagstone has invitingly fallen into place. Would the gods lure me here just to cast me like a tin can down the mountain?

Once a summer retreat for royalty, the resort town of Mount Abu is built around Nakki Lake, a marshy puddle

clawed from rock by a god using only his nails, or *nakh*.
A taxi transports me from the bus station to a large complex on the edge of town—a Brahma Kumaris centre but,
unfortunately, not the right one. "What you want is the
university," informs the white-robed receptionist. "It's
farther up the mountain."

Before I have chance to feel discouraged, a young man,
also in white, takes my bag. Another finds me a BK car
and driver. All these people smile gently, move slowly and
exude calmness like the inhabitants of the Dayananda
Ashram in Rishikesh.

Again the road loops upward through rough plains and
forests combining deciduous trees, evergreens and palms.
Unlike Delhi's toxic air, this oxygen tastes like freshly
uncorked lime fizzy. At the end of the road, a large sign
written in a jumble of colours and typefaces proclaims,

Hearty Welcome in
GYAN-SAROVAR
ACADEMY FOR A BETTER WORLD
(A Spiritual Educational Institution)
NOT A PLACE FOR TOURIST INTEREST

The gatekeeper waves us across a reservoir bridge into
a Shangri-La of multi-storied pastel buildings tucked
into the hillside and landscaped with lawns, gardens, fountains and a small zoo of topiary animals. *Aren't ashrams*

supposed to be humble places where you eat lentils in their infinite variety and sleep on the floor? Everything about Mount Abu seems too good to be true.

Though I phoned ahead to make and then to reconfirm a booking, I'm apprehensive as I line up in the Overseas Co-ordinating Office to register. Both calls generated confusion until I mentioned Robin Ramsay. "Oh yes, Robin. I'll put you on the list." And then, the second time: "Yes, I see. You *are* on the list."

But I'm not. Not the official list that comes on a formal printout accompanied by name tags and orientation kits.

"What delegation are you with?"

I speak my mantra to the woman in white. "Robin Ramsay invited me." *Will he even recognize me? Will I recognize him in this gaggle of white swans?*

"We'll put you in this building. The room is open. We don't use keys."

Still gliding on the grace of Robin Ramsay's name, I follow a white-clad Indian youth through a white maze as if drawn on a beam of light. He deposits my bag in a spacious white-marble room, spotless and airy with two single cots, plenty of shelf space and an attached Western bathroom. I stare at the one anomaly—a wall light like a drop of blood with a picture of a white-robed, white-haired man haloed like a saint. *Who?*

I tour the campus with other new arrivals, including my Chinese roommate, a young woman so neat, self-contained and private that I will hereafter experience her only in the millimetre shift of a toothbrush, the slight indentation of a pillow, the faint after-scent of tamarind. Like the rest, I'm wearing white—mine a two-piece outfit resembling a busboy's uniform, which I had stitched up in two hours the evening before. Unlike the Trinity in white, I do not glow.

Though the Brahma Kumaris World Spiritual University accommodates up to fifteen hundred residents, fewer than three hundred delegates, all foreign, are attending this Peace of Mind conference. More modern than most North American colleges, this complex has its own sewage-treatment plant, generates its own electricity, prepares meals with solar energy from twenty-four rooftop discs and recycles water for irrigation. Along with an auditorium seating sixteen hundred, it has fourteen seminar rooms, a library, a bank, a clinic, an art gallery, a phone and e-mail centre. However, the campus jewel is Baba Brahma's room—an ethereal, low-ceilinged, white-cushioned disc bathed in pink light, resembling a flying saucer. Open twenty-four hours a day, it allows devotees to meditate staring at a point of light haloed in misty pink or at an idealized painting of Baba Brahma, benign of face, with deep-set eyes, high forehead, close-cropped balding pate and thick white moustache. No matter where I squat on the luxurious carpet, Baba's eyes seem to follow me.

Though I assume this to be a trick of the artist's brush, I later experience the same sensation with Baba's portraits.

But who is Baba Brahma?

Each morning at six-thirty the conference begins in the Meditation Hall, dominated by another ethereal portrait of Baba mounted under another beam of pink light, with forty-five minutes of *raja yoga*. In the West, the word *yoga* usually refers to breathing and stretching exercises, but it is actually a more general term meaning "to yoke" the individual to God. For raja yoga, we are instructed to sit with eyes focused on that point of pink light beaming from above Baba's head while using positive thought to turn our minds from body-consciousness, meaning material desires, to soul-consciousness, or union with the Supreme Being. To be effective, this positive thought must be focused, not random or rambling. At the same time, the BKs reject physical exercises, mantras and breath control as distracting forms of body-consciousness, and they use open-eyed meditation as a logical step toward transforming one's whole life into a permanent state of soul-consciousness. Though I'm grateful for the hall's upholstered seats, sparing me the discomfort of sitting cross-legged, I find the open-eyed meditation unbalancing, even nauseating, until I learn to focus on Baba's face instead of the light.

Afterwards we embark on a walking meditation into the surrounding hills—a silent string of white-clad pilgrims threading through towering lantana bushes, clustered with modest pink and yellow flowers. It's an inspiring image with precedents spiralling back in time, reflected above in a sprinkling of stars like candles lighting up banks of still grey clouds. Sometimes thorns claw at the ivory shawls given to us by the *dadis* (senior sisters) as our "friends and comforters" leaving a collective weave on their branches. Away from the high-decibel clamour of Delhi, I can hear the wind, even a stir of breeze. I can catch bird notes, loud in contrast to inner silence and the scent of something shy and invisible with the sweetness of frangipani. As I gaze up at rocky green ridges, like the broken rim of a bowl outlined against a pink sky, I find myself humming childhood hymns—"We Are Climbing Jacob's Ladder," "Unto the Hills"—with an almost weepy fervour.

Twice a day we gather in Harmony Hall for lectures, simultaneously translated into eleven languages, on the conference's theme of *Om Shanti*—I am a peaceful soul—which also becomes the preferred greeting over the next seven days. Our 260 delegates from forty-five countries represent all continents, with large contingents from Japan, Russia, England and Australia, the conference organizers. The delegates' level of education and accomplishment is

high, including professors, lawyers, psychologists, doctors, CEOs, scientists, engineers, bank managers, computer
analysts and writers.

Against a backdrop of Baba embracing planet Earth,
white-robed dadis impart BK philosophy seasoned by
their own experience.

Who Am I?

I am a soul in a body. A soul is just a point of light but
it contains all our power. Though the soul performs acts
of karma through the body, joy and sorrow come and go
on the level of body-consciousness, whereas with soul-
consciousness we enter a permanent state of peace. Affirmation: "I am a peaceful soul, immortal and imperishable.
I was never born and I will never die. I have come from
God and I will return to him. The soul is a traveller, the
body is its case. I am an eternal soul."

How Should I Relate to Others?

The two words causing most problems in the world
are *I* and *mine*, arising from body-consciousness and representing ego and attachment. With soul-consciousness,
happiness is no longer based on possessions and status but
on inner wealth, which, if shared, is increased rather than
diminished. To have soul-consciousness means that we
value everyone the same, inspiring us to do service with
detachment out of unconditional love and not based on
transactions.

All relationships have limitations except the one with
God. Husband and wife partnerships are not wrong but

they represent an attachment. Sex, lust and possessiveness arise out of body-consciousness, breeding anger, conflict and dishonesty. Through celibacy, the mind becomes stable and clear. Our relationship to others is most harmonious when we perceive them as brothers and sisters.

What Is Our Purpose in Life?

All living things have karmic accounts to be cleared. Like the physical world of Isaac Newton, the moral world has laws stating that every action creates an equal reaction, and ignorance of these laws is no excuse for careless or harmful behaviour. The goal of raja yoga is not to withdraw from the world but to perform enlightened action within it. Meditation is a practical instrument for change. If you want to change the world, change yourself and then everything changes.

Three classic ways of clearing karma are through suffering, deep remembrance of God and selfless service to others. Repeated actions imprint on the soul. Anger reveals a lack of tolerance. Blaming others is a projection of weakness. Anxiety indicates a lack of faith in the future. Self-knowledge plus willpower create right action. Our inner voice is our guide, with God as our source of power without limit. Forgive yourself for the past and strive to correct the present. Make your expectations zero and happiness becomes 100 per cent. Know that all souls have come from the home of silence beyond the stars. Earth is like a dream. We play our role here, then return home.

Who Is God?

There is only one Supreme Being, and our relationship to him is one of belonging. He is our father/mother/friend. When linked to God by love, we experience deep bliss—a sweet and beautiful state of super-sensuous joy that can be felt but not described. When that happens, the Self becomes pure, the whole personality changes and the world becomes your friend.

In granting prayers, God is limited by your karma and circumstances. If you turn to God with selfish motives, God has no responsibility to answer. If your feelings are pure, God will fulfil your requests. Always you will get power from God for spiritual growth—that is guaranteed. Where physics ends, metaphysics begins; where science ends, silence begins. Inner silence is more than the absence of sound. Sound comes from matter, while silence opens us to a higher dimension.

But Who Is Baba?

I purchase a biography of Baba Brahma entitled *Adi Dev* (The first man), written by Raj Yogi Jagdish Chander, a devotee.

Known to his friends as Dada Lekhraj of the Kripalani family, Baba Brahma was born in 1876 in Hydrabad, then northwestern India, the son of a Hindu schoolmaster. Through the diamond trade, he became one of India's richest and most respected men. Though lacking formal education, he was a charismatic person of principle who studied sacred texts, went on pilgrimages and abstained from drinking and smoking. He was also a devoted family man offended by the low status of Indian women.

At age sixty, Dada Lekhraj experienced powerful visions of Vishnu and of Shiva, revealing to him that he was the original Adam and that he should allow his body to be the chariot, or medium, of Shiva. Successive revelations showed him that the Supreme Soul is a point of light and that human souls are sparks of that light. He also saw horrific visions of the destruction of civilization as we know it. Intoxicated by this knowledge, Dada Lekhraj retired from business and, as Baba Brahma, began attracting devotees. Soon two hundred people a day were arriving at his house for *satsang*, a spiritual gathering that took the form of ecstatic singing, dancing and lectures. Some who saw him surrounded by light experienced instant transformations. Most were young women whom he urged into celibacy, sending shock waves through the community. He also ignored caste restrictions, further arousing opposition.

In 1936, using his own fortune, Baba Brahma founded the World Spiritual University in Karachi, now part of Pakistan, to be run by nine of his female devotees known as Brahma Kumaris, or daughters of Brahma. For fourteen years, he and three hundred disciples lived as a self-sufficient community, spending much time in intense meditation. Outraged husbands and fathers continued their attacks—physically with rocks and fire and legally through high-ranking politicians and the media. Many women who wished to join were beaten and confined by relatives. A murder attempt on Baba was said to have failed when the paid assassin became frightened by the dazzling light emanating from him.

In 1951, after the partition of Pakistan from India, the community moved to Mount Abu. Madhuban—meaning Forest of Honey, and the complex where I first landed— was their original headquarters, now with an annex called Shantivan, meaning Place of Peace, providing accommodation for fifteen thousand. When sisters fanned out to Delhi and Bombay to establish other communities, some were so unsophisticated that they had to learn the use of money and trains. After Baba died in his sleep in 1969 at age ninety-three, the Indian government issued a commemorative stamp, and BK leadership passed to two dadis from his original group. Even today members of that core, now in their eighties, run the organization according to Baba's instructions received through a discourse known as the *Murli* (The flute). Several times a year they gather in Shantivan's twenty-thousand-seat auditorium where an elderly sister falls into a trance during which she channels Baba. Despite—or because of—their unorthodox CEO, the organization has become immensely successful, with four hundred and fifty thousand devotees worldwide and with thirty-five hundred branches of the Brahma Kumaris World Spiritual University in seventy countries. Now affiliated with the United Nations as a non-governmental organization working for peace with strong ties to UNICEF and UNESCO, the BKs are honoured internationally for accomplishments in the fields of culture, health and science, especially relating to youth and women.

Though I'm impressed by my personal contact with the dadis, some of the BK ideology makes me uneasy. When I was a philosophy undergraduate, liberation meant casting off the straitjacket of my literal-minded, guilt-inducing Christian upbringing for "agnosticism leaning toward atheism." Though deepening life experience has subsequently convinced me that the universe is intelligent, purposeful and meaningful, I've never become reconciled with the faith of my youth, with its reliance on miracles, revealed truth and a personal saviour.

During a seminar that I attended in the 1980s, the late Joseph Campbell struck a personal chord when he described Christianity as religious pathology. A Jungian scholar and mythologist, Campbell argued that the function of any religion—its observances, myths and storyline—is to serve as a metaphor illuminating a Truth so large that it can't be captured in words or reduced to historical facts. Traditionally, to have faith meant to have faith in the Mystery to which myth provides an ethnic gateway and bridge; however, when the Church of Rome insisted that the Bible was literally and historically true, it turned true myth into false fact, destroying the bridge from the known to the Unknowable. He defined this as religious pathology.

During the past dozen years, I've found myself attracted to the Eastern concept of God as a life force permeating the universe, located both within and without, to be worshipped through reverence for all things. This was the view I expected to have reinforced in India, but ironically, here at Mount Abu I'm being invited to re-ensnare myself in the dualism of my childhood. Once again God the patriarch is said to exist somewhere Up There. Instead of being represented on Earth for thirty-three years by Jesus the carpenter, he's supposed to have been manifest for thirty-three years in the body of Baba, a recently deceased jeweller. Despite these reservations, the BKs' core practice—meditation—is beyond the reach of ideology; reincarnation and the law of karma make sense to me logically, emotionally, practically and intuitively. Inspired communication through an *avatar*, meaning a godly incarnation, is part of the Eastern tradition, and I've come to India as a pilgrim to learn, not as a philosophy undergrad to judge. At Mount Abu I've missed the avatar by only thirty years instead of two thousand. For anyone raised a Christian, the question of how one might have felt and behaved if born during the time of Jesus remains provocative. Meeting the dadis is like meeting St. Peter, St. Paul and Mary. All that's asked of me

here, in return for everything I'm receiving, is to keep an
open mind.

Despite their dismissal of body-consciousness, our Indian
hosts do everything possible to make us, as conference
deligates, physically comfortable. We're served three delicious vegetarian meals a day and showered with small
gifts. Our rooms are cleaned regularly, and we're pro-
vided with free laundry service; BK cars offer transportation into town, and we're taken on local excursions. All
these tasks are performed by BK volunteers, usually Indian
women who've left their families for a month to serve conference participants, most of whom are white foreigners.
Since this arrangement seems to reinforce old colonial
stereotypes, I feel uncomfortable until I come to realize
that these volunteers—modest, gentle and attentive—genuinely do feel blessed in providing selfless service.

As Brother Surya, who is in charge of the BK kitchen,
explains, "Those who have dedicated their lives to experiencing God in this way accept everything with humility,
and they are free. They don't think of you as outsiders or
even as guests. They believe you are their own family, and
in a family no one can ask for payment. Water and food
are affected both by negative and positive thoughts, so all
who cook food must be pure. It's also important to keep
everyone smiling so we can cook in love and serve with

joy. Sometimes there are two thousand to be fed, but we work very fast and can do that in an hour, so we never worry."

I ask Brother Surya, small and lean with cropped head and appearing more youthful than his forty-nine years, "How did you, an advanced yogi with a reputation as a brilliant mathematician, come to be running the kitchen?"

Chuckling, he explains: "Food is important in our practice since food influences the mind, but if a man is a philosopher, he is not going to want to look after the kitchen. I was very fond of reading the Bhagavad Gita [The song of the Lord, a sacred Indian text], but I also wanted to turn this life into a laboratory, to bring to it the practice of selfless renunciation without attachment. When Baba asked me to run his kitchen, I surrendered my intellect so that I would not even question. Words and vegetables became part of the same practice."

As we watch a cluster of smiling women rolling chapatis—up to five thousand for a single meal when this complex is full—I ask Brother Surya what caused him to choose the BKs out of India's abundance of spiritual offerings.

"My family was Hindu, and while I was growing up I developed a strong feeling to become a yogi. I studied a book about that, which I couldn't understand, but when I practised, I had a very beautiful experience that pulled me in. I came to Mount Abu in 1968, just after I graduated from university. Hardly a hundred people were here, and Baba always used to be among us, not off in a room or cave like many other gurus, so I noticed everything about him, his personality and his face. As soon as he entered the class, it was as if a powerful current came through the hall, and all of us experienced it and became alert. When Baba started to talk, I had a clear feeling that some unique power was speaking through his mouth. Then, out of the class, he seemed an ordinary human being, and that power and that personality and that expression were gone. For seven days I noticed that, and everyone else noticed it too. One day in class I also had a vision. A light was coming down from above, and again not only I saw it but some other souls of that group. Then I came to hear that many people from different groups had had the same experience, so I had full faith in this incarnation, and that also compelled me to dedicate my life here."

While we stroll amid steaming, metre-wide cooking pots, I ask the question I find most compelling: "Who do you think Baba Brahma is?"

Brother Surya explains with characteristic precision: "In India we know the difference between a great soul and an incarnation of God. Many devotees call their own guru an incarnation, but while those souls may be very great, an incarnation is a different thing. An incarnation doesn't come with a book in his hands, and those others, they were teaching from books. Because I had studied philosophy I knew Baba's knowledge was completely different. He was not a scholar but just an ordinary devotee, so where was this knowledge coming from? The second important difference I noticed, and many others noticed it too, is that great souls can tell you to be good, but they cannot teach purity. When God incarnates, people receive an inspiration to become pure, and I saw with my own eyes many people who had an immediate transformation. Maybe they were drinking all the time—using alcohol instead of water, practically gargling with it—but in a second they gave it up, left it. That's the effect of God power, and we could see this difference, this greatness."

"I've been told that Baba continues to guide this organization through the Murlis, during which one of the sisters channels him. Have you experienced this?"

Brother Surya's face grows radiant. "Oh, many times! When Baba left his body he was not reborn because he had settled his complete karmic account, so then he came back to us in the body of one of the dadis who has been in this organization from the beginning. He enters her body, then speaks knowledge and instruction through her mouth. Eight times a year, ten thousand BKs come to the big hall in Shantivan to experience that sister going into trance and having the Supreme Soul enter her body. Such powerful and peaceful feelings spread throughout the hall, and everyone experiences those vibrations. I myself become bodiless, and my mind goes over into very deep silence, and such wonderful feelings come to mind, and I become perfectly steady, and many times I could not see even the sisters in front of me who disappeared for the moment. Afterwards, when the sister came down from trance and opened her eyes, the expression on her face completely changed, and she was back to being herself."

Smiling sweetly, Brother Surya adds, "All these things have given me faith."

At odd times during the day, even when I awaken at night, I slip into Baba's Room, glowing with pink lights, where I fall easily into a peaceful altered state. Sometimes under the intensity of my gaze, the soft colours of his painted face melt, then transform into the faces of persons living and dead with whom I wish to communicate, dredging up a ton of grief—old stuff, often attached to deaths insufficiently mourned. During this time I feel especially close to my sister, who died in 1990 from cancer of the eye. In family photos she is usually holding my hand—a friendly, freckled kid in gold-rimmed glasses who did her best to care for me with the wisdom of her extra four years. Her unexpected death at fifty-nine happened too quickly, given the false optimism with which we were living, yet too slowly, given the suffering she endured as she travelled from medical procedure to medical procedure like Stations of the Cross on a conveyor belt to death. Eight years later I still feel bonded, as if we are a single unit in a journey through more than one lifetime. Such thoughts are powerful and healing, sometimes elevating me into an experience of universal love. Yet waiting for me to emerge from this peaceful place, forever nagging at its shiny edges, is a feeling of self-dissatisfaction that I can't name or explain—a dark encrustation that smothers joy and absorbs light. It's the shadow of discontent that inspired this trip and that I experienced as restlessness in Rishikesh, now exaggerating my sense of illegitimacy at having slipped into Mount Abu through the back door. When I raise this issue with others, they're always reassuring: "It must be your karma to be here." And though I'm surrounded by people I'd be happy to know better, I find myself retreating behind a defensive thicket. Usually I'm comfortable in crowds, but having left my social masks and costumes locked in the closets of my now-empty Toronto condo, I'm forced to deal with the more vulnerable creature who wore them. Yet, embedded in this anxiety is the sense that I'm exactly where I should be and that some necessary part of me is creeping forward to be healed.

A lavish on-campus gallery initiates me through paintings, sculptures and several *son et lumière* shows into the BK cosmology, apocalyptic and cyclical. According to Baba's revealed truths, the Earth passes through five-thousand-year cycles, beginning with a Golden Age that slides into a Silver Age, then tarnishes into a Copper Age that deteriorates into an Iron Age—our present dark and destructive period—leading inevitably to cataclysm from which humans will emerge purified to enjoy a brief Diamond Age as the gateway to another Golden Age, repeating the cycle. Though many societies have embraced the concept of cosmic eras, usually their time periods are far longer. Plato theorized that a Great Year ended when all planets returned to certain key positions in the cosmos, which his disciples estimated to take thirty-six thousand years. Also using cosmic markers, the Mayans devised a Long Count calendar in which an age lasted twenty-six thousand years. In Hinduism, Brahma is said to dream the world in billion-year cycles divided into four ages, or *yugas*, with our current one, the most degraded, known as *Kaliyuga*, or the age of Kali.

Though the light shows are mesmerizing—especially the red laser drawing up the soul to God—the interdenominational art created by devotees is naive, literal and preachy. How, I wondered, were the other Western delegates—the university professors, the journalists, the lawyers, the scientists and the engineers—coming to terms with the kinks and quirks of BK revealed truths?

Though I've been eager to speak with Robin Ramsay since arriving in Mount Abu, we don't connect until a few days into the conference. A glance at the program demonstrates why: not only does he perform each morning with his former wife and daughter in a morality play called

The Tao of Truth, but the same talented trio also stages *The Accidental Mystic*, a witty evening production combining the hazards of travelling in India with the rewards of spiritual quest. When we do finally meet, Robin is still wearing silver gloss from his last performance, highlighting his already aristocratic features and halo of white hair. While we have tea on the dining-hall patio, I ask him how he discovered the Brahma Kumaris.

"I'd been on a spiritual search since the sixties when I lived in America as part of that New Age poets' wave, but I'd sort of filed it into the 'too hard' box—either it took too much time, or too much money, or you had to give up too much of what you'd already learned to receive someone else's little secret. Then, in 1984, some actors who found the BK program useful invited me to a workshop followed by a vegetarian lunch. I must also confess that my eye was caught by the fact that no fee would be charged for any of it, at any time. What did I have to lose? In my very first meditation, I experienced this euphoric silence, focusing on this loving dot, with a feeling that my negative tendencies were being burned away. After touching that for even a few seconds, I was skipping down the street."

"Do you meditate every day?"

"By now it's more like my being in a permanent meditative state—that accepting, generally loving, somewhat detached, peaceful state—so that when things come at you, as they do, you deal with them without getting upset.

That's why open-eyed meditation is so good. It's quite another thing, sitting in a corner, eyes closed, burning incense and chanting, then coming out into the real world and suddenly you're arguing with a taxi driver."

"How important are the BKs to your life?"

"They're major, which isn't to say I accepted everything with alacrity. The biggest impact was intellectual."

"That surprises me, since it's the intellectual part that gives me the greatest difficulty."

Looking thoughtfully into the rough, green Aravali Hills, Robin explains: "There's a huge logic in the physical world, but it's only through the laws of karma balancing the great differences in advantage with which people are born that I can see logic in the spiritual world. People in the West have a lot of trouble with the idea of divinely inspired direct knowledge—'What do you mean that God spoke through this old man, and now that old man speaks through this old woman?' To me that's all part of the logic—that God has to speak through someone—and I accept Baba as a pure soul who became an instrument of God. Either that make sense to you and the penny will fall or it doesn't."

"Perhaps that's so, but as a Protestant dropout I'm attracted to the Eastern concept of God being present in all things. When I think of the times that I've felt most spiritually alive, it's usually involved some natural setting—biking through Danish fields in the twilight of a storm; travelling by dogsled through an Arctic landscape of infinite white; speeding in a convertible through a balmy Arizona night with every star accounted for and native fires flickering from cliffside caves. Though I'm not a tree-hugger in practice, I am in spirit."

"Ah yes, 'I am God, God is me,'" sighs Robin, with cheerful forbearance. "I see that as avoidance of responsibility. If God is everywhere, you can just relate to everything, without having to make choices and so endlessly pursue nice places."

Recalling that Robin's former wife is also a BK, I ask, "How do you feel about the BKs' stand on celibacy? That must be even more of a sticking point than divine revelation to the organization's growth in the West."

"That's a sticking point everywhere!" admits Robin with a laugh.

"I'm surprised there hasn't been more discussion about it at the conference. People seem to be skirting the issue."

"That's probably because if it's introduced, that's all anyone will want to talk about. When I first heard about it, I said, 'Oh, give me a break,' but if you want to be in charge of everything, you have to run that part of your life too. There's nothing that takes you more completely into body-consciousness than that whole romantic thing. I won't say that it hasn't been a battle, but I didn't feel I could keep a foot in both camps. It's an individual matter. Lots of people with strong ties to the BKs aren't celibate, just as some BK couples are. For me, celibacy is a practical decision with clear benefits and not a morality one."

"There's another aspect of BK philosophy that's giving me trouble. Yesterday I took a tour of the art gallery. I don't dismiss out of hand the apocalyptic view of history. Perhaps there actually was a flood, though not the way the Bible lays it out in the story of Noah's Ark. Perhaps Atlantis did actually tumble into the sea. Perhaps Mars is the sorry remains of what was once an advanced civilization, as myths state, but . . . five-thousand-year cycles? I find that naive."

"Yes, the hardest piece of the BK world for me to take on was the Golden Age cycle, but I did some research into Darwinian evolution, and I found its scientific underpinnings are now considered very dodgy. The myth of the Golden Age is found in all cultures—even ours, as the Garden of Eden—so I do accept that part literally, but I don't pay a lot of attention to the numbers. That five-thousand-year cycle has symbolic importance in Indian mythology. It's a number that reverberates with them. Since about 95 per cent of BKs are Indian, there's a bit of a cultural divide in the organization. The Indians are used to accepting authority, whereas in the West we like to discuss things and we demand nuance. Just think of BK wisdom as a jewel box that's being offered to you, then take what you want and leave the rest. For myself, I said, 'I'll take the lot.'"

One evening we all climb into the cliffs surrounding Nakki Lake. Amid cactus clumps and jagged outcroppings, we silently watch the setting sun illuminate peak after enshrouded peak, then turn a pond into a rosy eye, like the one in Baba's Room, before extinguishing itself. When several of us tell Naoise Power, the leader of our seminar group, that we prefer meditating out-of-doors to staring at a pink light, he patiently responds: "You say you felt so peaceful watching the sun set, but that peace wasn't coming from the sun. The sun isn't peaceful. It wasn't coming from the rocks. Rocks aren't peaceful. That peace was coming from you. All the rest is just body-consciousness. It's the same when you feel anger toward someone. Even if the person has injured you, that anger isn't coming from anything or anyone but you. What you are experiencing from that other person is only that person's pain."

The next time I find myself growing annoyed—in this case, at a woman who sighs, fidgets and flounces during meditation—I concentrate on sending her peaceful thoughts to heal her discomfort. Within minutes she falls into a heavy, snoreless sleep. More important: Plan C leaves me liking both myself and her a lot better than Plan A, which called for me to nudge or glare, or Plan B—the most likely—which had me storing up anger for delayed release. Though this incident is a small one, I feel I've taken a signifigant first step toward changing a deeply ingrained response.

A tall, sturdy Irishman with cropped grey hair, Naoise and his wife joined the BKs within two weeks of discovering them. "That's all it took for us to give up smoking, drinking, meat and sex." He adds with characteristic irony, "We like to think that in another life we were a priest and a nun who weren't allowed to marry."

As a counsellor in the London prison system, Naoise has a knack for offering timely dashes of wisdom. When dealing with gender issues, he advises the women in our group, "Just look at that soul who is troubling you and think, 'He is my sister in a man's body.'" Before the final session in which delegates are invited to share what they've learned at the conference, he comments, "In my experience it's not such a good idea to compare. You may be feeling pretty good about what you've gained here, then someone will say, 'I had a vision of an angel,' and someone else will say, 'I saw the face of God,' and suddenly everyone's competing for the biggest transformation or to produce the shiniest halo, and you'll begin to think, 'I guess nothing much happened to me.'" Being forewarned, I held on to my modest victories.

Naoise's main credo, expressed in his every word, breath and movement, is "Slow down. Even if it's just a matter of crossing the street, be conscious of the pavement under your feet. When you greet someone, really look at that soul and let them look at you. Don't be afraid of silence." He tells us the Zen story of the sage who was chased over a cliff by a tiger. As he clung to a shrub halfway down, with the tiger leering above and the jagged rocks below, he noticed mice nibbling at the base of his shrub, which possessed a single wild raspberry at its tip.

Ignoring the tiger, the rocks and the mice, the sage picked the raspberry, savouring its sweetness.

The tiger represents the past, the rocks the future, and the mice the passage of present time. "We have only a few moments to grasp the wild raspberry."

On our last day, suggestions are offered for taking the conference home with us.

1. Meditate regularly by waking up half an hour early. Begin with ten minutes for the first month, then twenty for the next three and thirty thereafter. Finish the day the same way. By concentrating the mind for greater efficiency, you will find you gain time.

2. Take care of the body—as the food, so the mind. Respect it as the costume you are currently wearing, but make the intellect the ruler of the senses.

3. Practise traffic control: stop one minute every two hours for contemplation.

4. Forgive yourself for the past and do it right now. Live in the present and don't be anxious about the future. Whatever has happened until now has had to happen; what is happening now is good; what will happen tomorrow is the best.

5. Remain spiritually aware while performing even the smallest tasks.

6. Know that you are the one who can and must create change both within and without.

7. Know that Mount Abu is your real home. The country where you live is just your office, your service centre in this life.

8. Remember that peace is never more than one thought away.

I speak through an interpreter with Dadi Janki, one of Baba's original disciples, in her campus cottage. Now eighty-three, she's the BKs' international director responsible for their expansion into seventy countries, in constant demand as a speaker at world peace and health conferences. As broad as she is tall, she has a presence more dynamic than gentle and, yes, her white garments most certainly glow.

"I understand you were only twenty-one when you joined Baba. Have you ever regretted giving up a world you hadn't yet experienced?"

Dadi Janki's wide smile stretches between severe brackets of grey hair. "Worldly things never had any attraction for me. I had been searching for honesty and truth but couldn't find it because, in the community where I lived, they suppressed you by making you follow only the scriptures. Before Baba became an instrument of God, I knew him as a prominent and respected businessman. One day I was walking with my biological father when I saw Baba. Lights were coming from his body. He was transformed. I asked Father, 'Did you see what I saw?' My father had not, but for me it was a wonderful experience, full of truth and beauty. Something from Baba said, 'You belong to me,' and I took just one second to decide. After such an experience, so sweet and loving, I stopped reading the scriptures and visiting pilgrimage sites. Compared to it, everything else was perishable, so my advice to people is 'Don't think too much about divinity. Just experience it.' God says, 'Child, open your third eye,' and when you do, then you can renounce body-consciousness. There's no reason to hate worldly things. It's just that we don't need them."

"Did your family accept your decision to join Baba?"

Dadi shakes her head even before the translation is finished. "Since I was brought up in a well-to-do family, there were many obstacles. My parents were concerned about how I could manage if I went away to live, but I had faith that God would look after me."

"I have trouble accepting Baba as an incarnation of God in the same way as I have trouble accepting Jesus as the son of God. Do you ever have such doubts?"

Her deep-set eyes pierce. "No, because I knew Baba himself was not God. God simply spoke through him, using his body. Nobody should be considered God. Krishna was not God. Jesus was not God, though that's a mistake some Christians make. All are elevated souls."

"Can you describe your personal experience with the Supreme Being?"

With her right hand creating lyrical arabesques, Dadi Janki explains: "For the past sixty years I have been in contact with God, and if I tried to tell you that in detail we would have to spend many days and nights together. I had no trouble giving and getting love from God because I came as an innocent. This is an experience based on faith but not on blind faith. At first I thought that God sometimes didn't hear me, but now that the intellect has become clean, I talk with God. I eat with God. I walk with God, and whatever action I am performing, I am doing for God. This path is so easy. I am here before you as a practical example. It takes time to create your own path, but to see an example and follow it doesn't take much time."

As part of her spiritual apprenticeship, Dadi Janki nursed the seriously ill for fourteen years, and recently she herself underwent treatment for cancer. "Did you ever wish simply to escape from your body?"

"I've never had the thought that this is too much. No matter how bad the condition of the body, it never showed on my face because I was always in a state of happiness and positivity. If I have to leave my body, I'm not sorry to do so, but I have never had any desperation to leave it. Those who worry a lot or think too much waste time and lose energy. When energy is used in the right way, then the body span increases."

"There is a proverb that says 'Many paths lead up the mountain.' Do you agree with that?"

Again, the flash of sharp eyes. "That is a mistaken idea. The system Baba created for us makes us strong, but it is necessary to have faith in the rules and to perform actions. Meat eating makes people hard, with no compassion for themselves or others. Sex is body attachment—nectar and poison can't exist together. The success of the Brahma Kumaris organization is because of celibacy. If you don't understand that, it's because you are still trapped in body-consciousness. I know that it takes time for some people to leave the past. Never use the words *but*, *difficult* or *I'll try*. After fifteen minutes of powerful raja yoga, you see everyone with love. You are beyond the senses. When I sit with Baba, my eyes become blind and my ears deaf to any other person's weaknesses. If there is a bad smell, I will close my nose. Through science we understand only matter, but through silence we understand the soul. We travel beyond the stars. Always remember this is not an ordinary thing. Let others see the happiness your transformation brings to you. What you receive here you can't just keep to yourself. It must be shared—not given because the sense of giving can lead to ego. It's up to you how much you take from here. Listen attentively, examine carefully, and if it is useful, take it, but also take the key with you. Keep unlocking the treasures."

I ask myself how much I'm willing to change for spiritual beliefs: do I want them to direct my life or just to provide a reassuring sidebar? Do I want something extra or something more? And how do I feel about "the sticking point"?

At this conference I've found it subtly liberating to belong to a group in which celibacy makes sex irrelevant as a social motivator and mixer. Gone are the little flirtations, the exclusive duos, along with the anxiety of being selected when you don't want to be or not being selected when you do. This conspicuous absence of signalling demonstrates how pervasively sex acts as an underground determinant even in situations that aren't about mating. Sizing up another person as a potential sex partner is often an ingrained, adolescent habit that produces demeaning snap judgments: too old, too short, too fat, too bald, too hairy, not smart enough, not sophisticated enough, not the right race.

On the other hand, the BKs' denigration of "body-consciousness" also troubles me. As in North America of the fifties, I'm hearing soul pitted against body with body as the sorry loser. Once again the Virgin Mary is to be the female role model, this time with a Virgin Joseph as her consort. Though some dadis attempt to speak well of the body as if trying to see good in a close relative they really don't like very much, the words *impure*, *lust*, *poison* and *dirty* slip into the dialogue with disturbing frequency. Is this a translation problem? Perhaps. How about cultural bias? Probably. When the BKs formed during the thirties, celibacy was a courageous way for Indian women to renounce a social system in which they were brides for barter. For them—as for medieval nuns—celibacy was an expression of temporal feminist power, apart from its spiritual or moral value.

In the West, religions have traditionally also assumed the authoritarian task of ensuring social stability by branding sex apart from marriage and procreation as immoral. Because women were charged with maintaining the restrictions while men were allowed to celebrate their prowess, sex also became an instrument of male domination. The Roman Catholic insistence on celibacy for its priesthood is another form of power-mongering, as it ties loyalty to the Church. After growing up under the influence of the Christian Church and the virgin-obsessed fifties, I needed decades to free myself of the duality that branded the body as evil. My mother couldn't even say the word *fun* without specifying good, clean fun, always spoken with pursed lips. I belong to a generation of women for whom sex was initially so fraught with fear of both pregnancy and whore-branding that only the fortunate escaped with libidos intact. Therefore, as an individual sorting out my priorities, I reject the moral argument—the "thou shalt not"—as irrelevant and even offensive.

In the Eastern holistic model, sex and spirituality are said to be fuelled by the same biological energy, with procreation as a goal of life's first phase and Enlightenment its second. In the youth-obsessed West, sex is regarded as a lifelong affirmation of power in men and of desirability in women, while celibacy is feared as a harbinger of old age, loneliness and death. A blatant prosyletizer for this attitude is the recently divorced, seventy-something Hugh Hefner who boasted to the media that with his erection sustained by Viagra, he was delighted to discover "a whole new generation of women out there waiting for me," including twenty-four-year-old twins named Mandy and Sandy, with a "spare" of about the same age named Brande. Such suspect bravado aside, it's probably fair to say that serial relationships for most people, end in disappointment: expectations that weren't fulfilled, lifestyles that didn't fuse, attractions that faded, transactions that weren't worth the effort. Is celibacy an enlightened way of taking happiness into one's own hands through creation of a new set of values? Why does Western society promote the view that lack of sexual activity is dysfunctional? Is lack of tennis playing after sixty dysfunctional? Could the term *over the hill* reflect an immature view of what it's like to be actually standing on top of the hill? During the rush of youth and throughout the child-rearing years, having a partner with whom to share and to learn is probably the most satisfying way of experiencing life, but when does coupledom become a yoke holding back personal growth? Is sexual bonding the best or only way to retain love, tenderness, companionship and friendship? When does marital sex become a habit, an obligation or a substitute for real intimacy? How many couples would prefer to become devoted friends or BK brothers and sisters if that were considered an honourable option? If sex and spirituality are fuelled by the same energy, which reflects the greater maturity: a continuing sexual relationship with one person or a life redefined in terms of spiritual quest and community service?

I still have an aversion to the "thou shalt nots," even when self-imposed, and since abstinence has become part of the rhetoric of the so-called Moral Majority fond of telling others how to lead their lives, I'd hate to be mistaken for a member of that brigade. Nor do I wish to bunk in with the word teasers who believe in born-again virgins or who define celibacy as two weeks without opportunity. At the same time, spiritual self-determination, including celibacy, is gaining in attraction for me as a way of broadening rather than narrowing my horizons.

So where does this long discourse lead me? Still on the fence but with greater comfort and clarity.

Our meditations in Harmony Hall are led by a senior sister who sits on a dais facing us. Her presence is more than a courtesy, as even the sight of an Enlightened person, called *darshan*, is believed to transfer energy. When Dadi Janki replaces another sister halfway through our final session, my response is immediate and electric. Several times before I thought I saw auras around senior meditators but, given the suggestive stage lighting, couldn't be sure. This time, not only does Dadi Janki radiate light but I see light around myself so intense that my eyes burn and my body vibrates, drenching me in sweat. It's a pleasing experience that seems more natural than mysterious, lasting for about ten minutes and producing a refreshing afterglow. Curiously, at the end of this meditation, Dadi Janki comments as if brooding to herself: "After Baba left his physical body, it has been so easy to keep in contact. I was experiencing Baba just then, as if he were a dome of light and I was playing the role of lighthouse."

I've spent seven days in a warm, pink womb being spiritually, emotionally and physically nourished. Most of what I've received is useful, some of it is wise, some provocative and some merely idiosyncratic, but all has been offered with great kindness. It is highly seductive.

Much about the Brahma Kumaris seems cult-like: the presence of mommies and a daddy (or dadis and a baba) who love us. The pictures of Big Baba in every room. The group meditations in which we enter a suggestible altered state. The music broadcast over loudspeakers one minute out of every two hours during which we drop what we are doing to focus inward. The white uniforms we wear. The somewhat repetitive lectures delivered in soft melodious voices. The call to celibacy.

Yes, the BKs just miss being a cult, but it's a clear miss. No attempt is made to proselytize beyond the lectures. Though Baba's Boxes for donations are distributed about the campus, they're never mentioned. For "family members," the suggested donation is one rupee a person a day, which is about 2 cents American, and non-members aren't supposed to pay anything. Everything here genuinely is free, though I'm sure most delegates found ways to donate, as did I. The BKs' international reputation as a force for good is well earned and their integrity unassailable. I am not up cult mountain.

What I'm being offered is the portal to a beautiful and attainable Peaceable Kingdom, and perhaps it is my weakness and my loss that I can't bypass my intellectual censors and walk through it. As a college student I remember being appalled by the French philosopher Blaise Pascal's wager: believe in God, because if that belief turns out to be false, you've lost nothing, but if you don't believe, and it's true, you've lost everything. To my youthful self, that seemed like the shallowest opportunism, but now I understand that you can choose to have faith just as you can choose what to have faith in.

Perhaps all that is needed from me here and now is to choose to commit, to look beyond the BKs' sometimes eccentric trappings to the core of wisdom.

Perhaps.

brahma's
moon

"You see what you are"

NEW DELHI, India's capital, is the base from which I briefly explored this country during an around-the-world trip in 1977 and it's where my Toronto flight landed a couple of weeks ago. On my early-morning taxi ride in from the airport, I was charmed to find cows ambling up the expressway, just as I remembered. Despite possessing the world's largest emergent middle class, India is still India.

With a population of over eleven million, Delhi is historically eight or nine cities side by side with teeming seventeenth-century Muslim laneways to the north and broad British avenues to the south. During this stopover, I will be staying at an upscale guest house in the south. With astrologers having proclaimed October 31 an auspicious date for weddings, I, along with half of Delhi, am on my way to one, as a guest of the bride's aunt, a friend from Toronto.

The bride's parents' home—up a tree-lined driveway transformed for the evening into the Milky Way by tiny white lights—has been extended into the garden by a two-storey silk-and-canvas pavilion. Men in Western dress and women in beaded saris with jewel-encrusted gold chokers, bracelets and rings, stroll amid illuminated flower beds and fountains afloat with candles in petal boats. The bride and groom—regal in matching cream-and-white silk robes—receive their guests from a gold-and-orange enclosure, while a buffet for three hundred is served in a huge pavilion with round tables draped in yellow. This is the fifth night guests have been entertained with different menus, floral arrangments and table settings. I'm used to seeing my Toronto hostess in power suits in boardrooms. Wearing a sari, bindi and jewellery, she's as effervescent as a teenager.

It isn't until 2:00 a.m. that the ceremony begins, with bride and groom seated on cushions surrounded by a wheel of friends and relatives. Since the groom is a Bengali, this is a "mixed" wedding, officiated by priests from both cultures. Halfway through the Bengali priest's contribution, I'm surprised to hear women guests break into derisive laughter. A girl in a pale yellow sari with a flower-petal face explains: "He's saying things we're not used to hearing." She translates: "The bride must decorate herself only for her husband. When he isn't home, she must dress plainly. If she wants to visit a friend, she must ask his permission. If she tries to return to her mother's house, her mother must beat her off with a broom."

The bride is weeping copiously.

"Brides always cry," explains a matron in scarlet and gold. "They cry for months before and after the wedding. We have a whole culture built around the sadness of women over leaving their mothers to live with their mothers-in-law. There are many songs about this."

I'm offered *paan* from a silver tray—a mildly intoxicating mixture of betel nut and spices such as turmeric, pepper and cardamom, wrapped in a dewy leaf. "Are most Indian marriages still arranged?"

"Absolutely. That's the way we do things, and Indian women cry even more if they don't get married. A niece of mine had seventeen rejections in one month because she has a birthmark on her face and a bad astrological chart. She's very bitter about that, even though she has a good job working with computers. In India we're expected to fall in love with our husbands after the wedding."

The paan explodes with a taste both sweet and bracing. "And do you?"

She laughs. "It's best to try. If you're lucky you'll have a son too. From early childhood we're always telling our girls, 'You don't belong to us; you belong to your husband's family,' and pushing them away while we hold on to our sons. It may not sound very nice to you, but that's the way we were brought up."

Later during this trip an American woman, married to the eldest son of a prominent Calcutta family, will confide, "When I first met my husband's relatives, I wore a head scarf and kissed everyone's feet. I was only twenty and all I wanted was acceptance. I didn't get it. Everyone wished I would leave or die, and they worked full time on that, but I had a child my first year and had to stay put. Now a hundred people are dependent on my husband, so they pretend to accept me, but it doesn't matter any more. I don't care."

As the wedding ceremony ends, the matron in gold and scarlet shyly confesses, "I sometimes wonder what it would be like to fall in love the way they do in Western movies, but my husband is a good man who looks after me very well. In India we have a proverb: 'In bad times the family is a fortress. In good times it is a prison.'"

When I leave the party, Delhi is obliterated by a toxic yellow mix of fog, exhaust fumes and smoke from kerosene fires. As my car crawls through ghostly traffic that can be heard but not seen, a red light flares through the windshield like a bloody moon. When my driver brakes, a scrawny child of about seven flings herself at my window screaming, "No mother, no father!" Her face is dirt streaked, her hair spiky, her eyes fierce as she clings with hands like suction cups—poignant yet monstrous. My neck hairs rise: *I know you! For decades you clawed at the windows of my life, leaving dirty smudges and trailing blood from your soiled pants.* While my driver stares implacably ahead, I lower my window to give her all my change. Instantly, half a dozen other beggars hurl themselves against the car, scratching and shrieking like a frenzied multi-armed Kali. They expertly jump to safety as my driver pulls away. *So you've followed me here, have you? Is this trip to be a reprise of all the dark corners of my psyche?*

Before leaving Toronto, I spent a couple of months reading everything from travellers' guides like the Lonely Planet's *India* to the sacred Vedas, lyrically celebrating Brahma's Creation, and the Upanishads, exploring moral and metaphysical questions. Although this trip is a pilgrimage, I know that some truths are better gained indirectly, the way one catches an unexpected glimpse of oneself in a mirror while doing something mindless, such as shopping. For this reason, I intend to follow whatever path unfolds, paying equal attention to India's natural beauties as to her temples and ashrams in the belief that Spirit will find me if and when Spirit wants to. As the Upanishads verify, Brahma is everywhere: "He is invisible: he cannot be seen. He is far and he is near, he moves and he moves not, he is within all and he is outside all." He is us and we are Him. *"Tat Tvam asi"*—"Thou art That."

The invitation to the New Delhi wedding was a last-minute piece of good fortune, as is a second invitation, to Rajasthan's famous Pushkar Camel Festival, arranged by another Toronto friend. When I join the others in the group travelling in a convoy of three cars, I discover that my hosts, whom I am meeting for the first time, are treating me, along with a couple of dozen of their closest relatives and friends, to four days at Pushkar to celebrate their twentieth anniversary. That I—a stranger—am included in such an intimate event merely because we possess a mutual friend is one of those grand acts of Indian hospitality without a North American equivalent. When I express gratitude, I receive only a bemused and gracious "But it is our duty."

Nominally Indians drive on the left, like the British. I say nominally because I was in India for several days before I could be sure. Since most roads are narrow, vehicles take the centre. Where two lanes exist, the traffic weaves so incessantly that the impression of sliding across the road is more pronounced than that of moving forward. It isn't unusual to see a truck passing a car that is simultaneously passing an ox cart. It isn't unusual to see a car, speeding up the wrong lane, force an oncoming motorbike or camel cart onto the shoulder before darting back in line. Even when the highway is divided, it isn't unusual for a car to shoot across the boulevard to overtake a herd of cattle. A hill? A curve? Just apply horn and brakes.

The one saving feature is that everyone seems to be playing by the same rules, which to the outsider look like no rules at all. As the fumes of an oncoming truck fog our windshield, a space to the left opens, allowing our driver to squeeze back in line for, say, ten seconds before attempting the next leap of faith. Though the roadkill may be proportionally no higher than on a holiday weekend in North America, the victims tend to be larger and messier: pigs, dogs, gaily decorated transports lying on their backs with wheels spinning, bleeding oil and perhaps a ton of rice. Our youthful chauffeur has the reflexes of a Pan Am racer and the instincts of a Rajput warrior: he loves the game like blood sport.

During Pushkar's Camel Festival, held annually at November full moon, this town of thirteen thousand swells to two hundred thousand. To handle the influx, the tourist bureau erects a mammoth tent city on the outskirts of the fairgrounds. My hosts have arranged for their private village to be pitched in a nest of stony hills fringing Pushkar. Each tent is as comfortable as a small bungalow, with electric lights, single cots and a multitude of flaps to let nature in or to keep it out. These are supplemented by a dining tent and a bold yellow-and-blue latrine with sinks, showers and flush toilets. An abandoned Hindu temple marks the entrance to our camp, and a tribe of monkeys, who use the roadside chai stalls as trampolines, patrol our borders.

To my embarrassment, the dry cough that began in Rishikesh has developed into laryngitis. While blaming Delhi's horrendous pollution and Pushkar's dust, I probe my mind for deeper answers. My throat is the weakest part of my anatomy—the fuse that blows, forcing me to pay attention to things I might otherwise ignore. I first made this connection when I discovered that every time I finished a book, I caught laryngitis. Loss of book = loss of voice. Still, I haven't had so much as a cold in five years. *Why this? Why now?* An actor once told me that he found a character when he found the voice: did it issue from the chest or belly or diaphragm or sinuses? Were the lips shaping it flaccid or tight? With his breath under control and his mouth held just so, his body fell into line, bringing into focus the character who owned it. Deprived of my voice, I feel my persona dissolve like a papier-mâché effigy in a storm, leaving . . . what? As I gasp, wheeze and mime to my companions across what I hope to be a germ-free trench, I'm forced to realize how much my self-worth has always rested on my ability to perform, an activity dependent on my voice. In Rishikesh I strove to give up words. Now they've abandoned me.

I dream that I am sitting cross-legged by the Ganges, meditating, with a white stone in my mouth. When I try to spit it out, I hear my guru's voice: "Be patient. It will hatch."

Even one camel is a snorting, sliding oxymoron—graceful yet ungainly, dignified yet silly, obliging yet contemptuous. Pushkar has twenty thousand of them tarted up with red and yellow pompons, tinsel chains, elaborate tattoos and dangling silver earrings. Add herds of exquisitely groomed horses along with golden-hoofed Brahma bulls sporting silver collars the size of Elizabethan ruffs and delicate chains around their well-turned ankles.

We wander the fairgrounds over desert hillocks stretching from Pushkar Lake to distant ridges. Rajput men act out their warrior past in their confident stride, the proud shrug of their shoulders, the scimitar curve of their moustaches and their fluorescent turbans glowing like orange, raspberry and lime sherbets. Their women travel in flocks, plumaged in the loose-fitting pants and tunic called the *salwar kameez*, sliding their see-through veils across their faces when strangers glance.

"That's not shyness, that's because their men are present," one of my female companions confides. "It's their husbands and brothers they're really worried about, not strangers."

Out of a jumble of striped and tasselled tents, merchants sell camel saddles, bridles, wooden pitchforks, leather whips and cowbells. Towers of brass pots compete with bolts of hand-loomed fabrics in jellybean colours. Vendors sell sticky sweets twisted like pretzels or steamy curds stirred in giant vats. Squatting barbers shave faces, while dentists, surrounded by grinning false teeth and the fearsome tools of their trade, yank decayed molars.

In my Indian family I sort out who belongs to whom, not just couples but bloodlines, feeling the criss-cross of their relationships containing the group like a finely woven hammock. If I had a voice to question them, they might tell me of their differences, of the knots and snags in the ties that bind, but all I experience in my silent world is the strength of their connections.

My own family was something I wore like a hair shirt. Given my father's servitude to a lousy shift job and my mother's slavery to stove and ironing board, my older sister and I grew up feeling like supplicants in a dangerous world. What my mother craved for her sacrifice were good report cards to show off to the neighbours, while my sexually abusive father demanded services more sinister. To me families are killing fields. Yet I know I'm allowing these deeply buried thoughts to surface here and now because I do feel safe. I've come to India for an assault on the heart and I'm getting it. Melting into the arms of my Indian family, I gratefully accept the flow of kindnesses I can't possibly repay as we float from place to place, breaking into smaller groups, then reassembling. It's fun to forget my identity and to think in terms of the group, to submerge.

Once again I dream I am meditating by the Ganges with a stone in my mouth. This time, when I open my lips to complain about the dryness of my throat, a golden coin falls out. "See? Your silence is golden!" mocks my guru.

Wearing metres of hand-dyed Rajasthan cloth as turbans and shawls, we pile into three camel carts for a circuit of the fairgrounds, past jugglers, minstrels, snake charmers, acrobats and a child walking a tightrope with pails on her feet. In the rays of a dying sun, temple bells ring out, women harvest camel "bullets" for the cooking fires that have begun to explode from hillsides. With only one mirror in camp to remind me of who I am, I take my self-image from those around me. The foreigners at the fair have begun to look too white, too gauche. I see them in their shorts and baseball caps photographing each other on camels. Weird.

It's typical of India that this event, appearing to be a camel and cattle market, is actually a religious festival. According to myth, Pushkar, known as the Pilgrim City, was founded by Lord Brahma, who descends from heaven each year during the October–November full moon. Curiously, though Lord Brahma is Hinduism's supreme deity, Pushkar has the only shrine dedicated to him. As we approach his fourteenth-century temple, the ambush on our senses begins with the crush of devotees, the clamour of beggars, the shouts of vendors selling offerings. As the religion of 80 per cent of Indian's one billion population, Hinduism possesses no founder, no single authoritative text or formal structure and accepts no converts. Called *Sanatana Dharma*, or the Eternal Truth, by its adherents, it offers three paths to the Divine—wisdom (*jnana*), good works (*karma*) and devotion (*bhakti*). It's bhakti that brings Hindus by the millions to their temples to prostrate themselves before their gods, to bathe them, perfume them, dress them, sing to them, weep before them, thank them for past favours and plead for future mercies.

As I shed my sandals, adding the coolness of marble to the sensuous mix of incense, camphor and sweat, of bells and chanting, I remember the boredom with which I as a child attended church twice on Sunday, primly decked out in hat and gloves, kicking the pew ahead with my scuffed shoes as loudly as I dared, flanked by my sister, my mother and my father, smelling innocently of talcum powder. The United Church where I was confirmed went to considerable trouble to squeeze the emotion out of worship, the way our family Bible could be counted on to press the juices from the leaves and flowers I slipped beween its pages each fall for my natural science charts. Now as I enter this temple courtyard, old women clap and chant around a holy basil tree, an ancient rite deriving from worship of Devi, the earth mother who predates the power triumvirate of Brahma/Vishnu/Shiva.

"Indian women go to the temples as their club," comments the elegant matriarch with whom I've been sharing a tent. "It's the only place they can go without their fathers and husbands and brothers and sons telling them they shouldn't. Their daughters-in-law probably want them out of the house and they want to be out of the house."

As I gaze into their rapturous upturned faces I remember the eagerness with which my mother also fled to church, how ardently she sang the hymns, head thrown back so far that she threatened to dislodge her hat from its pins—"What a Friend We have in Jesus," "Rock of Ages"—the songs she rendered with equal fervour while changing sheets, peeling potatoes and running clothes through her wringer, sailing out of her prison on a treble clef.

A silver turtle on a marble floor embedded with silver coins guards Brahma's temple, while peacocks, symbolic of Brahma's daughter and consort, Saraswati, decorate its walls. Ahead I see a saucy red spire like an upthrust tongue. Though I attempt an orderly progression through outer

shrines to inner ones, I grow confused, which is just as
well since non-Hindus are banned from the most sacred
altars, and I'm never sure where that prohibition begins.
For me the archetypal excitement lies in the totality of
the experience—the thrill of this high-decibel chaos commanding all the senses. Unlike our slender gothic spires
shooting like rocket ships to heaven, the domes of Hindu
temples slowly spiral upward with their burden of gods
and demons, flowers, birds, humans and other animals, in
postures sacred and profane, more Chaucer than St. Thomas Aquinas. Life unedited. The unexpurgated version.

I rejoin my group at the ghats on Pushkar Lake, where
a few dozen pilgrims bathe in the twilight waters afloat
with lighted leaf boats like swarms of fireflies. Tomorrow
night at full moon two hundred thousand of them will
crowd into this lake, waiting for Brahma to descend for
his annual swim, washing away their bad karma.

The following day, a group of us drive eleven kilometres
through Snake Mountains to the city of Ajmer to visit
India's holiest Muslim shrine, containing the tomb of
Mu'inuddin Chishti, a thirteenth-century Sufi saint. With
130 million adherents, Islam is India's second-largest religion, and this Muslim population is the world's third
largest. In the eighth century, Islam—meaning submission
to God's will—was imposed on India through invasion.

Later it attracted Hindus eager to escape the caste system, especially the Untouchables, without caste, who still make up about one-fifth of India's population.

Once again, as we deposit our shoes we enter an electric forcefield with tension escalating the higher we climb toward the saint's tomb. A revered teacher, Chishti was credited with many miracles, and it is the yearning for such a boon that lures throngs of disciples to his tomb. In a courtyard of striped awnings strung between old trees, musicians known as *qawwali* sing poetry accompanied by drums and the harmonium while male disciples clap and sway. As the mystical wing of Islam, Sufism stresses personal experience of God over the law and ecstasy over ritual. If someone falls into a trance, the singers are supposed to repeat the last couplet until he recovers; if he dies they must repeat it until his corpse is buried.

At the tomb's entrance, bodies pressed flat against mine propel me forward. The crush in the small marble room is alarming. The *mullah*, or priest, squatting at one corner of the tomb hooks his scarf around my neck, yanks me toward him and, smothering my face in his robes, shouts a prayer into my ear. I give him a 100 rupee note. Tightening his scarf, he demands another 100. I give him 50. With a snort, he unhitches his scarf and thrusts me back into the stream like an undersize fish. While I'm still unbalanced, an anonymous hand attempts to unzip my purse. As I hug it to my chest, the mullah guarding the tomb's second corner hooks me, then prays over me. When

I give him 50 rupees, he demands 100. I refuse. He insists. I refuse. He too thrusts me back into the crowd. Though forced to continue around the tomb, I manage to avoid the mullahs at the other two corners. Once outside, I check for the reassuring textures of brocade (my wallet), suede (my camera) and linen (my moneybelt). It's then I discover that one of our group—a Christian who purchased a platter of petals in honour of her first visit to a mosque—was robbed of 5,000 rupees. As she lifted the platter onto the tomb's altar, her bag was slashed by thieves who are said to conceal razors under their fingernails.

Though this is my first unpleasant experience at an Indian place of worship, it won't be my last, convincing me that religion and spirituality don't necessarily mix and, in fact, may be opposed.

On our final evening, we gather after dark for a spectacular display of fireworks cut short when a nearby camp of tribesmen grows hysterical thinking we are shooting at them. Retiring to our bonfire, we sing songs, tell stories and offer toasts with my Indian friends unselfconsciously sliding in and out of English, as they always have. Even I join in, having recovered my voice just in time to thank them for the cornucopia of gifts that they have showered upon me. Our host, wearing a blue sweatsuit, white running shoes and a turban, is bent over a big-bellied pot, which he beats flat-handed like a drum, comfortable inside his own skin and within two cultures, joyful to be sharing his good fortune with good friends.

Taking my hand, a woman urges, "Come with me." She leads me down an aisle of tents to the abandoned temple beside a ruined brick farmhouse. "This is a sacred place. A very holy old man died here, and an old woman prays here every day." Now she leads me into the courtyard of the farmhouse. "At Pushkar you've been brought to exactly the right place at the right time for your healing. India has only one temple to Brahma because Brahma is the only Hindu god who committed incest and this is the night he clears karma, including his own." She points into a brackish well. "Here is your past."

I peer into the inky hole spiralling down into the earth, *into the fierce eye of the dirt-streaked, spiky-haired child who threw herself at my car shrieking, "No mother, no father!"*

She points upward to the moon wearing an iridescent halo.

"That is your future. . . . A voice in my head has told me I must tell you this."

It is then I realize that while I've been dreaming India, India has been dreaming me.

chakras

"It's the space between the spokes
that makes the wheel"

THOUGH I'VE BEEN travelling in the storybook state of Rajasthan since Pushkar and Mount Abu, it isn't till I head northwest by bus toward Jodhpur that I feel myself to be entering this legendary Land of Kings with its fabulous desert fiefdoms, historic forts and Rajput warriors. Now, as the landscape outside my window flattens, cracks and bleaches from brown to dull red and then to beige, the fluorescent pink and orange robes of women balancing water jugs and the scarlet turbans of men driving ox carts seem to burst from the fissures of this impossible garden like exotic cactus blossoms. Despite animal pens made of upright granite slabs, the area's few goats and sheep roam free, grazing on the yellow growth bordering the gravelly skeletons of rivers or cadging leaves from carob trees resembling pale green umbrellas. And, at intervals, the strident call of the wild peacock, once used as a royal guard dog, screeches like chalk scraped across the flinty face of this monochromatic land.

Because I was taught the British version of India as one nation bound by arteries of steel and an English-speaking bureaucracy, I'm surprised by how many of its citizens shun that collective word *Indian*, referring to their state as their country, to themselves as foreigners and to outsiders as double foreigners. It's in Rajasthan that the evidence for historical conflict in this nation with fifteen official languages from over sixteen hundred is most indelibly stamped on the land. Clifftop fortresses jutting out of the desert like tigers' teeth remind the traveller that the inhabitants of neighbouring cities now appearing as interchangeable bus stops might have spent three hundred years hacking off one another's heads. Yet somewhere in my six-hour ride to Jodhpur, jouncing over potholes on a listing bus with broken seats, I realize that whatever anxiety fuelled my Indian trip, then shadowed me from Rishikesh through Mount Abu and Pushkar, has now evaporated. I feel carefree and content, living fully in this moment and looking forward to the next, confident that an inner process has begun and will continue, no matter where I wander.

My centuries-old hotel is located amid the daunting twist of blue-painted Cubist houses and laneways that have earned Jodhpur the name of the Blue City. From the hotel's rooftop restaurant I look up into Meherangarh Fort, rising like the prow of an iron battleship over Jodhpur's azure waves. As I drink chai under an umbrella on this mid-November evening, clouds gradually pack up the heavens like a delicate Delft bowl while the setting sun torpedoes the red fort, sinking it into a dark sea. Instead of growing quieter, the city seems to find its voice. Hindi matinee music from a local café acquires a chorus of baying dogs, to which is added the Muslim call to prayer and a recording of Celine Dion singing "Life Will Go On" from *Titanic*.

Though the music eventually winds down, the dogs and the Muslims alternate until morning. I meditate for half an hour, sinking slowly through this disonant layer to rest peacefully like a clam in the silty depths of Jodhpur's blue world.

At sunrise I wander the cerulean alleyways of the old city—blue walls, blue balconies, blue arches, blue gateways, blue latticework, blue shutters—contained within a sixteenth-century wall. At every puddle and pump a half-dozen people line up to wash and shave. In one corner shop women embroider the jesters' slippers for which the city is famous; early-rising merchants sweep dust onto their neighbours' front steps, and a man with a cart harvests cow dung.

A sassy pack of schoolboys demand, "Where are you from?" When I tell them Canada, they shout, "Capital city Ottawa!" "Prime Minister Jean Chrétien!" "English or French? Hello! Bonjour!" Then a colossal boner—

"Madonna? Are you Madonna! Autograph, autograph!"

Each kid reveals himself to be a practised con with a specialty: "I'm collecting foreign money for my coin collection." "Do you have a pen? I need one to write my exams or I will fail." "Take my picture! Take my picture!" Then, "Send it to me, oh please! I need ten copies. I want to enter a contest." And "Come home with me. Take a picture of my mother and my grandmother!" "Do you have a baseball cap?"

An old man with skin the colour and texture of flypaper gestures from his balcony. Mistaking his vigour for hostility, I back away, only to discover he's directing me to a stone staircase leading up to the fort. The climb is exhilarating, offering stunning views over Jodhpur's flat-roofed blue houses and up to the majestic rust-red battleship. I am scaling the prow when I notice that I'm surrounded by pariah dogs. Aggressive from a night's carousing, they block my path, throats growling, lips curled, yellow fangs glistening. Vividly recalling the slashed leg of a Mount Abu woman who was attacked while hiking, I freeze, silently repeating, "Om Shanti." I don't know whether it calms the dogs but it calms me. They are no longer snarling but neither have they given way. This situation has become a matter of saving face—mine from the fangs of the alpha dog and his from the scorn of the pack should he back down. Shifting my eyes in search of the circle's weakest link, I see a female dog with dugs hanging like cow udders from providing so many feasts. Do I merely imagine that she has a friendly face? As I slink submissively toward her, the alpha dog barks ferociously, which I hope to be a substitute for leaping. It is. Sliding behind a clump of bushes, I break canine eye contact, then cautiously loop back to the path.

Towering above me on its 125-metre bulwark of turreted red sandstone, Meherangarh Fort looks like what it is: a lethal engine of war. Founded in 1459 by Roa Jodha of the kingdom of Marwar, meaning Land of Death, it contains a temple to the state's patron goddess, Durga, slayer of demons, who holds weapons in her ten hands and rides to battle on a tiger. To assure the goddess's co-operation, Maharaja Jodha—who gave his name both to the city and to the baggy-thighed breeches designed for riding horses—was said to have ordered the bloody sacrifice of his seventeen sons and fifty-two daughters while he looked on. Then, as a more practical measure, he interred his architect alive to protect the secrets of his defences.

The fort's walls are also marked by fifteen vermilion handprints of the widows of Maharaja Man Singh, who leaped onto his funeral pyre in 1843. Glorified by sacred Hindu epics, *sati* is a two-thousand-year-old tradition in which women immolate themselves out of love or pride or honour. The sacrifice of the mythical Sati, who gave the horrific custom its name, was for something as trivial as her father's social snub of her husband, Lord Shiva. With Sita, wife of the god-hero Rama, it was to prove her purity to her doubting husband after being kidnapped by his enemies. Inspired through such myths, Indian women have danced like moths around their husbands' pyres, sometimes leaping, sometimes being shoved, drugged and tied down. Among the volunteers, such a death often seemed preferable to being cast out and forced to beg for daring to survive their husbands. Though the British banned this custom in 1820, these highly revered vermilion handprints were made twenty years *after* the ban, and even today sati assures a glorious martyrdom.

On September 4, 1987, hundreds of frenzied spectators in the village of Deorala watched Roop Kanwar, an eighteen-year-old Rajput bride of seven months, burn on her husband's pyre. According to some eyewitnesses, the deeply religious Roop led a procession of her relatives to the pyre, then tranquilly climbed upon it. Cradling her husband's corpse on her lap, she chanted hymns while her brother-in-law applied the torch, villagers fed the flames with pails of *ghee*, or clarified butter, and sword-wielding Rajput youths marched clockwise singing, "*Sati mata ki jai*" (Glory to the Sati mother). According to other accounts, Roop—who was having an affair with a Jaipur man during her brief marriage—was dragged screaming to the pyre, forced upon it, then prevented from escape by a ring of sword-wielding Rajput youths. Undisputed is the fact that during the two weeks following Roop Kanwar's death, five hundred thousand people, including political leaders, came to worship at her shrine, from which the village of Deorala still profits.

The sati tradition finds a sordid epilogue in "stove accidents" in which brides with unsatisfactory dowries are dispatched with spilled kerosene and a lighted match, often by female in-laws with or without a husband's consent. Though such incidents are likely to be grossly underreported, in New Delhi alone official figures for 1983 placed the toll at 690. "Stove accidents" are also the way wives commit suicide to frame their in-laws as revenge for maltreatment. The hideousness of such a choice testifies not only to the cruel inequalities within the Indian domestic system but also to the romanticism still surrounding death by fire for Indian women.

As I place my hands over the small vermilion prints on the wall of Fort Meherangarh, trying to imagine the emotions of the fifteen women who made them, a shadow causes me to look up. Perched overhead, I see one of the buzzards that form a permanent black cloud draped like Dracula's cape over this fort with its walls the colour of dried blood, where historically they've dined so well. Continuing up the Hill of Strife, I come to a series of palaces and courtyards and then to the ramparts leading me back to the ship's prow. While I inch my way along the headland with sheer plunges on either side, the buzzards continue to spiral overhead, as ugly as hangmen, now joined by the jet fighters guarding India's Pakistan border.

The primal forces I'm experiencing here—the fierce wind, the giddy drop, the raw physicallity of Rajasthan's desert landscape and the elemental emotions fuelling its history—remind me of the Indian energy model with its seven chakras, externalizing as the seven glands of the endocrine system and controlling our basic drives. The root chakra, located at the base of the spine, manifests as the adrenals and governs the will to survive. The sex chakra externalizes as the gonads, controls the reproductive organs and governs the sex drive. The navel chakra externalizes as the pancreas, controls the digestive system and governs the power drive. The heart chakra manifests as the thymus, controls the circulatory and immune systems and is central to issues of love. The throat chakra externalizes as the thyroid gland, governs the lungs and is the source of creativity. The brow chakra between the eyes externalizes as the pituitary gland and governs the nervous system. The crown chakra at the top of the head manifests as the pineal gland and is the seat of consciousness through which humans contact the Divine.

As a Hindu matures, he or she is expected to shift energy and focus from the lower chakras to the higher ones, though individuals as well as societies often become fixated upon one stage or another. In journeying through historic Rajasthan, I'm revisiting chakras one to three—survival, sex and power. These are also the issues that govern American pop culture from the cult of the Wild West through James Bond, *The Godfather*, *Rambo*, *Star Wars* and *The Terminator*. It's a world where survival is always threatened, where narcissism reigns and where love equals lust, jealousy and obsession. This is certainly not the world I came to India to find, but it's one I recognize from once having lived through it myself: *the laurels that had to be won, the affairs to die for.* Though I don't begrudge my younger self her dramas, I'm grateful that the vermilion handprints no longer fit, that the warrior armour is too tight and the weapons too foolishly cumbersome. I'm grateful that the emptiness of such values as a lifetime pursuit has forced me to search for something better, deeper and—

"—even more dynamic."

The hand appears like a crab over the edge of the cliff, followed by the peppery head and grasshopper limbs of my guru. Though he seems to have climbed vertically up the rock face, his breathing is even as he continues: "A culture clings to adolescent passion when it doesn't have anything better to put in its place. Since you in the West equate spirituality with old age, impotence and a dying religion, it must seem like a very poor consolation prize."

"I wondered where you'd disappeared to!"

"You didn't need me, or at least you thought you didn't, which amounts to the same thing."

"What makes you believe I need you now?"

He chuckles. "You were sounding so pompous that I thought I better help out. If there's lecturing to do, best leave it to me." Squatting beside me, he arranges his lungi, the same rusty red as the rocks. "Where was I?"

"You were saying, I think, that in the West we confuse spirituality with religion, which has lost its formal power—"

"—entirely ignoring the biological spiritual power-house locked inside each one of us."

"I suppose you're referring to kundalini energy."

"Of course. By redirecting kundalini to spiritual use, Buddhists experience what they call *nirvana* and Hindus *samadhi*—an explosion of bliss far surpassing anything sex has to offer."

"Rather like a spiritual orgasm?" I tease him.

"With far more staying power!" he snaps back. "The late Ramakrishna of Calcutta spent six months in ecstatic union with the Divine. Since he had no detectable heartbeat or breath, his glowing face offered the only clue that he was even alive. Of course, this was the culmination of years of disciplined practice. For the foolhardy, unleashing the power of the third eye can be more dangerous than giving vent to an uncontrolled sex drive."

"The third eye? To Westerners that sounds like something used in a witch's hex."

My guru throws up his hands, scattering a flock of sparrows. "Perhaps that's because they're unaware that the human head actually does contain a hidden inner eye. When your nineteenth-century scientists dissected the pineal gland, they found that structurally it is a light-sensitive organ. It developed on the head of the reptilian creature that evolved into man, gradually sinking to its present location just above the brain stem. The pineal secretes hormones and neurotransmitters like melatonin and serotonin that control sexual maturation and sleep cycles including dreaming. It's also the brain centre most affected by drugs such as LSD and Prozac."

As I watch a returning sparrow resettle in my guru's wiry red hair, apparently mistaking it for a nest, I suddenly remember: "It was the pineal that seventeenth-century philosopher René Descartes thought was the centre of consciousness through which mind and body interact. Though that always raised a giggle in Philosophy 101, maybe Descartes was right."

Nodding, my guru continues: "It's not surprising when geniuses of the East and West come to the same conclusion, since both employ the same method. You call it intuition and don't understand how it works because you don't have a science of the mind, which is why you produce brain surgeons while we produce sages."

"What about psychology and psychiatry? They're sciences of the mind."

"Just the behavioural mind. Until your scientists put together biology, psychology, philosophy and religion, they'll never understand karma , kundalini or the third eye because these ideas are woven from the wisdom of all four disciplines. Even then, this is wisdom best acquired through direct inner experience." He fixes me with his yellow-flecked brown eyes. "Now that you've been meditating regularly, what's your personal experience of kundalini?"

Though caught off guard, I reply, "Sometimes I'm aware of heat rushes up the spine and an inner hum like a field of crickets—it's white noise, energizing and pleasant. Though both started years ago with the practice of yoga, recently they've intensified."

My guru continues like an examining doctor: "What about other signs, like radiant light, expanded consciousness, mystical experience, creativity, sharpened insight and genius?"

"In modest amounts. Except the genius."

He laughs: "All in good time—perhaps in another life! As you know, the awakening of kundalini may be gradual, through natural maturation, or explosive." Pulling a book entitled *Kundalini* from the folds of his lungi, he turns to the first page. "This is how the late Gopi Krishna of Kashmir, then thirty-four, describes his awakening after meditating for seventeen years:

> One morning during the Christmas of 1937 . . . I was meditating with my face toward the window on the east through which the first grey streaks of the slowly brightening dawn fell into the room. Long practice had accustomed me to sit in the same posture for hours at a time without the least discomfort, and I sat breathing slowly and rhythmically, my attention drawn toward the crown of my head, contemplating an imaginary lotus in full bloom, radiating light. I suddenly felt a strange sensation below the base of my spine. . . . I had read glowing accounts, written by learned men, of great benefits resulting

from concentration, and of the miraculous powers acquired by yogis through such exercises. . . . With a roar like that of a waterfall, I felt a stream of liquid light entering my brain. . . . The illumination grew brighter and brighter, the roaring louder. I experienced a rocking sensation and then felt myself slipping out of my body, entirely enveloped in a halo of light. . . . I felt the point of consciousness that was myself growing wider, surrounded by waves of light. . . . I was no longer myself, or to be more accurate, no longer as I knew myself to be, a small point of awareness confined in a body, but instead was a vast circle of consciousness in which the body was but a point, bathed in light and in a state of exaltation and happiness impossible to describe.

My guru has been pacing our narrow headland with the sparrow still camped in his hair, eyes glued to his book and gesturing expansively. Now, pausing with his toes balanced on the rock lip and the rest of him dangling in space, he exclaims: "Aha! I can see by the anxious look on your face that I've been successful in suggesting that unleashing the power of kundalini is like teetering on a precipice." Again squatting beside me but still with his rump overhanging, he continues. "If you read on, you'll discover that Gopi Krishna at first found the force he'd wakened a torture to live with. That's because it wasn't a gift of illumination from a personal god but the kick-start of a dynamic biological process that, like atomic energy, can be destructive or beneficial. Second, while he found himself possessed of unexpected creative powers that inspired him to write poetry in languages he didn't even know, he regarded this as just a by-product of radical inner and outer transformation leading to prolonged periods of radiance."

Handing me the book, my guru adds, "Gopi Krishna came to believe that mankind is slowly evolving toward a sublime state of consciousness that he himself had only glimpsed. Though that idea of progress is more Western than Eastern, I certainly hope that he's—"

My guru disappears in mid-sentence, leaving a startled sparrow sputtering in space. Whether he dissolved or tumbled over the cliff I don't know, and I refuse either to look down or to worry about it.

Six hours by bus northwest of Jodhpur, another fortification arises like a heap of shimmering pirates' gold. Whereas Jodhpur's red fort is all sharp angles, Jaisalmer's twelfth-century golden one has the sturdy, rounded turrets that kids love to build with sand pails. Whereas Jodhpur's is a museum, this one is inhabited. I wander through its maze of crooked lanes sprouting hotels and gingerbread mansions called *havelis*, like buds of a desert cactus. The honied stones smother the sound of my footsteps, creating a spell of deep peace—an ironic peace since Fort Jaisalmer must hold the medieval equivalent of the Guinness record for mass suicides. When a blockade toward the end of the thirteenth century paralyzed this community, Mulraj II and his brother Ratansi requested that their wives become sati, and at dawn the two queens were said to have dutifully led *twenty-four thousand* women in bridal finery toward the flames. Because no pyre could accommodate them all, many were slaughtered by their husbands, fathers and brothers, who then rode to battle smeared with their blood and ashes. Unlike at Jodhpur, where history is frozen at its most brutish hour, at Jaisalmer residents have spread a patina of twentieth-century normalcy over their fort's savage past: children chant rhymes, merchants hawk dhurries, beauty parlours offer massages. Through an open door I even spot a goat watching TV. No buzzards fly overhead.

From my table at a rooftop restaurant on the fort's main square, I gaze at the seven-storey royal palace, also of golden sandstone. With its fretwork balconies and lacy domes, it resembles a Victorian birdcage—not just to me but to the neighbourhood sparrows and pigeons. At a magical moment each evening, hundreds swoop from the clouds to nest, like the demonic flocks in Alfred Hitchcock's film *The Birds*, ruffling the air with their twittering long after sunset. When the cracks and crevices are filled, latecomers queue along ledges and domes till the palace is outlined in feathers, yet another unintended Hitchcock homage since this structure has a silhouette roughly like the Norman Bates house in *Psycho*.

A man in his thirties with a boyish face, round glasses and thinning blond hair asks to share my table. His name is David, he's from Minnesota, and a remarkably cheerful fellow, given the bad luck he's been trailing like Job's cloak. After he glances through the menu, he confides, with the quick ease and broad strokes that experienced travellers tell their tales, "I'm supposed to be with my brother, but we had a terrible row. I wanted to sink down into places and get to know them, but he wanted to keep moving. After we split I caught a viral infection while hiking in Nepal and had to be airlifted out by helicopter. Then the day I was discharged from hospital I was bitten by a dog. That's meant rabies shots a couple of weeks apart."

"How have you found the Indian medical system?"

David rolls his eyes. "I've been in dispensaries where pigeons flew in and out and nobody seemed to notice. In the hospital here in Jaisalmer, a cow was wandering through the halls."

"Do you have health insurance?"

"No, but that didn't matter. I did have to pay for the helicopter—$400 U.S. for twenty minutes—but everything else was free or close to it. It's in the States, where medical treatment is prohibitive, that you need insurance. In India the best defence is a ticket home."

"Perhaps, but under certain circumstances I'd come to India for healing, especially if the Western medical system had given up on me."

"It would take a lot of convincing to get me to do that!" he says with a grin.

"Something odd happened to me when I was in India twenty-two years ago. It's one of the reasons I returned."

David looks at me expectantly.

"It's quite a long story. . . ."

He signals the waiter. "Good. The chef here takes all evening."

We place our orders and I begin my chronicle: "It was my last full day in India and I wanted to see more of the countryside before leaving, so I picked a local train running at random out of Calcutta. A few stops down the line, at a town called Chandernagore, I glimpsed what looked like a festival in progress. Unfortunately, by then we were already pulling out of the station. For weeks I'd been watching locals all across the Middle East jump on and off moving vehicles. Without thinking, I leaped for the platform just as the train was gathering speed. Even in midflight I realized how stupid I'd been, and before I hit I was already praying: 'Not here! I can't be injured so far from home!'

"The next thing I heard was the sound of something overripe and pulpy smashing against concrete: my head. Yet even as I lay in shock, with a ring of sober Indian faces gazing down at me, my strongest emotion was one of embarrassment. Forcing myself to stand—amazed that I could—I assured everyone I was fine, then stumbled out of sight into a banana grove where I collapsed, still mindlessly repeating what had become my mantra: 'I am well. I am not injured.'

"About an hour later I awoke, surrounded by half a dozen giggling children who were daring each other to touch my blond hair, reminding me of Gulliver among the Lilliputians. Again I managed to stand, though my right side was too injured for me to straighten up. My right leg was scraped from thigh to ankle, my right arm was bleeding, and I had a plum-size lump on the back of my head. Despite my pain, I kept repeating, 'I am well. I am not injured,' as I willed myself to walk.

"A procession of young men was hauling a twenty-metre goddess down to the water with the intention of hacking her up and dumping her in, as part of a religious ritual. Though I should have gone directly back to the train station, I followed them, almost in a trance. After that, I was carried along by the crowd to a temple where dignitaries were conducting a ceremony. Probably because I was the only foreigner, I was propelled up onto a platform chair. Though I still couldn't straighten, by now I was so detached, so swallowed in euphoria, that I hardly noticed. During the speeches I could see members of the audience staring to one side of the dais. The silken draperies framing the stage had caught fire. Half a dozen boys started beating out the flames with their bodies. Though we were soon framed on three sides with fire, nobody screamed, nobody moved, nobody tried to escape. In fact, nobody could. With thousands of people pouring in from the station, the bodies around the platform were packed solid.

"Against all odds, the youths managed to smother the flames. Now, when I tried to return to the station, I could only move with the crowd rushing from it. For hours I tried to travel five blocks, only to be swirled backward by the human river. Half of Calcutta seemed to be here, shoulder to shoulder and thigh to thigh. The streets were unpaved, about four lanes wide, and thick with bodies. Over my shoulder I saw a fleet of three-storey goddesses, outlined in blinking white lights and mounted on flatbed trucks, coming my way. No question of watching the parade. I *was* the parade! Along with everyone else I had to keep walking at the same stately pace, arms and legs rising and falling in unison. To go faster was impossible. To stop or to slip meant being crushed. I doubt any North American crowd could have stood the tension without imploding, but by now I was a will-less part of the human flow. Then, a few minutes before midnight, the crowd impulsively surged back to the station, pitching me onto the last train to Calcutta. An hour or so later, I was stepping out of my cab on the unlit street in front of my hotel. All of a sudden I had the powerful urge to look down, as if someone were tugging on my skirt. Just under my foot yawned an open manhole somewhat inkier than the rest of the road!

"Next morning I had trouble remembering where I was. When I finally did, I began exploring my arms and legs, hoping I'd be able to crawl out of bed. Everything seemed in working order. In fact, I was pain-free. More remarkably, I had no bruises or abrasions. The bloody scrape from thigh to ankle had disappeared, along with the cut to my right arm. My only souvenir was a tiny scab where the lump on my head used to be."

As I pause to accept a lassi made of yogurt from the waitress, David carefully inquires, "Are you sure you were as injured as you thought?"

I shrug. "It's a long time ago now, but I certainly examined all that at the time. I do remember that the colour was scraped off my shoes and my skirt was ruined—the fabric had been burned right through. It was quite a full skirt in a bright print, but I was embarrassed to think I'd wandered around all day in it."

"So what are you saying—that you experienced some kind of faith healing?"

"Not in the Western sense of the laying on of hands. At that time I didn't know anything about energy fields or energy healing, but now I believe that the shock of the accident, plus the euphoria generated by the crowd, put me into an altered state that allowed for deep healing on a cellular level."

David's guarded face breaks into a grin. "If I were back in Minnesota I'd have trouble accepting that, but I had a weird experience in Nepal, too. All the time I was delirious I had the powerful feeling that a monk was sitting by my bed, even though I couldn't actually see anyone. I'd quarrelled with my brother, and I'd nearly died, but I never felt happier, and some of that feeling has stayed with me. I'm convinced now that things happen in India that don't happen anywhere else. "

What has lured me and most other travellers to Jaisalmer is the desire for a camel safari into the Thar desert. Safari-leader L. N. Bissa, also known as Mr. Desert, is an imposing figure with deep-set blue-green eyes, a glossy black beard and a sweeping moustache. He won his title in a government-sponsored beauty contest in 1988 for the élan with which he wore tribal dress, and when he won twice more, he was promoted to Mr. Desert Emeritus. By then he was also a poster boy for Jaisalmer cigarettes, India's version of the Marlboro Man.

Because of last-minute doubts over my ability to endure desert heat and to handle a camel, I reluctantly sign up for a half-day safari instead of the overnight one. At two in the afternoon eight of us set out in two jeeps—a preppie couple in Gap shorts and Banana Republic hats and five flower children, bareheaded and barefoot with dreadlocks, skimpy clothes, tattoos and anklets. After two hours of jouncing over flat, arid terrain with patches of sagebrush and a few thorny cactuses, we come to a spot no different from any other, except that it contains a troop of turbaned tribesmen with our camels, already saddled and loaded.

My driver, a cheerful, weathered man named Ishak, reassures me: "Babaloo is a happy camel." Though I'm lightly clad in T-shirt, cotton pants, sandals and wide-brimmed sun hat, hoisting me onto Babaloo's cushioned saddle takes only a little less effort than seating a medieval knight in full armour. When Babaloo stands, haunches first, I find myself looking down a slope as acute as on any roller coaster and quickly learn the use of the saddle horn for clutching. After Ishak adjusts my stirrups, he hands me the rope reins and we're off, first at a walk and then a trot.

Fifteen minutes later, I've grown used to the peculiar sliding gait of my beast with its skinny legs working as if by elastic bands, ending in splayed hooves with pulpy centres that sink into the sand, providing traction like high-end Nikes. The sun is beginning to hunker down for the night; a soft breeze blows; Babaloo is, as advertised, a happy camel, and the preppie couple are slower than I am.

During the next couple of hours we travel over pools of yellow grass grazed by stray goats and puddles of sand shaded by trees stunted from their struggles with the niggardly soil. Occasionally someone shouts, "Howrah!" sharply whipping his camel into a trot, causing a chain reaction. By now I know I'm the only one returning by jeep after dinner with Mr. Desert instead of staying overnight, to the disappointment of both myself and Ishak, who will be scratched along with Babaloo.

We stop for dinner on an exquisite stretch of *café au lait* sand that deepens to cappuccino as it ripples in shifting peaks and valleys to the horizon, unmarked until I run across it, sinking to my ankles, surprised at how silky, sensuous and cool it feels. After watching the drivers lead off our camels to be fed and watered, I join Mr. Desert on a wind-puckered dune. "I don't want to leave. I've bonded with Babaloo."

He nods. "There's enough food and blankets. I can pick you up tomorrow afternoon."

I've brought no nightclothes, no warm socks, no toothbrush, no extra toilet paper. More problematic: "I have a train ticket to Delhi for tomorrow."

"I'll try to change it."

"Then I'll stay."

He smiles in approval. "I love the desert. It's so quiet, so far from the crowd and it doesn't change. It makes me feel very relaxed, very deep. You see shooting stars and falling stars and those new sparkling stars—"

"Satellites?"

"Yes. Many of those."

He will not let me take his picture until he has curled his black moustache: his image is his collateral, and it wasn't until the promotion following his title win that he found the confidence to trade in his truck for a jeep to conduct camel safaris. "I had only four customers in my first month. I was ready to give back the jeep!" Fortunately, his commercials—for an Indian paint company, for Coca-Cola, for MasterCard, for anyone wishing an icon of Rajput manhood—kept him in the public eye while he built up his business by word of mouth. "I still have to work hard, but I am now a success." He supports this with scrapbooks of testimonials in English, Dutch, German, Italian and Spanish.

My bedroll has now been added to the others around a wood fire where our chef is preparing dinner—a varied and delicious feast with subtle flavours ranging from spicy through savoury to sweet. Afterwards, as I snuggle into my mound of blankets for what may be a cool night, I watch darkness give birth to the night sky—first the planets, no mere pinpoints of light but crystalline chunks, followed by the bolder constellations. I watch Orion shoulder his way over the eastern horizon chased by Sirius the dog star, with the moonless sky so pure and black that I can easily make out the fuzzy nebula below his belt. I count the seven sisters—old friends from childhood now obscured by light pollution in most Western skies—then a half-dozen satellites and a dozen shooting stars. As I gaze up at the Milky Way lumpy with stars—more like porridge than spilled milk—I hear a voice express exactly what I'm feeling: "No wonder our ancestors were such happy sky gazers." My guru is sitting in a nest of embers with his orange lungi spread around him, indistinguishable from the flames.

Hiding my surprise, I nod in agreement. "Imagine the thrill of early explorers when they found they could navigate by the stars!"

He chides me goodnaturedly: "Of course someone as restless as you would think in terms of travelling. I was thinking of the benefits of staying put to observe from a single still point." As if to prove this argument, he stares fixedly into the sky for a full minute before continuing. "It was from centuries of observing heavenly cycles that the ancients developed the idea of the Great Wheel of Life that still governs Eastern thought today. In the East we always pay attention to what happens together."

When I draw closer to the fire to warm my hands, my guru teasingly makes room for me in the embers. "Our sages, just like your scientists, noticed that when lightning flashes, then thunder booms, and that tides ebb and flow with changes of the moon, but they didn't conclude that the one caused the other, just that they happened together. That's one of the major differences between Eastern and Western thought."

"How do you mean?"

"Think of an orchestra playing a symphony. Though all the flutes and violins may stop and start together, it isn't because they're acting upon each other through cause and effect. They play in harmony because they're following the same score. Astrology works the same way: the sun and moon and planets don't *cause* human events but may be co-ordinated with them because of some underlying harmonizing score."

"Now that's a leap!" I protest.

My guru smiles enigmatically. "To the ancients it seemed self-evident. Doesn't a woman's menstrual cycle have the same rhythm as the phases of the moon? The words *month* and *menses* come from the same root in many languages. As above, so below." Taking a coal from the fire, he holds it in his palms, staring into it as if into a crystal ball. "In the latest scientific model of the universe as a single cosmic web of energy outside of space and time, the pairing of a comet with a king's death or an eclipse with war is no less rational than the pairing of the phases of the moon with rising tides or—"

"But those things *don't* happen together," I interrupt impatiently. "Not comets and kings, not eclipses and war."

"What makes you so sure?" My guru hurls his live coal so that it looks like a comet with fiery tail staining the black sky. "For hundreds of years your scientists believed they could chart and measure the world objectively, despite the fact that all their observations were performed through the small window created by their five senses. By contrast, the ancients accepted that everything is subjective, then looked for patterns that were meaningful to them. Now, which of the two groups would you say was the more deluded?" Without waiting for an answer, he continues: "It was Isaac Newton's concept of cause and effect that entrenched Western scientists in the Grand Illusion of Objectivity. That also hooked them on the idea that time was an irreversible arrow flowing smoothly from something called the past through the present to the future. The great irony is that Newton didn't completely endorse this model based on his own concepts. When the astronomer Edmund Halley twitted him about his continued belief in astrology, he replied, 'Sir, I have studied the subject. You have not.' Newton sensed the presence of a deeper organizing principle underlying the materialistic, linear model of the universe created in his name."

"As relativity and quantum theory are proving!" I concede.

My guru points up at the sky. "What do you see?"

"Stars, planets, constellations."

"What *I* see is the blackness and infinity of space. Remember, in the East we think in terms of fields, the totality of things—not just the words but also the silence between them. As the great Chinese sage Lao-tzu once said, 'It's the space between the spokes that makes the wheel.' "

When I awaken, the flames are gone and so is my guru. I know that it takes two hours for one of the twelve constellations along the band known as the zodiac to rise over the horizon, yet the sky seems to be spinning much faster. In fact, my sense of being in motion is so palpable that I feel precarious, as if I were clinging to Spaceship Earth as it rotates through the heavens, praying I won't fall off. I begin to feel queasy and then sick enough to impel me from my bedroll. Without a flashlight, I stumble over one dune and the next, avoiding the campsite, as requested. Even while I'm gagging and retching, I sense I'm not alone. An animal is watching me, a vague but ominous shape glowing in starlight. It comes closer. As I hesitate between bolting and freezing, it sits down at a respectful remove—a lone dog of the greyhound type, probably a hungry dog waiting patiently for what I can produce for him. I've seen too much of this on the streets of India— one animal's droppings are another's banquet. Cautiously, I back away, over this dune and the next, shivering in my cotton slacks and shirt as I circle back to the campsite.

What campsite? All dunes look alike in the dark. Can I, like ancient helmsmen of old, chart my way by the stars? No, as it turns out, but by sheer luck I lurch around till I find myself surveying a circle of bedrolls. The last thing I notice before falling asleep is the upside-down dipper poking over the horizon on its handle, tugged by the northern star.

As the sun rises like a pink grapefruit, I gaze mournfully at breakfast, feeling woozy and apprehensive. Skipping the toast, boiled eggs and chapatis, I settle for a banana and an orange, saving even these for later. We have a four-hour ride till lunch, then an hour after that before Mr. Desert will be picking up me and the preppie couple, leaving the five flower children, who've been rebelling against the stately pace set by our guides, to gallop on for another day.

The first two hours are endurable: my stomach, though delicate, is reasonably stable; however, after another hour under a shimmering, burnt amber sky, I falter. The defining moment occurs after I watch an oasis of trees take shape on the horizon, see it grow to include a pond, imagine myself sleeping on its shady shore, then watch in disbelief as our guides saunter past. I know I must stop anyway and belatedly look for a suitable bush. When someone hollers, "Howrah, howrah!" setting the camels off on a jog, I swear they are shouting, "The horror, the horror!" No longer able to keep up the pretence of normalcy, I lag feverishly behind with Ishak patiently plodding beside me. While I'm still searching, time runs out. "I have to stop—now!" Clumsily leaping off Babaloo while he's half standing, I run to a spare little shrub struggling as hard as I am for survival and pretend quite shamelessly that it's a spruce forest. By now I'm delirious and living on borrowed toilet paper, and I have to stop twice more before I catch up to the others camped for lunch.

Lunch in name only. All I want is rest and shade, and this spot offers precious little of it, though I'm surprised by the difference even a few twigs between my head and the sun can make. Unfortunately nausea has made me careless and I've tramped on thorns. One pierces the ball of my foot, shooting needles up my spine whenever I apply pressure. Though it's invisible, I can feel its rough tip as I picture my tweezers on the dresser in my hotel room. No one else has a pair, but Ishak has something better—native ingenuity. On the principle of "the hair of the dog," he skilfully uses another thorn like a tiny scalpel to dig out the offending one. His hands are soothing, his presence reassuring. I recall the story of Androcles' lion with a thorn piercing its paw with much deeper understanding: Ishak's Fables.

Since we lengthened the morning ride, the afternoon one is only half an hour. By the time we meet Mr. Desert I'm in recovery and by next morning, when I board my train back to Jodhpur and Delhi, the memory of my few hours of discomfort has grown remarkably dim, knocked out by the splendour of the desert and Ishak's gentle humanity.

In retrospect, I believe that it was useful for me to become ill, even that I was supposed to. Though I don't think of myself as a mistrustful person, I realize now that I strenuously avoid situations where I may need help, which is why I signed up for the half-day safari when I yearned to stay overnight. As it turned out, the worst happened: my body humiliated me, pride took a fall, my vulnerability was exposed and I became helpless among strangers. Yet nothing dreadful transpired. The environment proved trustworthy, teaching me something about gratitude, humility, trust and the short-sightedness of decisions based on ego.

In Jodhpur, where I transfer to an overnight express back to Delhi, I meet a porter who reminds me of Ishak—of indeterminate age, spare of body, with a face fissured like the desert. Because of a last-minute track change, the simple task of settling me and my baggage in my coach grows more complex. Instead of cantankerously demanding more money (which I'll give him anyway), this obliging soul reassures me over and over not to worry, and when I discover my ticket isn't where it should be, he seems more upset than I. In my last view of him, he is standing framed outside my window, hands folded in prayer, unwilling to leave his post until his task of consigning me to the care of the Indian railway system has been completed. When I find my ticket in a wrong pocket, he weeps with relief, a gesture so endearing that my eyes water too. Eventually his face blends with Ishak's to create an archetype of humble people who do tough jobs with care, eagerness and kindness because that's the way they should be done—practitioners of karma yoga, like the serving women of Mount Abu, as common as clay but more precious than gold.

karma

"The thought is more powerful than the deed"

I SPEED NORTHWARD out of Delhi toward the Golden Temple, the centre of world Sikhism, at Amritsar in the northern state of Punjab. My interest in this religion began in the early eighties when I studied yoga with a Western Sikh teaching foundation located in Toronto. Almost two decades later, I find myself eager to visit the home of this discipline that continues to have such a healthy impact on my life.

Now as Delhi's urban chaos gives way to fields and ponds, peacocks and water buffalo, I remember that I've travelled this particular route before. In 1977 I journeyed even farther north to Srinagar in Kashmir, once the summer playground of Mughal emperors and British colonials. While this Shatabdi Express with its reclining seats, free newspapers, hot meals and water service promises to deliver me to Amritsar in seven hours, my 1977 trip required an overnight train followed by a twelve-hour bus ride. A railway ticket-seller had boasted to me that India had no third-class travel while neglecting to explain that first and second had so many subdivisions that the ticket he sold to me was, effectively, fifth class. Even before the train had fully stopped in New Delhi station, I was swept aboard on a tide of shoving, churning bodies. To my surprise, I managed to snag one of the few wood slabs in a standing-room coach, and it wasn't until we were under way that I understood why: I was the only Westerner and the only woman. Gallantry had prevailed amid primal struggle.

One detail nagged me: my ticket was clearly stamped "Sleeper," suggesting that somewhere in this never-ending train was a horizontal slab with my name on it. Though life in steerage fascinated me—the stream of beggars and entertainers, the companionship of an occasional goat, the cooking and sharing of food—this coach had no toilet and I wasn't keen to join the men who leaped off at each station to squat in the fields; some of my fellow passengers were already asleep in the rope luggage racks, and it would soon be too dark to see out of my window. More worrisome: its frame bore the only English I'd seen since embarking—"It Is an Offence to Fall Out This Window." Because it was without glass or grating and cut almost to my waist, I took this as a friendly warning.

After waiting four hours for a conductor, I decided to go in search at the next stop, even though this train was so long that I couldn't be sure of reaching the station before it pulled out. After sprinting a couple of city blocks, I encountered a uniformed man with the snappy bearing of a general. He studied my ticket at great length. "But you are four hours late!" he chided in perfect English. "This is for Delhi. Where have you been? This has been cancelled."

He listened to my explanation as if it were the most

remarkable he'd ever heard, then called to a colleague: "This girl . . ." He repeated my story in slavish detail before summoning another colleague. "This girl—"

Interrupting, I pleaded, "Is there anything you can do for me?"

He shook his head. "The train is full." A dramatic pause. "I will try."

"Will I have time to get my luggage from my coach?"

Soberly, he consulted his large pocket watch. "Maybe. Maybe not."

By good luck I recognized some of the heads sticking out of my car, even though I'd neglected to memorize its number. After thanking the guardians of my bag, I raced back to the conductor, who still seemed in no hurry. Decorously he ushered me onto a coach subdivided by rows of three-tiered bunks, then paused to chat with a family that was sitting on one slab while stewing vegetables over a portable stove on the facing one. With cheerful nods toward me, they consolidated their belongings onto a single slab.

"You can have this place," announced my now-smiling conductor, gesturing toward the empty one.

My guilt at displacing the Indian family was tempered by my suspicion that this was my bunk in the first place. Thanking the conductor, I gave him a 100 rupee note, which I assumed, cynically, to have been the point of this whole drawn-out exercise.

My slab, I soon discovered, made a better cooking station than a bed. Now I understood why passengers had been renting bedrolls in the Delhi station; however, when I went in search of a toilet, I was gratified to find a cubicle with a hole bracketed by metal footprints. En route back to my bunk, I again encountered my conductor, who seemed to want to speak to me. He was holding my 100 rupee note, folded so only the denomination showed. "Why did you give me this?"

Wasn't it enough? I chose my words diplomatically: "Because you helped me and I had nothing else to give."

With a kind smile he returned the note. "You have suffered enough."

In contrast to Rajasthan's rough, untethered landscape, most of the Punjab seems under cultivation. Carpets of golden mustard are neatly bordered by trees, while small tractors instead of oxen work the soil. This flat and orderly land—the most prosperous in India—hides its wounds well. At Independence in 1947 it was hacked in two to create Pakistan, with the Punjabi capital of Lahore becoming the capital of the new Muslim state, leaving the rest as a Hindu-Sikh state. Sikhs fled eastward from Pakistan while Muslims fled west, resulting in an exchange of some seventeen million people with death estimates from atrocities on both sides ranging from one to five million.

Ironically, Sikhism was founded five hundred years ago as an idealistic link between Hinduism and Islam. A mystical faith, it was the inspiration of a Hindu quester named Guru Nanak who travelled tens of thousands of kilometres throughout India and the Middle East in search of Ultimate Truth. At age thirty he leaped into a river for his morning bath, then emerged three days later, transformed. Ultimate Truth, he proclaimed, cannot be found in sacred texts. Like God, it is latent in the heart and soul of every human in every station of life, awaiting only selfless, prolonged endeavour to discover it. From Islam, Guru Nanak took the concept of one God without form, while rejecting its militancy, formal ritual, the mediation of priests and all religious authority. From Hinduism, he adopted karma, reincarnation, the concept of God existing in all things and knowable through direct experience, while rejecting idol worship, the caste system and asceticism based on beggary. Since God reveals himself in everyday life, Nanak maintained that it was not necessary to renounce the things of this world. The best way to serve him is through helping others as an ordinary householder, and the best way to worship him is through devotional singing and meditation on his name.

After Nanak's death in 1539, Sikh leadership passed to a succession of nine other gurus, all regarded as his incarnations. The last, Gobind Singh (1666–1708), formed a brotherhood called the *Khalsa*, or Pure Order, creating the ideal of the *Saint Sipahi*, or saint-soldier. He did this by assembling eighty thousand followers and demanding with drawn sword who among them would be willing to sacrifice his head. During the startled silence, one man stepped forward. Seizing him, Sri Guru Gobind Singh dragged him to his tent, emerging minutes later with blood-stained sword. He did this four more times before revealing that all five volunteers remained unharmed. He then initiated these five into his Khalsa, giving them and all Sikh males the surname Singh, meaning "lion," along with their distinctive dress known as the five K's: *kesh*, or uncut hair, which he taught was a source of strength, to be drawn into a topknot and covered by a turban; *kangha*, or comb, to remove dead hair; *kara*, or metal bracelet, symbolizing perfection; *kancha*, long drawers, symbolizing sexual restraint and preparedness for activity; *kirpan* or ceremonial sword taking its name from *kirpa* (kindness) and *aan* (self-respect). He also compiled the Granth Sahib, or sacred scriptures, out of the poetry and songs of Sikhism's ten gurus, along with selected Hindu and Muslim writings. This holy book, which begins with the words *"Ek Onkar Satnam,"* meaning "There is one God who is everywhere and whose name is Truth," was declared by Gobind Singh to be his final incarnation.

As I have mentioned, I created a personal link to Sikhism in the early eighties through members of a Western Sikh teaching foundation called 3HO, meaning Happy, Healthy, Holy. Though none of my instructors were Indian, their guru, Yogi Bhajan, had arrived in Canada from the Punjab in mid-winter of 1968 to discover that his luggage had disappeared in transit and his sponsor had died. Without money and with newspapers tied around his sandals, he made his way into blustery downtown Toronto, where he stayed for several months attracting adherents, before leaving to establish his main headquarters in Los Angeles. During the eighties when other boomers had discarded long hair and natural fibres for clean-shaven faces and power suits, the Toronto community still wore the five K's. At a time when aerobics and weightlifting were the workouts of choice, they taught yoga and meditation in a white room with sky blue carpet and a picture of the Golden Temple on the wall.

Now that I am actually standing before the Golden Temple, I see that its glories could never be captured by camera because the whole structure confronts, embraces, surrounds and overwhelms. Afloat upon the Tank of Nectar, the Holy of Holies has a lower storey of white marble inlaid with arabesques of semi-precious stones, but all the startled visitor can see is its dazzling upper storey, plated with sheets of copper covered by one hundred kilograms of pure gold leaf and domed with an inverted lotus symbolizing the Sikhs' dedication to earthly service. Though the Taj Mahal, which I visited in 1977, is advertised as India's most perfect building, the Golden Temple must be its most dynamic. Whereas the famed Taj is an ethereal monument to a dead queen, the Golden Temple is the fiery heart of a living religion. Whereas the first is an individual expression of grief, the other is the collective celebration of faith. Whereas the Taj takes its aesthetics from the curved line, the Golden Temple represents the triumph of the square. While one is feminine, the other is masculine; while one seduces, the other conquers. While one is fleshed in white marble, the other wears armaments of gold. Both are splendid.

Much of the Golden Temple's impact derives from its lavish use of space. Around the Tank of Nectar—once a forest pool, now an enclosure of white marble—runs a broad marble terrace contained inside a shaded colonnade. This, in turn, is encased in a square of gracefully arched and domed administrative buildings that blush from white to pink and mauve with the setting sun. It's the whole grand complex—the white container, the placid reflecting pool, its flashing golden core—that stir awe, reverence and a sense of serenity like a golden ship assail on a marble ocean.

Along with thousands of Sikhs (literally, "disciples"), I stroll around the Nectar Pool, head covered, feet bare, as required by custom. As in Jaisalmer I experience the madness of the birds as they swoop and wheel before settling like grey blossoms in the branches of the sacred Jujube Tree, causing its boughs to quiver and bend. While volunteers wash down the marble promenade with large hoses, pilgrims bathe in the sacred waters filled with giant carp. It is here—not the Ganges—where the world's twenty million Sikhs purify themselves for union with the Divine. At the four corners of the complex, elders continuously read aloud from the Granth Sahib. As chanting accompanied by sitar and harmonium undulates across the water, I feel a powerful desire to meditate. Sitting cross-legged on the marble floor of a shady colonnade, I fall into a light trance. When I open my eyes half an hour later, I'm ringed by Indians staring at me as if I were a corpse lying in state. As I scramble self-consciously to my feet, three young men ask to have their pictures taken with me. "We want you to come to our residence tomorrow," says one. "My father is the police chief. We're touched by your reverence." It's when he adds, "Are there any other nice ladies you would like to bring with you?" that I decide this is an invitation best refused, with thanks.

Attached to the Golden Temple is a hostel offering accommodations with payment by donation. I'm assigned a bedroll in the Foreign Women's Dorm—a windowless high-ceilinged concrete cell accommodating eight sleepers in two rows. Completing the amenities are an efficient overhead fan, two banks of lockers, two poorly strung clotheslines, a dangling light bulb and a door opening into the Foreign Men's Dorm.

On my arrival four young women are in residence: a Norwegian who's been backpacking since '93; a French teacher who has just completed a three-year contract in Pakistan; an American who's winding down after a year of wandering; a vacationing Australian who has just spent eight hours with thousands of ecstatic pilgrims climbing a mountain to view what turned out to be three sacred rocks bearing crowns.

In keeping with Sikhism's commitment to charity and equality, a twenty-four-hour kitchen outside the temple offers free food to all comers. Periodically, the gigantic doors swing open to allow one group to depart and another to enter. As we squat in long rows on straw mats, prayers are chanted, then volunteers distribute chapatis and ladle lentils onto steel plates, feeding up to forty thousand every day. While the Indians around me take advantage of the "all you can eat" manifesto, the food is too anonymous in colour, flavour and texture for most pampered Western tastes. Henceforth, I and my tribe eat at the local Burger King, which produces a mean veggie burger.

Awakening around five in the morning, I stumble over the thirty bodies in the Foreign Men's Dorm to join pilgrims trekking barefoot to the Golden Temple. The half-moon and a top hat full of stars is no competition for the flash of the floodlit Holy of Holies resting like a crown on its liquid black pillow. Pilgrims already jam the courtyard of the Akal Takhat, Sikhism's seat of authority, and the

Divine Throne where the sacred Grantha Sahib is placed each evening. Accompanied by drumbeats and devotional chanting, a procession carrying the scriptures on a golden palaquin proceeds across the narrow marble causeway over the Tank of Nectar. Though I'm tempted to turn back when the shoving begins, I persevere, eventually reaching the upper floor of the Holy of Holies. Despite doors marking the four directions symbolizing that all are welcome, it's only at the urging of several Sikh women that I squat on the plush carpet. In this small gold-domed room, exquisitely inlaid with shards of red, midnight blue and mirror, everyone is chanting from the Grantha Sahib. The air is super-charged like that inside a chiming bell. Feeling claustrophobic, I eye the four exits, now blocked.

"I guess you'll have to sing in self-defence," suggests a cheerful voice. Though my guru, dressed in white kancha, tunic and turban, is seated several metres away with the men, his steady voice continues in my ear: "We're all musical instruments wanting only breath to start us vibrating."

I move my lips but my throat is parched.

"Health is harmony, disease and depression are discord," he reassures me. "Everything in the universe has its own vibration from particles to pulsars. Our seven chakras are tuned to the musical scale with the lowest being C, the second D and so on up the scale. The universe is structured as a symphony."

Though I don't understand the chants, individual phrases are familiar. Gradually my windpipe opens, and without conscious thought, I seem able to pluck the words wrapped in notes from the throats around me.

Ek Onkar: There is only one God who is everywhere.

Satnam : His name is Truth.

Karta Purkh: He is the Creator of everything.

Nirbau: He is beyond fear.

Nirvair: He is beyond anger.

Akal Murat: He never dies.

Ajuni: He is beyond birth.

Saibhang: He created himself.

Gurprasad: He is realized by the Grace of the True Guru.

Jap'u': Repeat His name again and again.

Ad Sach: He was true in the beginning.

Ju gad Sach: He has ever been true.

Hai Bhi Sach: He is true now.

Nanak Hosi Bhi Sach: Guru Nanak says He will be true in the future.

As I sing, fuelled by a powerful surge of kundalini, all the gold and mirror bits in the room seem to vibrate with their own special sound, turning it into a glittering wind chime. After what seems like ten minutes, I check my watch. More than an hour has passed. I continue to chant, envisioning my third eye as a pink jewel haloed in gold, feeling as if I were inside the crown chakra of the universe.

Given my gentle introduction to Sikh wisdom through ex-hippies, I'm disconcerted by how like a military monument the Golden Temple appears, beginning with its plaques commemorating war heroes and climaxing in a museum of paintings of Sikhs being boiled in oil, scalped, drawn and quartered, crushed joint by joint and broken on spiked wheels. Even more gruesome are photos of the bloodied and beaten corpses of contemporary Sikh martyrs.

Though originally Sikhs donned their turbans and swords like Knights of the Round Table in defence of the oppressed, the Golden Temple has been ransacked and desecrated so often—by Mughals, Muslims and, latterly, by the Indian army—that defending it has become a pre-occupation. In the 1984 Indian attack, which was the culmination of Prime Minister Indira Gandhi's attempt to consolidate control of the Punjab, many Sikhs were shot inside the Golden Temple, and its great library was burned. In vengeance Sikh members of Indira Gandhi's bodyguard assassinated her four months later, resulting in the torching and sacking of Sikh temples and businesses throughout Delhi, leaving four thousand Sikh casualties. Subsequently, divisions within the Sikh community itself have led to bitter power struggles for control of the Golden Temple.

Today, mention the word *Sikh* and most people think war rather than peace. Aggression is also evident in the fierce bearing of the Sikhs who patrol the Golden Temple complex, pouncing on anyone guilty of a minor infraction.

And, despite Guru Nanak's championing of sexual equality, Sikh women (who bear the surname Kaur, meaning "princess") seem relegated to menial tasks like sweeping, while the men assume the leadership roles. Instead, I prefer to associate this faith with an event that occurred in Delhi before I left for Amritsar, during a celebration marking the birthday of Guru Nanak. All day Sikhs ladled out generous portions of free food from soup kitchens while marching bands led a parade of schoolchildren uniformed in every style from pink saris and orange tunics with turbans to plaid skirts and shorts with ties. As I watch from a doorway, a slight teenager carrying a child begs with practised, listless gestures. Horrified, I stare beyond this pantomime to her little girl's face so deeply ripped from eye to lip that I can see bone. Though the wound has begun to heal in what will be a nasty, barbed-wire scar, bloody flesh still hangs open with flies buzzing inside. Unconvinced that any money given to this mother will go to heal the child, I cast about for a pharmacy. Suddenly a Sikh truck covered in marigolds heaves into view with signs offering free first aid. After trying in vain to get the mother to understand the meaning of the red crosses, I conscript the Sikh beside me. Without hesitation he scoops up the wounded child in one arm, the mother in the other and, unmindful of the blood staining his sturdy barrel chest, carries them through the crowd. Such service demonstrates the intention of Guru Nanak's teachings and that is the context in which I place my visit to the Golden Temple.

The early-morning rickshaw ride through Amritsar to the train station feels romantic, even thrilling: the murky sky with its few leftover stars, the still-glowing night fires churning the air into halos of luminous fog, the creak of my wallah's bicycle through the ominous silence make me feel like a character in a black-and-white spy movie featuring cunning villains, rumpled anti-heroes and dangerous women. The occasional electric light casts the same yellow glow as the street lights of my childhood that summoned me home from a day's play, marking the limits of the permitted, while a few dogs, working the night shift, strut and sniff through garbage dumps. It's the sort of melancholy tableau expected afterhours in a city that runs on sun time, but what am I to make of the eerily deserted Amritsar train station? Where are the porters, the ticket-sellers and the passengers for the 5:30 a.m. Shatabdi Express to Delhi?

A single porter, rising groggily from the floor, tells me my train has been cancelled. A frustrating hour later this is confirmed by the appearance of a single ticket-seller. A serious accident occurred last night on the Amritsar-Delhi line and the next Delhi train won't be leaving till 9:00 a.m.

I become fixated on making that train. For the next several hours, during which the sleeping station turns into a buzzing hornets' nest threatened with evacuation, I sprint from wicket to booth to office, receiving a chit for a

refund, having it signed, cashing the refund, buying a pro-
visional ticket for an unreserved seat, getting that signed.
Half an hour before departure, I'm installed in a still-
undesignated seat in a second-class coach into which
people pour, carrying the contents of their houses. My
compartment, intended for six, becomes the headquarters
for a Sikh family of seven—a toddler, a teenage son and
daughter, two parents and two grandparents—plus baggage. I settle in as best I can on my straight-backed bench,
feet propped on my luggage, knees scraping my chin for
what I'm sure will be a miserable seven hours. Even my
drafty window is a doubtful blessing. On this chilly late-
November morning, it's too cold to open and too dirty to
see through.

As the train leaves the station, the Sikh mother un-
packs salads and cooked vegetables in plastic containers.
After serving the adult males, she offers me a chapati filled
with a spicy potato mixture. Because I've just spent two
nights in the friendly, claustrophobic Women's Dorm, my
desire for separateness remains stubborn and strong, but I
accept out of politeness. Since the teenage boy is the only
one who speaks English, the genial family chatter flows
around me, embracing me without obligation. Relaxing,
I observe how much genuine pleasure the Sikh mother
takes in serving her family, even in sharing her food with
me, a stranger. *Service* was not a word that acquired much
cachet in my family. To my immature mind, it had meant
my mother's turning herself into a dutiful doormat for my

irascible father and performing all sorts of tasks for me in the spirit of self-sacrifice that I didn't want done. Service became a double yoke to be avoided—both the right ox of doing and the left ox of being done for. Now I see that it's a shiny word, full of power. I have confused it with servitude, and my present servitude lies in being yoked to infantile ideas. According to the Bhagavad Gita, giving and receiving are the same when performed with disinterest, whereas in the West *what* is given and *to whom* are usually paramount, creating transactions that are isolated and specific. When the act of giving itself takes precedence, what would have been a straight line joining two people is expanded into a bountiful circle embracing strangers as well as friends.

Meanwhile, the countryside crawling past my window is much lusher than I remember from the journey north—lily ponds, rice paddies, blue flowering vines, banana and palm groves with flocks of jade parakeets. As I discover during one of several half-hour unscheduled stops, this train has been rerouted onto secondary tracks because of last night's collision between an express and a mail train. Cars from the mail train are being hoisted from the tracks, while those from the express, still containing crushed and dismembered bodies, have yet to be dismantled. Though I was told when I purchased my ticket that this train would arrive in Delhi around four, I can see I'll be lucky to get there before dark. Small matter: a rumoured two hundred people didn't make it at all, and if I hadn't spent an extra day in Jaisalmer camel riding, I could have been one of them.

"Do you really think that's true?"

I look in the direction of the voice. My guru is seated on the luggage rack—at least his head is up there, his turban scraping the ceiling. The rest of him appears seconds later, one leg followed by the other as if stepping through a curtain.

"Why not?" I persist. "I admit the chances were small: most days thirteen million people ride India's 62,900 kilometres of track in safety, but last night two hundred of those for whom the statistics against death were the same did die."

"You weren't killed because it wasn't your karma," insists my guru. "It has nothing to do with chance."

"Are you saying life is predetermined?"

My guru allows his legs to dangle over the luggage rack. "I'm saying the opposite. In Sanskrit, *karma* means "action"—that which is self-created. Each of us has the power to choose, but once choice has been exercised the law of cause and effect takes over."

I stare at my guru's bare feet trying to figure out what's odd about them. "In other words, everyone who was killed last night deserved to die!"

"Not in the sense of being punished. In the East we don't employ God as our judge. Each death was the sum total of that person's karma flowing through many lifetimes and no more good or bad than the falling of an apple from a tree. The system of karma is self-sustaining, which is why Buddhists often consider God an unnecessary complication, like adding pedals to an airplane."

I see that my guru's soles are smooth, without markings, which is why they seem strange. "I remember a study of train crashes done in the sixties by a U.S. mathematician named William Cox. He compared the number of passengers in damaged coaches with those in other coaches of the same train. Then he compared the number of passengers in the damaged coaches with those same coaches for several weeks previous. In every case fewer passengers occupied the damaged coaches than would be expected by chance, suggesting that passengers had unconsciously sensed and avoided the danger. How does that fit with what you're saying?"

My guru smiles. "Perfectly. What you in the West see as coincidence, chance or luck, we see as the manifestation of deeper karmic patterns." He shifts as if he's about to leave, then turns back. "Why haven't you ever asked my name?"

I stare at his unlined feet. "I never thought you had one."

Drawing them up under his lungi with great dignity, he announces, "Everyone has a name. Mine is Moonji."

My Sikh family debarks, bequeathing me a bag of food. By now most coaches have emptied, leaving only a few of us rattling around inside as our ghost train lurches from station to station. An Indian woman wearing a serviceable brown sari moves into my compartment. She's composed entirely of curved lines, boneless, with rounded shoulders, pendulous breasts and a heart-shaped candy-box face containing chocolate-cream eyes and a bindi like a ripe cherry. She settles languidly across the three seats opposite, then begins to peel an orange. Covertly I watch her childlike fingers methodically skin and section the fruit, staining the air with a juicy citric tang. Since I assume her absorption in this task reflects her desire for the fruit, I'm surprised when she extends the orange on her palm, open like a blossom. "Take it." When I hesitate, her smile deepens. "*Please.*"

Once again I've missed the point: sharing the orange was an anticipated part of her pleasure in peeling it. I accept one section, and then, having witnessed the loving birth of this small world from its rind, I taste it with the same attention, feeling the succulent fruit split under the pressure of my teeth, releasing a sweet, acidic squirt that bathes my taste buds before swelling to fill the cavity of my mouth. When she offers me another section, I accept that as well, but refuse a third and a fourth, not wishing to overdose on sacramental wine.

In halting English, she tells me her name is Lakshmi and that she has just visited her daughter, who is pregnant with her first grandchild. Then, closing her eyes, she falls into a deep sleep, like Alice tumbling down the rabbit hole into Wonderland.

Lakshmi awakens as our train is pulling into Delhi. It's 9:00 p.m., with my seven-hour trip having taken twelve. When I wonder aloud if my reserved room will still be waiting, Lakshmi impulsively clasps my hand. "Come to my place! My husband is meeting me. You come to us." Though she is insistent, I am even more adamant about refusing. We bid an affectionate goodbye, then head in different directions.

Since this is my third return to Delhi, I'm expecting a three-minute pedal-rickshaw ride to deliver me to my hotel. Instead I find myself in a strange, jarring landscape without landmarks. I've detrained at the Old Delhi station instead of the New Delhi one, now a devious hour away through twisted, foggy, unnamed streets. What follows is India's version of the chariot race from *Ben-Hur* with my pedal-rickshaw alternately locking wheels with pushcarts carrying flour and donkey carts weighted with marble, while swerving to avoid the aggressions of auto-rickshaws and transports spewing noxious fumes. Instead of utilizing north and southbound lanes, one-way traffic floods the street until a policeman gestures for everything to push to one side for a surge in the opposite direction. Though not many vehicles have lights, everyone has a horn and a vigorous right hand for signalling. Twice my driver asks me to debark so he can push his bike uphill.

Twice our rickshaw almost overturns, once while careening on two wheels around a pothole, the second time around an animal carcass. *How ironic to have avoided a fatal train crash only to be offed by a dead donkey!*

My room *is* waiting. The instant my head touches the pillow, I tumble down a deep well, just as Lakshmi did. *In my dream she is waiting for me at the bottom. Extending her hand, she urges, "Come, Morris." When I look behind me, I discover we are alone, so assume that I must be Morris. Lakshmi leads me into a cavern where I see the blind boy from Rishikesh. He feels my eye sockets with the absorption of Lakshmi peeling her orange, his hands moist and pulpy like the orange, causing me to draw back in apprehension.*

In the fog of awakening, I remember a short story by D. H. Lawrence titled "The Blind Man" from a college English course. As I now recall, the blind man attempts to get to know his wife's intellectual friend more intimately by feeling his face. Repelled, the man of letters flees.

On my return to Toronto, I look up "The Blind Man" in my *College Survey of English Literature*. My recall proves accurate, with this exception: it's the blind man who is named Morris, which Lawrence spells Maurice. By then my computer's spell checker has already spewed up Morris as a questionable word, offering *Meyers* as a first alternative. Though the linguistic connection between these two names seems remote, perhaps my software was accessing a pool of deeper karmic meaning, since my maiden name is Meyers.

During stopovers in New Delhi, where my plane landed five weeks ago, I usually stay in the colourful Paharganj area, squashed between the Muslim laneways of Old Delhi to the north, where I accidentally detrained last night, and the broad British avenues to the south. It's inexpensive, convenient to the railway station and possessed of its own energetic charm, with its coat-hanger alleys creating a grand bazaar offering everything from religious posters to the latest rap videos. One moment I'm being nudged by a cow into the path of a motor scooter, the next I'm sending e-mail to Toronto from a cyber café or being robbed of a bag of bananas by the monkey colony at the train station or fending off a hawker trying to convince me that a drum will fit easily into my suitcase or eating French fries with lime prepared by a turbaned man with a cart.

The closest place for Western-style brand-name amenities is Connaught Circle, about ten blocks away, consisting of a scraggly park ringed by broad avenues offering such travellers' friends as American Express and Thomas Cook, Pizza Hut (with a doorman who checks reservations), the ubiquitous Bata Shoes, ice-cream parlours, coffee houses, banks and airline offices. While I'm running errands for my next journey—south by train to Madras, which I plan to make my headquarters for exploring southern India—a young man tugs on my sleeve. "Madame, your shoes need cleaning."

I've grown used to being importuned by cobblers when wearing my vintage desert boots with sponge soles that often come unglued. Then their challenge is to dramatize the need for extensive repairs while convincing me the shoes are still worth fixing. "Throw out *these*, madame? These are masterworks! Feel that suede."

But I am not wearing my desert boots. I'm wearing black-canvas-and-Velcro sandals. To confirm the absurdity of cleaning them, I extend my right foot.

I gape.

Resting impudently on the toe strap is a glob of fresh excrement. Instantly my shoe man is on his knees attacking the pile with liquid detergent and a small brush. Thanking him, I give him 50 rupees. He is outraged. "Madame, I am not a beggar!" He demands 300—about the cost of new sandals.

By now I've grown suspicious: I've been walking on pavement for an hour and the pinpoint placement of that stinky stuff is a little too perfect. When I stride away, he follows me, complaining vociferously for a block before falling back. Almost immediately I regret not having been more appreciative of such a clever, entrepreneurial ploy— a make-work scheme to counter Sunday downtime.

As it turns out, I have another opportunity to express my appreciation. The next time I'm at Connaught Circle, the same thing happens—same shoes, same foot, different shoe man. As I now know, this is a standarized con among the cobblers of Delhi, almost a franchise operation with a spray can as part of the start-up kit.

It's also while wandering Connaught Circle that I discover the saddest merchants in all of Delhi—Kashmiri carpet-sellers, displaced from their beautiful northern state by ten years of bloody border disputes, now exiled in windowless, airless downtown rooms, draped and piled with the handwoven rugs for which their area is renowned.

When India and Pakistan gained their independence in 1947, both coveted Kashmir, which was 90 per cent Muslim but ruled by a Hindu maharaja. While Maharaja Hari Singh vacillated, Pakistan attempted a military take-over, causing Singh to opt for India. Though the Indian government promised a plebiscite, none was forthcoming. Discontent simmered until 1989, when Indian troops put down a Muslim-led rebellion of separatists fighting for an independent Kashmir, with casualties of twenty-five thousand. Since then, skirmishes along the ceasefire line dividing Pakistan-controlled Kashmir from the two-thirds controlled by India has become a way of life. In the once-picturesque summer capital of Srinagar, mosques have been burned, along with blocks of historic wooden houses. The bodies of separatists, headless or with gouged eyes, have been found in lakes and rivers once noted for their lotus blossoms and floating vegetable gardens. Srinagar's famous carved houseboats, with their tourist-friendly names like *Queen Marry*, *Kashmir Hilton*, *White House*, *Young Mona Lisa*, *Holiwood*, *Rolls Royce*, *New Taxas*, *Heaven Lovely*, have been drydocked or commandeered for the 450,000 Indian troops and paramilitaries stationed in Kashmir. Though tourists have not been banned, they're advised to stay away. In July 1995, six foreign trekkers were taken hostage by separatist guerrillas: an American escaped, a Norwegian was found beheaded and the others are still missing.

When I travelled to Srinagar in November of 1977, it still possessed a romantic aura. After an overnight train followed by a magnificent twelve-hour drive through peaks and evergreen forests, I arrived after dark as the sole person left on the bus. A single light outside the closed depot was the town's only illumination. As I disembarked, about thirty men hurled themselves at me, shouting the prices of their houseboats. One yelled, "Houseboat *and* taxi!" and minutes later I was speeding along twisting, dirt roads into the Kashmiri night in an unmetered cab driven by a paunchy, balding man named Abdul.

Even by moonlight I could tell Abdul's houseboat was not top of the line: listing hull, slimy gunwales, spongy floors. Worse, I was the only guest and my tiny cabin—now revealed by kerosene lamp—had a curtain instead of a door. As I weighed my limited options, a line of shadowy figures boarded from the houseboat moored next door: Abdul's father, son and wife.

First light revealed my houseboat to be half-aground in a swampy cul-de-sac of the Jhelum River rather than afloat on Dal Lake. Flat bottomed and about thirty metres long, it had a musty, Victorian parlour featuring a Second World War portrait of King George VI and a dozen chairs in as many patterns of faded chintz. Though Srinagar was gloriously set amid snow-peaked mountains, it had the poignancy of a resort out of season. The willows, poplars and chestnuts bore only a few brown-pocked yellow leaves and it was snowing.

On the family's houseboat, Abdul's wife—a pretty, plump woman in her thirties—tended heavy metal pans over a low stove. As she poured ginger tea from a pewter samovar, Abdul's mother handed me a clay pot of live coals in a wicker basket. When I tried to warm my hands, everyone laughed. Kashmiri women keep these *kangris* under their skirts and between their legs. I continued to warm my hands.

The breakfast conversation conducted by the men in broken English set the agenda. Grandpa—a tall, craggy patriarch—was determined to lure me to one of Kashmir's famous weaving factories to sell me a carpet on which he would collect a 15 per cent commission. Abdul's ambitions were tipped by his "guest book," consisting of photos of himself with his arms around a rather gangly Western girl. "My British girlfriend," he whispered slyly. "She was our last guest."

It wasn't until I attempted to leave the houseboat that Grandma revealed her passions. Falling to her knees, she began rubbing her cheek against my beige velour slacks. Grandpa translated: "She wants your trousers."

"They're the only warm ones I have."

"She says she will wear them for the rest of her life."

"Tell her I'll send them to her from Delhi."

By the second day Abdul was wooing me with gifts. "I will take you for a meal of Persian food. Do you want to smoke hash? I will buy you a dress."

Grandma had upped the stakes on the slacks. "She says that if you give them to her now, she will pray for you five times a day."

Grandpa had acquired a second obsession, triggered by a Canadian calendar I gave him to distract him from the carpets. He pointed to a photo of the Rockies with snowy peaks and evergreen forests much like those of Kashmir. "Monkeys in the trees."

"No. No monkeys in Canada."

He reran the conversation, thinking I'd misunderstood.

I repeated, "Monkeys in Kashmir but no monkeys in Canada."

By the third morning, Grandpa was waiting for me with both a carpet he'd brought from the factory and the Canadian calendar. After sneaking up on me by a back route—"It snows in Canada like Kashmir?"—he ended with the refrain, "And you have monkeys in the trees!"

The presence of the carpet warned me that it was dangerous to lose even a trivial exchange with this gang of rogues. "No, no monkeys in Canada."

When I tried to leave the boat, Abdul blocked my path. "Where are you going?" When I returned, he greeted me like a jealous husband. "Where have you been? Were you alone?" Grandma had taken to snatching at my slacks. "Now! Give them to me *now*!"

I decided to leave Srinagar next day on the noon plane.

Grandpa, realizing he had lost all chance for the carpets, gambled his full authority on that business of the monkeys. Thrusting the calendar under my nose, he exclaimed, "There are monkeys in the trees!"

My answer was truthful but conciliatory: "Well, I've never seen any monkeys."

Triumphantly he thumped his palm against the calendar. "Ah, monkeys in the trees."

As I left the houseboat for my taxi, Abdul's docile wife spoke her first word to me: "Stop!" Peeling off her sweater, she unhooked her American-style bra. "You want a gift?"

"No! No gift."

In the twenty-two years since my slapdash, slapstick trip to Kashmir, during which this serenely beautiful land has become a flashpoint between nuclear powers, I sometimes wondered what happened to Abdul and his family. Did his sons take up arms and, if so, for whom? Are Grandpa and Grandma still alive? With tourism smashed, is Abdul selling carpets in Delhi?

Though I'm not likely to learn the answer to those questions, in a shop up one flight in Connaught Circle I encounter another Abdul whose family also owns a Srinagar houseboat. He's not yet middle-aged, but already his skin looks sallow against his dyed black hair, while a mole like a teardrop exaggerates the droop of his eyes. As we sit cross-legged drinking chai, he confides, "I am a man with two hundred people on my shoulders. Why else would anyone be in Delhi living like this? Our family boat is in drydock in Srinagar and I must support them all."

When I tell him I'm on a spiritual quest, his face brightens. "My guru lives in the mountains." Gloom descends once again. "He's ninety years old. I may never see him alive again."

Abdul sets a white mat on the carpet before me. "My guru gave this to me. Sit on it, please." When I do, he urgently inquires, "Can you feel the power?"

"I'm not sure. I find sitting cross-legged difficult."

"Bend one leg flat against the floor and stretch out the other. Relax the muscles, get used to that, then try the other leg."

I follow his instructions. "What do you think will happen in Kashmir?"

"Who can say?" He offers me a cigarette, which I refuse, still choking on secondhand smoke from his last one. "The longer it continues, the worse the karma. By now many people have been born on both sides who know only the conflict. Others who were killed have been reborn."

"Do countries have karma as well as people?"

"Of course. When war continues for more than one generation, karma increases many-fold because the plot-lines of everyone's lives from generation to generation become tangled and knotted like the strings of puppets in the hands of a mad puppeteer. My guru tells me that my sons' sons too will fight."

While we've been talking, I've been shifting position on Abdul's rug. Now I stare in disbelief: my left foot is resting on my right thigh in a half lotus. "I've never been able to do that before!" I exclaim. My limbs feel soft, like heated plastic. My right foot seems to want to imitate the left, completing the lotus. I couldn't be more astonished if I'd levitated. "You're a master teacher!"

Abdul firmly shakes his head. "I am a nobody. That mat has the power. . . . Let me see your palm." He examines my left one first. "Where is your husband?"

"We were divorced and now he's dead."

Abdul shakes his head. "Only in America do people throw out things when they are still good. That was a good marriage. It had a maximum of tolerance. He knew you better than you thought." He draws my palm into the light. "You are lucky. You have a very big life, if you want it. Over a hundred years. Or you can close your eyes after eighty years and die in your sleep. Not so many people have that choice. Only those who are old souls. When is you birth date?"

"March 8, 1935, just before noon."

He writes astrological symbols on what looks like an X's and O's graph but with lines also criss-crossing from the corners. "You are a lady of a very complex and mysterious type and very determined in your philosophy. You always accept a challenge and you can protect yourself without aid by anyone. I see that you have collected much food out of your sufferings, and while you are very emotional and romantic, you also want to know things and you will sacrifice to that."

"You said that I was an old soul. Can you tell me more about that?"

Reaching into a bureau, the only piece of furniture in the room, he hands me a box. It contains burnt matches. "Throw these in the air."

Abdul eliminates all that are not touching, leaving about a dozen. "These are the important ones for this life, especially where the burnt ends meet. I see that you and your husband have been together several lives before but this is the first one where you marry. You will marry in another life but you may take opposite sexes. . . . I see you in white robes. You have lived in India many times and you have known the Buddha." Squinting at the matches, he adds,

"When you leave this world, you will know where you are going."

"What does that mean?"

"It means you are going to a higher level, but it is a place that you will first see in a vision. Do you paint pictures?"

"No. I write books."

"You will write one that sells like hotcakes."

Abdul stares into his empty chai cup as if expecting to find the next instalment of my life.

"How is it that you can see the past and future?"

He sighs. "I myself do nothing." He points to my palm. "When I look into the small I see the large, which is you." He points up at the sky. "When I look at the big I see the small, which is also you. When you throw matchsticks you are saying to the universe, 'Show me what you want me to know.' Everything is connected to everything else. I do not need matchsticks. I could throw the beads you are wearing and study the pattern of their falling if you had not forced them to sit side by side on a string. The stars themselves have been tossed by Brahma."

We hear people ascending the stairs, a man and woman speaking French.

"Customers," announces Abdul, climbing wearily to his feet.

Back at my hotel I try to sit in the lotus position. I don't come close—not then or ever again.

After two days in Delhi, I check out of my Paharganj hotel at noon for my trip to Madras. Since my train isn't leaving till nine this evening, I decide to spend the afternoon at the Red Fort, which is Delhi's most imposing monument, representing the height of Mughal power.

For the first five minutes of my auto-rickshaw ride, I see more of my driver's face than the back of his head, even though we are manoeuvring through vicious downtown traffic. His voice is as seductive as a lounge singer's as he croons, "Beautiful carpets! Beautiful saris! Good prices—cheap, cheap Indian prices."

I've heard this sales pitch hundreds of times before. "I'm *not* interested!"

"Just come and look," he pleads. "Look—it costs nothing."

"I know you expect a commission, but you're just wasting your time and mine. I will *not* be buying!"

"You don't have to." He confesses with a sheepish grin, "I get 20 rupees, even if you just go there."

The emporium is large and grand—several stories of jewellery, saris and carpets—aesthetically arranged in glass cases or framed in glowing wood. Meticulously groomed salesmen converge on the lobby, forming a reception line to pass me, like some rare ritual object, from chamber to chamber.

I see only one other customer in the carpet room. An engaging fellow in his twenties, he's wearing a funny, floppy, multicoloured knit hat over cropped dark hair, a green vest, a blue plaid shirt and heavy knee socks outlining sturdy legs that end in thick boots.

"He's Canadian," confides my salesman, who insists on introducing us.

We shake hands, then exchange the banalities of travellers forced to converse: "Hi, I'm Chuck. From Winnipeg."

"Have you been in India long?"

"Three months. I was studying Buddhism in the Himalayas, but I'm going home this evening."

I gesture toward the mounds of Oriental rugs. "By flying carpet?"

He laughs ruefully. "The plane is cheaper."

Early that evening, I see Chuck again in a juice bar in Delhi's Main Bazaar. He's added a sweater-of-many-colours—notably, fuchsia, yellow and blue—and he's talking to a clean-cut young man in jeans. As I wave, his companion shifts, revealing the logo on his T-shirt: "CBC Saskatoon." Given that we three Canadians are the only people in the juice bar, we elect to share a table.

Apparently Dustin just arrived today from Saskatoon and is leaving this evening for a Buddhist centre in Bodhgaya, which is southwest of Delhi. Instead of exchanging travellers' tales, we talk about the difficulties of explaining to uncomprehending folks back home the things we're seeking here. Though both young men are close to their families, they've rebelled against their well-intentioned middle-class programming. "Just go through one more hoop, my son, and you will be a man."

Sometime during the next hour, Chuck produces a Sony Walkman and a Neil Young tape. Huddled over the yellow Walkman as if it were a prairie bonfire, we listen to songs by Neil Young followed by a tape of "The Future" by Leonard Cohen. It's a quintessential Canadian moment, three expatriates—one just arrived, one just leaving, one poised in mid-flight—listening to two Canadian singers in a Delhi juice bar while waiting for a night plane/bus/train. Sealing the occasion, Chuck gives Dustin his Neil Young tape and me his Leonard Cohen one. He also presents me with his *vipassana* schedule.

"Vipassana?"

"It's a ten-day course in Buddhist meditation. It's offered all over India."

Several hours later, while waiting in the train station, I read Chuck's pamphlet on vipassana, meaning "insight" or "to see things as they really are." Based on techniques taught by the Buddha twenty-five hundred years ago, it promises "total liberation and full enlightenment" through self-purification by introspection. According to Western standards, this discipline is a severe one. To the usual ashram restraints—no smoking, no drinking, no drugs, no meat eating, no lying, no killing, no stealing, no sex—has been added no "high and luxurious beds," no bodily decoration, no talking, no reading, no writing, no musical instruments, no radios, tape recorders, telephones or cameras. All other spiritual or religious practices are also forbidden: no incense, no mantras, no beads, no praying, singing, fasting or yoga. Participants must bathe daily, keep their clothes clean and dress modestly, which for women means that backs and legs must be covered and bras worn or chests draped with shawls.

More important: students must surrender totally to the teacher and to the technique of vipassana, requiring eleven hours of meditation a day. Everyone must agree to stay for the whole ten days, during which foreign students must hand over their visas and passports. As the pamphlet sums up, "The rules are not for the benefit of the Teacher or of the Management, nor are they negative expressions of tradition, orthodoxy or blind faith in some organized religion. Rather they are based on the practical experience of thousands of meditators over the years and are scientific and rational. Keeping the rules creates a very conducive atmosphere for meditation; breaking them pollutes it."

No charge is levied for the course or for accommodations, and vipassana teachers are not paid for their services. My eyes slide back to the pamphlet's most telling phrase: "eleven hours of meditation a day." Is that possible? I pocket the schedule, thinking of the unlikely chain of circumstances that placed it in my hands, already knowing I will accept its challenge: karma?

miracles

"Miracles do not happen in contradiction to nature,
but only in contradiction
to what we know of nature"

IT TAKES thirty-three hours to travel from Delhi to Madras by train. Having purchased a ticket for air-conditioned class at four times the cost of second class, I intend to sleep, read, listen to music and meditate, supported by all the luxury I can get, as two-thirds of India slides past my window.

Though the Tamil Nadu Express looks down-at-heel from the outside, its compartments prove well designed and well maintained, with facing blue leather seats that convert into four curtained bunks. My upstairs mate is an Indian businessman who wears double whites with a sparkle I haven't seen since Mount Abu, while across the aisle is an odd couple I noticed in the station—a Japanese man in his thirties with neatly trimmed beard and wire glasses and his German girlfriend, a raw-boned blonde, probably ten years older and at least a head taller, dressed in voluminous hippie-style skirt and peasant blouse.

As soon as the train leaves New Delhi station, a porter arrives with crisp sheets, bouncy white pillows and good-quality wool blankets. Minutes later a steward takes our breakfast orders. Politely avoiding eye contact, the four of us settle down for the night.

In travelling south, I'll be entering the heartland of Hinduism. Faced with the inevitable profusion of temples, ashrams, gurus and pilgrimage sites, I've decided to focus on an element unique to India: its living goddesses. Before Jesus, Allah and the God of the Old Testament; before Jupiter, Zeus and Zoroaster; before Brahma, Shiva and Vishnu, there existed an agrarian Euro-Asian society that worshipped the Great Mother goddess of fertility. Rivers were her veins, rocks her bones, hills her breasts and the sacred caves containing her altars were her womb. As evidence, archeologists point to an abundance of clay, stone, amber and bone goddess statues dating from 30,000 B.C., discovered in burial sites from France to Siberia and throughout the Middle East to India, depicting a woman with pendulous breasts, massive thighs and distended belly. Other clues to this matriarchy, which seems to have lasted for thousands of years, persist in the Great Mother myths of early Mediterranean societies: Cybele of Rome, Demeter of Greece, Nut and Isis of Egypt, Ishtar of Babylon. However, it's only in present-day India that this goddess tradition has retained its vitality with its own archeological sites, temples, myths and even its own incarnations.

In her earliest Hindu form, Mahadevi, which is Sanskrit for the Great Divine, stands alone as creator, sustainer and destroyer of the universe. During the Aryan invasion of the Indus valley more than three millennia ago, her triune of powers was doled out to three male gods: Brahma, Vishnu and Shiva. Female energy was embodied in Shiva's first wife, Sati, who later incarnated as Parvati, the divine feminine power that activates male power while remaining subservient to it as the hideous custom of sati demonstrates.

Eventually, repressed female energy manifested as Durga, whose name means Beyond Reach, a beautiful, tiger-riding temptress brandishing weapons in her ten hands. To win this warrior goddess, whose sacred task is to slay demons, her lusting enemies must defeat her in battle, which none could do. When one demon attempted to rape her, she grew so angry that Kali, meaning Black, sprang from her forehead. A wild woman with unruly hair wearing a necklace of severed heads, a girdle of dismembered arms and serpents for bracelets, Kali dances naked in cemeteries, drunk on the blood of her victims. When she challenges Shiva, she often wins, and during intercourse she usually takes the superior position. Though her devotees once worshipped her through human sacrifice, now they slit the throats of black goats or engage in tantric rites that incorporate the taboos of sex, meat eating, wine and drugs. Some historians make a connection between Kali worship and the repressed rage of Indian women; others see her ferocious form as a projection of male fear of female power.

When I awaken at dawn I find myself looking into a burnished bronze sky with the sun balanced like a copper ball on a sheet of red-hot iron. An hour later the sun is still coppery, the sky bronze, the earth iron red. It's then I realize that the coach's hermetically sealed windows are so deeply tinted that I might as well be wearing Coke-coloured glasses. By contrast the folk in second class will be enjoying a blue sky, a yellow sun and clefts of forest green. Instead of shivering in air-conditioned luxury, they will be in shirt sleeves basking in a warm breeze.

The rough, flat countryside seems uninhabited, reminding me that India, despite her teeming cities, has a population density only slightly higher than Germany's and considerably lower than Japan's. As usual on these trips, I'm the only one in my compartment who bothers to try looking out the window. When the Indian businessman isn't sleeping, he's smoking in the vestibule between coaches. The Japanese-German couple functions as a self-contained unit more mother-child than lovers. She makes his bed, she plumps his cushions, she feeds him from little jars. They have their own bedding and cutlery, and the only thing they accept from the porter is hot water to make tea in their own pot. They move easily from German to English to Hindi, and both are studying Spanish. As the hours pass with no acknowledgement between us, I remember a story once told to me by a Canadian actor who lived with a musician in a New York walk-up. When their slum landlord removed the wall between their flat and their neighbours' during renovations, all the tenants behaved as if the barrier still existed, refusing eye contact and even greeting in the hall as if they hadn't just brushed their teeth together. Now I'm amused to see how long the Japanese-German couple and I can go without noticing each other's existence. We make it almost into Madras station, when the steward drops a bowl of soup, causing the three of us to shriek in unison. Catching each other's eyes, we burst out laughing, admitting the game between us.

Though it's been a relief to spend a day and a half free of touts and travel decisions, it's even more of a pleasure to step from my air-conditioned coach into the warm, moist Madras morning. Outside the station, rain puddles pock the pavement—the first I've seen since Toronto. In southern India, the southwest monsoons start around the first of June, then sweep north till July, when the whole country becomes inundated. Withdrawal of the rains from north to south starts in September, so that by the beginning of December, Madras has all but shaken itself dry like a dog stepping out from the spray of a garden hose. Though I've planned my trip to avoid the monsoons, I happily splash through a few puddles to christen this new adventure.

Every city has its quirks—the inconsequential details only travellers notice. With Madras, known in the south by its Tamil name of Chennai, it's discarded lottery tickets that litter gutters like fall leaves, money changers who work the streets like scalpers and an abundance of candy shops. On a grander scale, it's British Victorian architecture and giant billboards like those on L.A.'s Sunset Strip advertising Madras as the world's film capital, providing quantity is the criterion. After running errands, I take an auto-rickshaw to the Marine, where vendors selling pineapples, roasted corn and strings of boiled crabs lure a procession of families to the golden sand of Bengal Bay, wrapped in a line of misty ships like a wallpaper border. In any Western city, the balmy ocean on this sticky day would be churning with bodies, but in India water is treated more as a necessity or a sacrament than as an amusement. Only a few youths in swimsuits challenge the waves, occasionally joined by darting girls in saris or school uniforms who giggle uproariously when they are drenched. As I paddle along the shore with my long skirt soaked beyond the knees, I see only two other foreigners—a young couple posing for photos as I am constantly being asked to do.

By now I realize that I don't have time to explore sacred sites down both coasts of southern India; therefore, I decide to make the inland city of Bangalore my headquarters for focusing on the west coast. However, when I enter the Madras train station to catch the 6:00 a.m. Bangalore

Express on which I'm booked, I discover it has been cancelled because of flooding. Again I ricochet about the station with a porter, cashing in my ticket and making inquiries. This time I discover no trains will be leaving before tomorrow.

As I'm reviewing my options, a baggage handler grabs my arm. "Bangalore?" He points to a travel booth where an enterprising agent has just chartered a bus. Though the agent's price—200 rupees—is almost triple that of the train, I pay up with alacrity, then wait two hours, during which the price climbs to 300 rupees with the agent gleefully threatening to hike it to 500.

Unlike most of India's luxury buses, this one deserves the name. As we jounce westward, I realize how inconsequential the frequent travel hitches have become when measured against my joy in India, as tangible as a beautiful silk shawl that only occasionally slips from my shoulders. When I visited here twenty-two years ago, it was the exoticism of the country that excited me, the fantasy come true. Now, oddly, I feel at home.

From paddy fields and tropical forest, we climb rugged hills marked with rocky outcroppings resembling forts. It's this elevation that gives Bangalore its equitable climate, accounting for much of its post-sixties success as a business centre. With its shady streets, paved sidewalks, malls with tenants like Colonel Sanders, downtown "sin strips" featuring wine shops, pool halls and bars with names like Cloud 9, Bangalore is more a Western city than any I've visited so far. Though its name means Town of Boiled Beans for reasons lost in legend, today it's best known as Cyber City, the capital of India's Silicon Valley and a magnet for the 250 million members of India's emergent middle class. As proof of its modernity, signs posted on brick walls warn "Urination will attract administrative charges," or more euphemistically, "It is an offence to commit a nuisance here."

My hotel, the Mahaveer, is proud of its commercial status. A tower built around an atrium, it offers rooms with phones, colour TVs with movie channels and such amenities as shampoo (for black hair), soap, Kleenex, matches, bath towels and *two* clean sheets instead of the one supplied by many Indian hotels. And yet, on my first morning in my second-storey room, I awaken to the sound of a mooing cow.

One factor spurring my move to Bangalore was my decision to take my vipassana meditation course here in three weeks' time, from December 24 to January 4, providing a Buddhist resonance to Christmas and New Year's. A second is my desire to visit the temple of Sri Karunamayi, described by her devotees as an incarnation of Devi, the

Divine Mother, and a rising star in India's flourishing god industry. According to her official biography, *Sri Karunamayi*, published in 1992, Karunamayi's 1958 incarnation was the fulfilment of two visions: exactly a year before her birth, her devout mother was praying in a Mysore temple when she saw Devi descend over a lotus lake and then felt the goddess enter her body; at the time of Karunamayi's birth, her father was meditating, when he also beheld Devi surrounded by sixteen lights.

Even as a child, Vijayeshwari, as she was called, displayed unusual poise, meditated regularly and donated her belongings to the needy. At age three, she was declared Divine by the priest of Tirupati temple when he found her asleep under the sheltering hood of a cobra. Around that same time, Vijayeshwari's mother was anointing her when she became blinded by light from the child's eyes. "After that I was even afraid to touch my own daughter."

At age six, Vijayeshwari is said to have rescued several people by stopping a charging elephant in its tracks. When she was eight her mother was awestruck to discover her again asleep in the garden under the hood of a cobra. "The tender rays of the early morning sun matched the colour of the child's face, and they both looked alike. Seeing this cobra in such close proximity naturally created fear and anxiety in me. However, when I knelt and offered my prayers, the cobra calmly disappeared and could not be traced in any nearby areas."

At age eight, Vijayeshwari reportedly lifted an iron safe that eight men had struggled to move, allowing her father to retrieve some lost files. She also displayed an uncanny ability to read minds, to prophesy and to heal, including curing a maidservant of cholera.

As a college student, Vijayeshwari possessed a photographic memory and was a skilled artist and singer. Along with her academic work, she studied sacred texts, practised kundalini yoga and fasted for weeks at a time.

In 1980 Vijayeshwari left home to live in a remote forest north of Madras. After a decade spent meditating and enduring severe austerities on behalf of humanity, she founded an ashram on the outskirts of the forest, to which she has added an orphanage, a school for children with special needs, a food depot, free medical clinics and classes for the preservation of India's cultural heritage. Now known as Sri Karunamayi, meaning the Compassionate One, she teaches such precepts as:

Service to man is service to God.

There is no need for another lamp to see the Sun. It is enough to remove the curtain between the Sun and ourselves.

You speak to God in prayer, God speaks to you in meditation.

In practice it is very hard to control the mind immediately. . . . For example, the wild horses never listen to our words, but by training them constantly, then only are they able to listen to our words.

Wealth is like small dust particles before the power of the mantra.

As the arrow that leaves the bow cannot be taken back, what we talk senselessly about others causes us great harm.

A friend in need is a true friend, and one or two such friends are enough. Even relationships should not be cultivated in excess.

Compassion opens the door for real wisdom and expands the heart. Compassion melts the heart of worldly people and makes them as soft as butter.

At five-thirty, I arrive at Karunamayi's recently constructed suburban temple for her evening service. At the top of a steep marble staircase, I'm greeted by the only Westerner I will see this evening—a youthful man with a greying blond ponytail drawn back from fine features. Introducing himself as Joe from Alaska, he enthuses, "Sometimes when Karunamayi comes into a room you feel her energy immediately. It just pours out of her. Other times it creeps up on you."

"Do you think that she's Divine?"

"I'm absolutely convinced of it! I've rented a room nearby so I can attend all her services—well, see for yourself and judge."

"Have you ever visited Karunamayi's forest retreat?"

"Yes, but Westerners aren't usually allowed there because it's still too rough. I was sleeping on a dirt floor with mosquitoes in clouds around me. It was the best time of my life!"

About two hundred devotees sit cross-legged on straw mats in the temple, men to the left and women to the right, facing an altar featuring goddess sculptures with their gaudy colours softened by firelight. Some adherents, including Joe, create private altars of flowers, food and candles that they address through personal rituals. A woman with a microphone, accompanied by a male percussion band, leads the chanting of Devi's one thousand names expressed in 182 rhyming couplets, which Joe told me he is memorizing.

Though I attempt to meditate, I find myself sneaking peeks at a wall clock. I arrived around five and now it's seven—the time I told my auto-rickshaw driver that I'd be finished. Since his face lit up when I promised him a bonus if I went overtime, and since I don't mind paying the extra fee, my growing anxiety makes no rational sense. Focusing my mind through controlled breathing, I try to trace to source the habitual impatience that, since arriving in India, has so often bedevilled my efforts to meditate. The vivid image of a crying baby in a crib flashes to mind. The crying goes on a long time, till I've given up hope. When my mother does come, it's too late since I'm so upset that I throw up. *Is this a genuine memory?* Vaguely I recall my mother once telling me in a tone somewhere between regret and defensiveness that the experts of her day advised feeding infants on a strict schedule since picking up a crying baby was guaranteed to spoil it. Knowing my conscientious mother's intense respect for authority, I'm sure she would have stayed the course, no matter how difficult or calamitous. *Why would she tell me that story after thirty years if it weren't true, and why would I remember it for another thirty unless it were significant?* Once again I'm awaiting mother—in this case, the Divine Mother—and fretting like a hungry infant for whom a second seems a minute and a minute an intolerable hour. . . .

My eyes fly open. Karunamayi is seated on her throne, having entered through a door bearing her full-size likeness. At forty-one she appears younger and smaller than I expected. Her olive skin is unlined, her features pleasant, her black eyes arresting. As she speaks intimately to her rapt flock, exuding a femininity as silky as her gold-and-orange sari, her melodious words play through my mind like musical notes, and I see the face of the plaster goddess beside her appear to soften and to move. Though I know it's just flickering candlelight, in the dream I'm living perhaps this means something asleep in me is coming awake.

A devotee reads an English translation of Karunamayi's speech—a timely one for me, since it's all about

putting aside impatience, which Karunamayi labels a serious block on the path to self-realization. "Calming the
breath calms the mind," she continues. "Meditation is the
highest and hardest form of spirituality, but there's nothing it can't achieve if practised with patience. You must
keep at it. Silence is the key. Without meditation, everything we do is motivated by ego. Meditation goes beyond
religion. It purifies us by focusing our attention on what
we need to know."

Afterwards Karunamayi walks among us, carrying fire
for purification, then water for cleansing. Her eyes, rim-
med in kohl, are so dark that the pupils and irises coalesce.
When I look down into them, I see a reflection of her
candle: *the moon in the well*, as deep as all of India.

It's eight-thirty by the time I leave the temple. My driver is overjoyed with his bonus, heightening my own suddenly celebratory mood. As we pass restaurants, temples
and dance pavilions ablaze with lights, he tells me that this
is yet another day declared by astrologers to be lucky for
weddings, inspiring one half of Bangalore to marry the
other half.

*That night I dream I'm a baby crying in a crib. After a
near-fatal bout of choking, I cough up a snake longer than myself. When I stare at it on my pillow, I see that it is a jewelled
snake. Gazing at me with emerald eyes, it slithers away.*

As I lie in bed brooding about my dream, I hear a noisy
click. My television set has turned itself on. Mesmerized, I
watch the centre point of light enlarge into the black-and-

white image of an Indian sitting cross-legged: "Moonji!" Now fully awake, I slide up on my pillow, eager to converse. "I need your advice. Every time I think I've made a little progress, it's snatched away. I'm especially bothered by my restlessness in the temple."

Grinning, he replies, "That's because you think of meditation as a celestial staircase carrying you ever higher, when it's actually a cratered road that sometimes lurches downhill. It's the same with kundalini—sometimes it functions as a magic wand, and sometimes that wand turns into a snake. What's more, the snake has two heads, one jewelled and full of Mystery and the other poisonous."

I remember, suddenly, the cobra that convinced a temple priest that Karunamayi was Divine. "I'm also having trouble with the idea of god incarnations and the miracles that dot their biographies like raisins in a hot-cross bun."

Moonji's eyebrows shoot up into an inverted V. "What's your definition of a miracle?"

"Something that happens that couldn't possibly happen, I guess."

"Ahh, something that contradicts the laws of Western physics. A Miracle with a capital M."

"Sure. Anything else is just an illusion—a magician's trick."

Moonji's image has begun to rotate, requiring me to turn my head to look into his face as he explains, "Since we in the East already view the physical world as an illusion, miracles don't upset our framework of knowledge.

In fact, they support it by stripping away that sensory veil to uncover a deeper Truth."

"What truth?"

"The Truth that lies beyond material cause and effect."

Moonji now appears to be balanced on his head. "This is what you must do."

"Stand on my head?"

"Something more difficult. Stand your beliefs on their head. You know that television images are a two-dimensional illusion based on material reality. Now think of material reality as but a three-dimensional illusion based on an even more profound Reality."

"Plato argued that over two thousand years ago in his famous allegory of the cave! He compared the material world, which is all humans can perceive, to shadows cast by firelight on the walls of a cave, in comparison to the sun, which stands for the highest Reality."

"Of course. Sages through the ages have reclothed the same wisdom in different words and images to suit their times. To be understood, they too must be fashionable! The late physicist David Bohm, who claimed both the Eastern mystic Krishnamurti and Albert Einstein as his mentors, uses the image of the holograph. He describes the physical world as a three-dimensional holograph projected from a Reality with many more dimensions than we can grasp. Breakthroughs into that deeper order produce inspired thought while breakouts produce psychic phenomena."

"Such as miracles! But how come India has so many more than its fair share?"

"Perhaps that's because our people have learned to recognize them. Your physicists know how to split atoms through their understanding of physical laws. That's one way of manipulating matter. Do you suppose that through the course of many lifetimes, our sages may have learned to manipulate matter by going beyond those so-called laws?"

"It's still a lot harder to produce a miracle than to convince yourself and your devotees that you have."

Moonji's voice grows stern. "It's not your job to decide who's a miracle worker and who's a magician. It's enough that you open your mind to all possibilities. What may prove rarer than witnessing a miracle is being willing to accept one as such. We're all the product of conditioning. We see what we expect to see and reject the unfamiliar. When a tribe of African pygmies who had been brought up in dense jungle first encountered a herd of gnus thundering across the plain, they were thunderstruck. They didn't understand the gnus were coming closer. They thought they were *growing larger*. Similarly, when the eighteenth century British explorer Captain James Cook brought his ships to shore in Hawaii, the natives literally could not see them because nothing in their experience told them ships could be so large."

Moonji's image shrinks until it disappears from the screen, giving him the last word, as usual.

I take an overnight train from Bangalore down India's west coast to visit Mata Amritanandamayi, India's most famous female avatar, known internationally as the Hugging Saint. Since I've rejected air-conditioned class for second class, I occupy a lower bunk without bedding in a coach with all the amenities of a tin can. Nevertheless, I'm content. My open window delivers a salubrious breeze along with a first-class view of Kerala—India's most tropical state, stretching more than five hundred kilometres between the Arabian Sea and a crusty mountain ridge called the Western Ghats.

Kerala is also India's most progressive state, as the Christian minister sharing my coach is pleased to tell me. "Did you know that Kerala is 20 per cent Christian? We also have 90 per cent literacy, for which I credit both my church and the Communist Party."

"That seems an odd combination!"

"Not in Kerala. In 1957 we voted in the world's first freely elected Communist government. They were people who took land reform and wealth redistribution very seriously. They empowered ordinary people, and now it's impossible to go back."

My companion also takes pride in Kerala's infant-mortality rate, which is the lowest in India. "Not coincidentally, Kerala is also the only state with more women than men. To understand that sad connection, you have to understand the effect of the dowry system on Indian families. Most parents must start saving for a daughter's marriage the moment she's born, perhaps putting aside several times their yearly income, then hoping to get back that money with a son. If another daughter is born instead, that is an economic tragedy, inspiring a flood of sympathy cards from relatives and friends. Unfortunately, it's human nature to neglect such an unwanted child and to let events take their course. Though one family can hide its sin, when a whole state has significantly more boys than girls, such a statistic reveals its collective shame, which is why I take heart in Kerala's surplus of women."

"Do you think the dowry system is dying out?"

"I'd like to say yes, but, if anything, people are becoming greedier, especially the educated middle classes who should know better."

When I learn that Mata Amritanandamayi won't be at her ashram for another twelve days, I decide to spend a few of those at Kovalam Beach on the Arabian Sea, about seventy kilometres north of India's southernmost tip. I choose to stay at Simi Cottages because they remind me of those bungalows called Seabreeze, 4E's and Dew Drop Inn that my family rented on Lake Erie for two weeks every summer. From the veranda I can hear the Arabian Sea, smell its briny bouquet, glimpse surf down a lane running past the Ganesh Tattoo Parlour.

The beach itself consists of two sandy crescents sheltered by three rocky headlands. Fishermen's Beach to the north is dominated by the Ashok Beach Resort for people who wish to play tennis and lounge around a pool in international space that could be Florida or Cuba or the Algarve. Much the wider of Kovalam's two beaches, it's also the place where local fishermen sow the tides with finely textured ten-metre floating nets that they haul in, a couple of dozen to a rope, chanting and singing. After squishing out excess water by trampling the nets bulbous with jellyfish, they reap their silvery harvest, leaving thousands of fry for the gulls.

Lighthouse Beach to the south, where I and most other tourists stay, is a narrow strip backed by palm groves, lagoons and rice paddies, twisted with red-sand paths connecting resorts from modest to luxurious, massage parlours, herbalists, Internet services, money-changers, yoga schools, book exchanges, clothing boutiques and shops stocking whatever else tourists can be convinced that they need. On sand shading from golden to black, you can relax on a straw mat with the help of a masseur or rent a boogie board for surfing or dine on bowls of bananas, pineapple and mangoes prepared by one of the sari-clad women who work the beach with fruit stores piled on their heads. Toward evening, everyone shifts to the cheerful open-air restaurants with names like Velvet Dawn and Serenity to eat the catch of the day chosen from tables of tuna, calamari, butter fish, tiger prawns and barracuda proudly displayed by maître d's who beckon from their sandy porches. From then on, a tourist's only task is to watch the tide roll in.

My first purchase from Kovalam's hawkers is a cotton sarong featuring black and white elephants, which I tie over my bathing suit as my costume of choice. Since most foreigners on package tours from Europe come in pairs and seldom leave their beach mats, they're spared the perplexing problem I must face: what to do with my passport and money while swimming? Simi Cottages isn't the sort of place to have a wall safe; every brochure warns against hiding valuables in a cabin or hotel room and my only other choice—a towel on the beach—loops me back to my first bad alternative. Reluctantly I decide that I will leave my purse in my cabin but only after changing the door's padlock.

Still suffering separation anxiety, I wade into the long, rolling surf, the same soft temperature as the air. Since the waves are breaking quite fiercely, I dive through them, revelling in my first ocean swim in two years. The occasional school of jellyfish—harmless, colourless swatches with no discernible features—just add texture to the water, as if I were drifting through clouds of invisible butterflies.

All of a sudden I'm struck sharply on the calf by what I take to be a rope from a floating net. I search the cove for fishermen but see none. Deciding they must be across the rocky spur on their own beach, I resume swimming. Again I'm struck—another jarring slash. Again I scan the cove, and still failing to find the rope's source, I swim away, toward the candy-striped lighthouse marking this beach's southern boundary.

While floating on my back some twenty minutes later, I hear a distant frenzy of whistles. On shore I see gesturing lifeguards in blue shorts and shirts. Though I'm not sure this is for me, I'm much farther out than I imagined, so begin a determined swim toward them. Five minutes later, I check my position. I'm no closer. I redouble my efforts. When I look a second time, I'm farther away. Though I'm now certain the lifeguards are blasting whistles at me, I'm powerless against the current sweeping me out to sea. I've heard this cove is ribbed by dangerous riptides, but until now I thought they operated like undertows with a warning tug that alerted a person to withdraw to safety. This surface countercurrent caught me so smoothly and irresistibly that I felt I was floating in whipped cream. As I will later learn, about the only way to outswim a riptide is to cross it on the bias, but my logical mind is fixed on what looks like the shortest route to safety. The lifeguards have no boat, and I can see none in this cove. If one attempts to rescue me by swimming, he too will be swept away. Though my situation appears hopeless, I'm still more bewildered than panicky, even forceful in my denial. *This isn't supposed to happen. I'm not supposed to die at this time in this place.* I remind myself: *Surely every drowning person has this same thought, 'Not me, not now.'* As I continue to lose ground, a chill creeps through me. *There's no solution.* And then: *I could die here.* I've always imagined that in such a circumstance, I'd experience a super-surge of energy, allowing me to swim to shore, but all I feel is peaceful surrender: *so be it.*

Suddenly, I remember: *the rope!* At that instant, I feel it slash my thigh. Snatching it, I pull myself handhold by handhold toward shore, grateful for the abrasive feel of its fibres against my palms. My mind remains detached, my thoughts weirdly convoluted, as I experience myself being pulled forward. *It's not fair to the fishermen to have to haul me in imagining I'm a big catch.* Like a guilty child, I'm glad the rope is hidden so no one can see that I'm hitching a ride.

A wave washes over me, breaking my grip and tossing me in a loop-the-loop. As I sputter to the surface, my toes brush bottom. Opening my eyes, I see three lifeguards, like a trio of glistening, dark-skinned angels, arms interlocked against the tide, bobbing toward me. As they catch and then float me to shore, my mind continues its queer little flight of fancy: *It would be impolite for me to undermine the drama of this rescue by mentioning the rope.* Jocularly I remind myself, *This is the only time in India I've taken a ride without first asking the price.*

A crowd has gathered. Though I'm feeling more hyperactive than tired, I let my rescuers lead me to a chair under an umbrella to rest. After a polite ten minutes, I announce, "I'd like to go back to my room to change."

A lifeguard not involved in the rescue asks, "Will you sign our book first . . . to say you were rescued?"

As I follow him through a palm grove with my feet not quite touching ground, he catches me in a conversational current as subtle as the riptide: "Five of us lifeguards work together. Those who have been rescued like to make a donation." The sum of $300 U.S. is mentioned.

Accepting his book without comment, I write a fulsome note of gratitude. "I'll come to your station after I've changed."

Back in my room, I find my passport and money, undisturbed, including some foreign currency. Three hundred dollars U.S. is a huge sum in a country where the annual per capita income is $370, but by now I've been in India long enough to know everything is negotiable, even this, with the asking price usually three to ten times the final one. Didn't the Minnesota traveller I met in Jaisalmer rent a helicopter for twenty minutes for $400 U.S.? I wish to be generous without letting the situation deteriorate into a payoff or a shakedown. I *know* I couldn't have made it to shore without the rope. Though I probably could have without the lifeguards, I'm grateful not to have had to try.

An hour later I count out $100 U.S., in the form of five crisp twenties, into the hand of my rescuers' agent. Then, to sweeten any shortfall between expectation and reality, I explain, "I'm a writer. I'd like to take your pictures and

interview you on my tape recorder for a book or a news-
paper article I may write." My rescuers seem content with
the money and thrive on the attention while I'm satisfied
the deal is ecologically sound: a significant sum for them
while respecting local values and not selling out the next
tourist. As for what I'm supposed to learn from the experience, I decide that this must be a cosmic joke: after all
the attention I bestowed on my "valuables," they were
perfectly safe while I was not. Still . . . I can't shake the
feeling that this experience remains unfinished. That this
joke may have a second punchline. . . .

That evening it rains hard—the first storm since my arrival in India fifty days ago. The downpour feels energizing, even thrilling, as water pummels the makeshift plastic
roof hastily erected over the surfside patio where I'm
drinking white wine. Again I'm reminded of summer cottages—of myself as a child staring through tear-drenched
windows as phosphorescent lightning bolts struck the
lake where I'd just been swimming, shivering with elation
to be so close to so much raw God power. Now, as towering breakers slash this shore, I watch the beacon from the
red-and-white lighthouse sweep the cove, illuminating
ordinary objects so they glow like the landscape in a
Magic Realist painting . . . God's finger pointing toward
me. I know I came as close to death as the red candle now

sputtering on my table, but I can't feel anything beyond a light-headed, surreal sense of detachment. I try to picture my bloated body snagged on a reef somewhere in the Arabian Sea, already an object of interest to nibbling fish. I imagine the surprise of the fishermen, perhaps in one of those boats now strung like Christmas lights across the horizon, as they open their nets to find . . . a mermaid with blue skin, crabs for eyes and seaweed hair. I try to grasp the finality of deadness, of eternity, and manage to conjure up a shudder or two. Was I right in believing it wasn't "my time"? The fact that I'm sitting here eating the catch of the day instead of being eaten by it suggests yes, but the millions who did drown when they were sure it couldn't happen to them aren't here to answer their questionaires.

As a gust of wind snuffs out my candle, leaving only its carbon ghost, I think about the rope—the impossible solution to an unsolvable problem. What were the chances of my reaching down into the ocean and finding a lifeline exactly where and when I needed it? With gooseflesh rippling up my arms, I even play with the idea that I might be dead. In ghost stories the corpse is often the last to know. *How can I be sure?*

Smiling, the waiter relights my candle, then presents me with a bill. *That's how. I guess not.* I lay down my money, which he accepts with enthusiasm. *Not this time.*

Despite such broodings, when I leave Kovalam three days later, I assume this must be the end of the story. But it isn't. Two months after I've returned to Toronto, I awaken early one April morning with a sense of urgency . . . something I've been dreaming . . . something puzzling, something not quite right . . . *something about Kovalam*. I lie in bed trying to figure out what it is that's bothering me . . . *something about the rope.*

I look at a map of Kovalam. I've never before tried to figure how far out the riptide carried me because I didn't see how I could. Now I realize that I should be able to establish the minimum angle that would allow a rope from a net in Fishermen's Cove to clear the rocky spur separating it from Lighthouse Cove where I was swimming. With a tape measure, I establish that if the fishermen were in their usual place just over the spur, the rope would have had to be at least eight hundred metres out when I caught it—more than eight football fields! Now, as I measure from the farthest arm of the cove to establish a minimum distance, my heart begins to thud. *None of this matters!* At last I grasp the simple fact that's been eluding me. *If I were hauled in on a rope from Fishermen's Cove, I would have ended up in Fishermen's Cove, which I didn't. My rope pulled me straight into the middle of Lighthouse Beach.*

I'm so dizzy that I have to lie down. As I flop onto my bed, struggling against unconsciousness, my mind feverishly reviews all I can remember about the rescue, especially its oddities: though I had no contact with the rope for at least thirty minutes, the instant I thought about it, it slashed my leg; it was exactly the right depth for me to grasp to propel myself forward; it was low enough to remain concealed from everyone on shore so that I would have looked as if I were breast-stroking; it was taut, meaning it was secured at both ends, not something floating in the water; it was moving as if being pulled—I felt a firm tug at all times, spawning my inane sense of guilt about hitching a free ride. The rope disappeared the moment I didn't need it any longer.

Lighthouse Beach, which is only a few metres wide, was filled with sunbathers. Two dozen men pulling a ten-metre-square net isn't something you can overlook. I saw no fishermen when I emerged from the water or when I sat under the lifeguards' umbrella. *There were no fishermen on Lighthouse Beach.* I move to my next realization. *There was no rope.*

the
sound
of
silence

"Each atom is constantly
 singing a song"

THE WAITERS are sleeping on their tables when I leave Kovalam at first light. It's a twenty-minute hike across the two coves, then up a cliff, where I'm hoping to find an auto-rickshaw to take me twelve kilometres to Kerala's capital of Trivandrum. While bent low under an improvised backpack, I'm feeling un-hurried, upbeat and well rooted in the sensuous universe as my sandals rhythmically bite the sand. Since I still have another week before Mata Amritanandamayi, the Hug-ging Saint, returns to her ashram, I've decided to detour inland to the Periyar Wildlife Reserve.

An auto-rickshaw *is* waiting at the top of the cliff, with the result that I arrive two hours early at Trivandrum's dilapidated, fall-down-drunk bus depot. Installing myself on a broken bench, with feet propped over a puddle cov-ering half the floor, I munch my breakfast, consisting of a spicy dried-bean mix along with some bananas, the trav-eller's friend: ubiquitous, nutritious, filling, cheap and delivered in their own sanitary wrappers. A young woman squats facing me, mimicking the motion of my hand to my mouth with a soulful theatricality that's both mawkish and mocking. Offended by what I experience as aggression, I change my seat. She moves with me. When I spill some dry-food mix, she scoops it up and eats it, including the bits that landed in the puddle. If her intention is to shame me, she succeeds. Since most beggars make it clear they want money and not food from foreigners, it never occurred to me that she might be hungry. Giving her both the package and the bananas, I escape in the direction of the reservation booth.

Though I've already been told by its agent that I can't prepurchase a ticket for Periyar, I approach him again with the same question. When he shakes his head, I persist: "The man I talked to last night told me I could make a reservation."

Shrugging, he uses the word *coupon*, then points out the door. Behind the depot I discover a bank of windows and a mob scene. I join the ladies' line, though it's as long as the other six, hoping for gentler treatment. It's only 8:00 a.m., but already I'm caught in the clammy grip of what will be a torrid day. At the point when I realize my line isn't moving, a woman carrying a baby tugs at my sleeve. As I'm handing her a 10 rupee note, a sweet-faced woman approaches me, wearing a pale blue voile gown. "The crush today is because of yesterday's general strike," she explains. "Some of the long-distance buses haven't come in because they weren't travelling."

Though Indian, her ethereal dress has features that seem Quakerish. "Does that mean the Periyar bus?"

"We'll have to wait and see. It hasn't been called yet."

As if reading my thoughts, she adds, "But you *are* in the right line. It isn't moving because they don't sell coupons until a bus has been called."

"What are coupons?"

"They let you on the bus, but you still have to buy a ticket from the driver. They cost 2 rupees." She stops to listen to an announcement. "That's *my* bus." Smiling, she returns to her place near the front of the line.

As so often happens in India, my two-hour lead has melted to half an hour. While I'm calculating the time it will take to reach the wicket, the woman in blue returns. "I've made a place for you up with me. Come." Gratefully I follow her to the front of the line, where I'm greeted with smiles from those I displace. "You needn't worry. I'm going to look after you. I'll wait with you till your bus is called." Identifying herself as a member of the Little Sisters of Jesus, she adds, "Yesterday's strike was to raise the minimum wage. We take strikes seriously in Kerala."

By now the line is moving steadily. As we reach the wicket, another announcement is made. "That's your bus," says my blue lady, beaming. Taking my 2 rupees, she buys me a coupon.

"I'm going on that same bus!" exclaims the vivacious young woman behind me. "I'll look after you now." Introducing herself as Kamini, she guides me to platform number 2, where her father, who has come to see her off, is saving waiting-room seats. Since I don't put much trust in my flimsy 2 rupee coupon, I elect to join the boisterous scrum at the bus stall. A porter snatches both my bag and my coupon. While I'm still protesting, he leads me onto an empty bus and installs me in seat 39. This is the first I've noticed the number scrawled on the back of my coupon, indicating I do have a reservation. The dénouement comes, as always, when he asks for 100 rupees. I give him 50. When he protests, I give him an extra 10. Satisfied, he leaves.

As the bus driver pulls into platform 2, passengers claw their way on board, showing as little faith in their coupons as I. Following politely in their wake is the owner of the still-empty seat beside me: Kamini, cool and unrumpled in her mint green salwar kameez.

By the time we leave, the aisles are jammed. As I glance through the horizontal bars that substitute for windows, I catch the eye of my porter and we exchange spontaneous smiles. Now that I no longer have a gun to my head, I hand him an extra 20 rupees through the bars, and now that his values are in line with reality, he accepts with joy. I remember the words of the dadis of Mount Abu—*Make your expectations zero and happiness becomes 100 per cent.* When the porter set his sights on 100 rupees, he was discontent with 50; after he'd adjusted to 50, he was satisfied with 60 and thrilled with 80. If I had an advance reservation, I might be annoyed to be stuffed with two others on a bench comfortably seating two, but since I thought I wouldn't get on, I'm grateful for this skinny slot with my luggage shoving my knees to my chin. This is especially true when I count only twelve seats behind me, meaning that if the blue lady hadn't rescued me I'd be jammed like a smelt in the aisles.

I also ponder the laws of karma. When I gave the beggar in the depot my breakfast, I found out about the coupon. The instant I gave rupees to the young mother, the lady in blue claimed me. Is this some principle of order at work, or am I projecting meaning onto chance? Either way, India with its endless negotiations demonstrates how character and destiny are shaped by moment-to-moment choices just as dabs of paint create a pointillist portrait. In the West our entertainments, our politics and our therapies flatter us into thinking that our lives and characters are fashioned from grander brushstrokes.

As the bus shunts through Trivandrum, Kamini tells me she's a civil servant who commutes three hours each weekend to her in-laws' home. "My husband saw me at my sister's wedding and asked for me, so it was an arranged marriage. He's jolly and kind, though he prefers to live with his parents, and my mother-in-law is very nice—just like my own mother. She even prefers her daughters-in-law to her sons, which is very, very unusual. A friend of mine was treated so badly that her family pleaded with her in-laws to stop beating her. That's unusual too. Generally a woman is expected to accept what she gets."

When Kamini debarks, I acquire a much plumper seat-mate. Though I'm three hours into a nine-hour trip, the aisle is still solid with people who've been standing since

Trivandrum. As I stare through the window bars, enjoying the verdant countryside and the occasional gust of wind, I'm jolted by a sharp retort followed by the disappearance of both breeze and view. The young man in front has slapped down a pleated, black leather curtain so he can sleep against it, leaving me with a narrow slot of vertical light from the window behind, accessible only by twisting my neck almost backward like the devil-possessed child Regan in *The Exorcist*. I am furious. I can't believe how furious. My arms ache with the suppressed urge to pummel him. Where is this rage coming from?

When the bus slides into a crowded terminal, about half the passengers file off, including Mr. Shades. *Nothing* could persuade me to leave my seat. I'm planning to be cremated in it. Just as I'm reaching forward to lift that infernal black hood, another youth slides across the seat and raises it for me: sun bursts in like a giant sunflower. I'm breaking open a bottle of distilled water to celebrate when—*bam!*—the shade behind me crashes. Now the slot through which I've seen the world for the past hour has been blacked out, but that's merely an irritant, not a reason to kill.

When the driver revs his engine, most of those who left the bus return, including Mr. Shades, now forced to stand in the aisle. Unfortunately, in this take-no-prisoners world, a blind youth has also been dispossessed. The sight of him clutching his white cane while grappling with the bumps and twists of the road is intolerable. Signalling to the peasant woman crushed against him, I indicate he can have my seat. She drops her eyes, apparently too shy to speak with a foreigner. As I'm repeating my message, the large woman sharing my bench departs, allowing the peasant woman to deftly guide the blind youth into the vacated seat. He's a skinny lad and she's barely a handspan. By sliding forward I make room for her as well.

Though we're supposed to arrive at Periyar by four-thirty, we're running an hour late and it has begun to rain. Because my hotel is inside the park, which closes at six, this concerns me. As the bus has climbed northeast from the coast into the Western Ghats, the countryside has grown spectacularly beautiful, with deep forest rifts giving way to tea plantations of a startling green. I've never before seen a colour in nature like this. It glows even through the mist, as if brushed with luminous paint, with the flat-topped tea bushes so densely packed that the whole valley seems expensively broadloomed. Women draped in pink, blue and yellow plastic sheets flutter among them like giant butterflies, harvesting leaves. As I crane to see out both sides of the bus, shades slam down, two by two, then three by three, until we're in a hearse with one open window. Curiously, it's the window in front of me now once again in possession of the youth who closed it earlier. The wind is whipping through its bars and he's getting wet, as I am. I have a raincoat. He doesn't, but he doggedly hangs in, perhaps having sensed my ferocious attachment to the window. As the weather worsens,

I begin to think I've laid a curse on it or him. The poor fellow can't close it, though he's shivering. At last he departs the bus. His seatmate doesn't move over, and he doesn't close the window. The aisle seat on my bench is also empty, but the scrawny peasant woman who was once too shy to speak remains glued to my side like a second skin. Even to draw my raincoat around me I have to struggle against her sharp bones. Perhaps she's so used to existing in small spaces that she can't accept the luxury of larger ones, like a bird that stays in its cage after the door has been opened, like all of us imprisoned by delimiting habits and viewpoints.

We arrive at Periyar Park ten minutes before it closes.

I know I'm in a wildlife reserve when I open my casement and a monkey pops in. I also know that whatever he snatches in the next thirty seconds I'll never see again—passport, money, camera—they're spread across my bed like a monkey's smorgasbord. However, just as my possessions weren't my immediate concern when I was caught in the riptide at Kovalam, so they aren't now. My floor-to-ceiling double French window was apparently already unlatched when I leaned against it to open it. As it swung outward, I clutched at its frame to keep from falling, so that I am now clinging precariously to the window two storeys above concrete. Refusing to look down, I manage to hook my closer foot across the sill and into the room, then to swing back on the window just as the monkey leaps out the other side, triumphantly waving a paper bag. Sitting in a tree crotch he defiantly displays, then devours, its contents—some orange rinds that I righteously refrained from tossing out of the bus as everyone else was doing.

Monkeys have a special place in the psychology of India, partly because of the Hindu fondness for their monkey-faced god Hanuman. However, while Hanuman was the selfless and sober servant of Lord Rama, an avatar of Vishnu's, India's monkeys are her court jesters—privileged, mischievous and quick to capitalize on human error. Periodically, communities plead to their state governments for help in controlling them through relocation. This week students of Lucknow University in Uttar Pradesh took to the streets for three days to protest their loss of clothes, shaving kits, books and food to marauding monkeys. Since the monkeys had also crashed the prime minister of Uttar Pradesh's computer system by chewing through the wires, the students seemed assured of a favourable hearing. Still, a delicate hand is needed, since Hindus and animal activists will not tolerate cruelty. A few years back a resident of Lucknow, angered by a pillaging monkey, shot the bandit dead. Not only was he arrested, but protest demonstrators established a fund for public cremation of the monkey.

My room at the government-run Aranya Nivas Hotel is decorated in the hunting-lodge style of the twenties, with a wine velvet settee, a matching outsized bed, a mirrored dressing table and a spacious marble bathroom. However, I'm far more interested in the world outside my window— wet and foggy but clearing to reveal the heavy limbs and high canopy of an old forest. Since it's been raining two days here, I feel lucky for this modest reprieve, especially when I read about the flooding to the southeast, turning streets into rivers that sweep cars and cows into Bengal Bay. Leaning very, very carefully out the window, I breathe in the loamy jungle odours, listen intently to the monkey chatter, the songs of birds and the cough of something large, which I hope isn't just another tourist with a cold.

Ten minutes before the departure of the morning wildlife cruise, the jetty downhill from the Aranya Nivas has attracted about a hundred passengers, mostly Indian. We board one of several peeling, flat-bottomed, double-decker boats, then arrange ourselves in rows on chairs with cameras and binoculars. The lake itself is magical, twenty-six square kilometres set amid vegetation so freshly tipped that it's as if one can watch it grow. At the same time a russet-flowering tree, prominent in the rolling hills, and the brown water heavy with reflections produce an autumnal cast. The signature of this hundred-year-old lake is its dozens of dead trees poking up like skeletal hands, the ghostly remains of the forest flooded to create it.

Though Periyar is sometimes referred to as a tiger reserve, the closest any of the present park personnel has come to seeing one of these fierce nocturnal cats is a dusty plaster cast of pawprints kept in the Tourist Information Office. During a couple of hours of cruising, we glimpse a dozen boar and some bison—a pleasant, low-key introduction to Indian wildlife. Then, just as we're returning to the jetty, we're summoned by boisterous trumpeting. Drawing closer to its source, we see one chocolate brown elephant and then another grow visible in the dense shore foliage. They're small in comparison with the grey African giants more usually conscripted for zoos, circuses and Hollywood, but still substantial enough to rip down trees, as they're doing now. While we watch, enchanted, they ford the channel, stately and unhurried, ears billowing like ancient sails, displacing a keg of mud at each step, some prowed by gleaming white scimitars, some shepherding their babies with their corrugated trunks as sensitive as hands. On the far shore, the jungle opens its green mouth, engorging them one by one.

In the afternoon I hike the forest road to Kumily, a one-street town still specializing in the spices that Kerala has exported for hundreds of years—cardamom, ginger, pepper, cloves, nutmeg and turmeric. Through broad-leafed teaks, filigree bamboos and fragrant balsams, I glimpse blue sky and spirals of mist like fairy smoke. Following a yellow butterfly as it hovers over orange lantanas, I spot one of the weirdest birds I've ever seen. Though its sleek blue-black chassis is of standard size and shape, its tailfins sprout drooping, fifteen-centimetre tendrils fancifully ending in tufts. Minutes later at a souvenir shop, I leaf through a bird book until I find its picture, unmistakable: "Greater racket-tailed drongo. Seen in semi-evergreen and deciduous biotopes. Sexes alike. Feeds on insects and moths. Excellent mimic of other birds."

Though some of my friends are ardent birdwatchers, I've resisted until now, preferring wildflowers, which stay still long enough for positive identification. With these feathered things, my specimen has departed by the time I've found the right subsection in the manual. Even when one does stay put, deciding whether it's fifteen centimetres or twenty, whether its top feathers are grey or taupe, its breast cream or beige defeats me. Here in India where birds are as inclined to be fluorescent green as sparrow brown, where they have dangly bits like my greater racket-tailed drongo, I'm softening for the challenge. I buy the book for my evening cruise.

Identification proves easier than I dared imagine, with many candidates posing on the lake's stump forest as obligingly as if stuffed and mounted. Here's a duck-billed cormorant spreading its wings to dry like clothes on a line; a fish-eating darter with striped neck so slender and supple that it looks uncannily like a striking snake; a grey heron as skinny as a supermodel with punk blond hairdo; a rusty, curved-beak kestrel; a green parakeet with blossom pink head; a turquoise-and-orange-and-white kingfisher with rapier beak; a white-breasted, jade green barbet; a pink-breasted, blue-winged blackbird and the ubiquitous speckled doves and jungle crows. It's as if a chunk of sky has opened like a skylight, welcoming me to a world where to know a bird's name is to possess its spirit. As the sun sets, leaving erratic orange splashes, the air fills with intense nesting sounds followed by silence so complete that I'm assured by the information officer that we can easily hear a single bird from the twin peaks half a kilometre away.

From the moment I arrived in Periyar I've been warned by park and hotel personnel that it's too wet for a jungle trek. Since dozens of alluring green tunnels fan out from the road, this seems a serious deprivation. When I pressure my hotel manager, I receive a series of "yes, buts" which I counter with "yes, buts" of my own.

"Yes, but you'll need boots."

"Yes, but I have desert boots, and if it's too wet I can always turn back."

"Yes, but what about the leeches? The paths are crawling with them. They'll get up your trousers."

"Yes, but I've got thick knee socks. I can tuck my khakis inside them." Fortunately, no one mentions the cobras and other vipers that routinely float from rock crevices during flooding.

The paths into Periyar's rain forest are of red mud, a little slimy but hard packed. Like most jungle creatures, my small-boned young guide is obscured by facial foliage in the form of swooping moustache and bushy hair. Though he's kind and knowledgeable, he's more used to experiencing nature than talking about it. Once we're passed the poinsettias and morning glories planted for tourists, the quiet green of the jungle takes over. It's the green of a thousand shades from lime to almost black, and of a million shapes from vine tendrils and grass and needles to a myriad of lobed, spiky, scalloped and serated leaves. Green that creeps, that tangles, that drifts and flutters and towers. Green that feeds and houses. Green, the colour of the transmuted sun, of life on earth. I love it all, the pungent smells, the hoots and whistles, cackles and squeals, played against an electrifying hum of crickets.

We ford a muddy channel by bamboo raft lashed with vines, paddled by a dhoti-wearing local who lives with his family in a tent. Now the forest is all-embracing, leaving only irregular swatches of sky between the white-trunked birches draped in black moss, the banyans dripping with long-fingered parasites, the twisted teak bowls turned ghostly white by layers of fungi. We hear the squeals of wild boar and the rustlings of something fast and brown, the size of a raccoon, that my guide calls a Malabar giant squirrel. We see tracks of deer and the leftover bones and fur of old kills, while the sky-high canopy shakes with the antics of monkeys and flying squirrels.

The leeches are as bad as advertised—not the fat, sluggish kind one finds under Canadian docks but black, needle-thin wrigglers, about five centimetres long. By perpetual motion they worm their way into tightly woven socks, between the soles and uppers of shoes, through shoelace holes, gouging flesh and leaving fiery wounds. Fortunately we're carrying a bag of leech napalm—a red-brown powder that we smear over our shoes and socks, killing them on contact. It has a common name—tobacco powder.

When we arrive at a swollen creek, my guide traverses it by fallen log, then reaches back for me. Though this improvised bridge supported his slight frame, it crashes under my North American poundage, giving me a soaker and a fresh crop of leeches. Then, just as we arrive at the place where our circular path is supposed to close, we encounter a swamp, meaning we must return the way we came—another hour's trek instead of five minutes. We also find fresh elephant droppings like the horse manure left by the milk wagons of my childhood, except these are the size of bowling balls. Sniffing the air, my guide announces matter-of-factly, "The herd is coming this way."

It's already growing dark in this place of stingy sky. As the forest stealthily closes in, I concentrate on the red-mud path, following my guide at a purposeful yet unhurried gait, lulled by a serene sense of oneness with nature. Jerking out of my meditative doze, I see that the footprints ahead of mine are bare. Someone in green robes and trailing vines is walking behind my guide. Falling into step with me, Moonji passes noiselessly through the brush beside the path.

"There's something different about you," he offers. "Do you know what it is?"

"That I have tobacco powder from my feet to my knees? That leeches are boring through my soles?"

"Something good. Your ears. They're as big as an elephant's. Ever since you chanted in the Golden Temple, I've been watching them open up. Listen! What do you hear?"

"I hear birds. I hear monkeys."

"Listen deeper."

"I hear the wind."

". . . *the breath of God.*"

"It's rustling through the trees."

". . . *the web of life.*"

There's a Sanskrit saying, *Nada Brahma*, 'the universe is sound.' Everything in creation is vibration, rhythm, waves, harmony."

I stop to apply more tobacco powder. "I guess that's what Pythagoras meant when he said, 'All is numbers,' then spoke of the 'harmony of the spheres,' though I'm not sure exactly what music and mathematics have in common."

"Relationships!" exclaims Moonji. "It's not one number but the entire equation, not one note but the melody." He scoops up a stone. "Atoms also sing. This pebble contains a whole percussion band waiting only for someone to listen."

I put it to my ear.

"I see you close your eyes to listen. Very good. Before we had eyes we had ears. In the darkness of the womb they were all we knew of the outer world, and they are the last sense to desert us in death. Though our eyes are wonderful instruments, they encourage us to notice differences as well as our own separateness. Our ears invite us to connect things, to find inner and outer harmony."

"I guess that's why the blind boy in Rishikesh played his flute so beautifully."

Moonji's voice slows to match the rhythm of our feet, as if his words were notes and our footsteps a metronome. "It's only when God turns out the lights and the stars burst forth that we can comprehend the vastness of the universe and our place in it. The sun illuminates our own ego-planet, blinding us to the rest. When scientists want to know what's happening in the farthest reaches of the universe, it's to their radio telescopes that they turn."

We pause while my guide repairs the bridge I crashed through on the inbound trek. "Did you know that scientists can now hear the distinctive hum of each planet?"

continues Moonji. "In fact, the late Hans Kayser, who founded the scientific study of harmonics, argued that the musical relationship between the planets is so perfect that scientists could have predicted the outer planets and the asteroid belt between Mars and Jupiter before they were discovered."

While I cross the bridge, Moonji walks on the water, never missing a beat: "Ptolemy and Kepler, those great pioneers of the sky, also thought of the cosmos as an orchestra, the solar system as a symphony, the Earth as a movement and each of us as chords made up of billions of notes." He stops, cupping his ear. "Listen. What do you hear?"

"I hear . . . the trees like a thousand harp strings, their leaves like tiny bells."

"Listen . . ."

"I hear the sun sliding sonorously behind the mountains. I hear the mist settling with a sigh over the swamp and the moon rising, dark and sombre, inside a tinkling sliver of light."

"Listen deeper, what do you hear?"

"I hear . . . Silence."

In the four days left before I head for Mata Amritanandamayi's coastal ashram, I decide to push farther inland to the hill station of Munnar. The seventy-kilometre four-hour bus trip north from Periyar delivers on the promise cut short by rain and falling black blinds on my earlier journey. Celestial peaks enshrined in mist, crashing falls with their watery feet clotted in trumpet lilies, emerald forests dotted with trees crowned in salmon blossoms are revealed during one switchback, only to be snatched away by the next. What does it matter that the pokey town of Munnar, sixteen hundred metres above sea level, has little to offer when I can stand on the balcony of my hotel gazing up into 150,000 hectares of tea plantations and down into an idyllic river valley. Though the whitewashed workers' bungalows lose some of their charm when their red roofs turn out to be rusty metal, I'm captivated by the emerald sea of tea catching every nuance of sun and shadow, then playing each back with virtuosity. Even after the narrow road turns to red clay, the hike is easy and rewarding with loops skilfully engineered to provide maximum lift for minimum effort.

According to legend, tea originated many centuries ago in Assam, northeast India, when a holy man was told in a vision that he could enhance his meditations with a drink made by boiling the leaves of certain bushes growing in abundance around him. As the guru's fame spread, he attracted more and more visitors, to whom he offered this stimulating brew. Some took home dried leaves for themselves and friends, unwittingly passing on the simple recipe. When it reached China's Szechwan province, a tea craze was launched among the aristocracy that spread toward the end of the seventeenth century to Europe, and especially to Britain. As India's colonizers, the British were attracted not only to places like Assam, where tea was indigenous, but also to the jungles of Munnar, where it might be coaxed to grow. When the first twenty-hectare tea field was planted in 1888, accommodations consisted only of mud-and-wattle huts protected by elephant trenches.

Since the Parsi-owned Tata Tea company purchased most of this area's holdings in 1983, it's presumably on Tata property that I'm now trespassing. The switchback road is so seductive that I couldn't stop even if I wanted. Though all I see are tea fields broken by the occasional creek or grove or herd of black boulders, the contours of the land are too spectacular ever to grow dull. The faintly acrid smell of tea conjures up memories of my grandmother, a British widow who died when I was eight. Everything about her two-room suite tucked upstairs in our house owed something to the habit of tea drinking: the carefully displayed Worcestershire and Wedgwood cups that staked our family's claim to gentility despite their chips and cracks, the old tea tins containing buttons, the oak parlour table where she told fortunes from tea leaves for the perfumed strangers who paid $5 each and the rickety card table where she read for non-paying friends, with me hanging over her shoulder, pointing out images in the mysterious clusters, earning the praise that I had the Gift.

Perhaps it's because of my English ancestry that I glory in the perpetual greenness flung in all directions, yearn to dance on it, dive into it: if I'm away from green landscapes for more than a couple of weeks, my eyes feel parched. I remember magical spring walks through Derbyshire pastures dotted with flocks of sheep and freshly dropped lambs, but here I'm genuinely alone without Bentleys churning dust behind me or demon motorcycles knocking me sideways with their aggressive roar. Occasionally I do hear a gentle swish, like gusting wind, of the hand clippers with plastic bags attached, like the grass catchers on old lawn mowers, used by women to harvest the leaves. Some call to ask my name or where I'm from as the road unfurls like a ball of ribbon, always racing around the next corner before I can catch up, sometimes even splitting in two. I try to memorize landmarks, knowing all will be reversed on the way back, converting what I hoped would be familiar into green anonymity.

Once or twice I encounter an ugly fissure: a belching processing plant like a blackened metal pot polluting the fresh mountain air.

I turn, in surprise, at the sound of a voice: "I wonder what our Assam holy man would make of this extension of his vision," comments a figure wrapped in a cloak the colour of the earth.

It's Moonji, of course, sitting by the roadside drinking tea brewed in a Brown Betty teapot covered with a crocheted cozy. As he pours some for me in a cracked

Wedgwood cup, I ask, "How come it's all right for gurus to stimulate their meditations with tea but not with alcohol, tobacco, drugs or even coffee?"

Smacking his lips to exaggerate his enjoyment, he replies, "Tea protects the human system, whereas coffee weakens it, tobacco poisons it, alcohol addles it and hallucinogens take the brain far faster and farther than it knows how to travel."

"Oh, I don't know about that," I protest. "My one LSD experience was a great adventure and a hugely valuable one."

Moonji's disdainful look, delivered without comment, only makes me more eager to continue. "Shortly into the experience, amid the usual swirls of coloured light, I suddenly heard myself ask some real or imagined Higher Force, 'Who created the world?' I couldn't have been more astonished when an answer came back, 'God created the world.' Then I asked, 'Who created God?' The answer came back, 'Who's asking?' I replied, 'Who's asking who's asking?' The reply, 'Who's asking who's asking who's asking?' Then again, 'Who's asking who's asking who's asking who's asking?'"

Widening his yellow-brown eyes over the rim of his cup, Moonji makes them spin like psychedelic discs, in a manner designed to tease me.

"I know all this sounds banal," I protest, "but in the silence between each question and the unexpressed answer, it was as if I were delving ever deeper into myself in return for a more profound experience of Reality."

Betraying his first glint of interest, Moonji replies, "Did you know that 'Who's asking?' is a koan that Zen monks sometimes present to their students?"

"The only koan I know is the one everyone knows—the sound of one hand clapping."

"As paradoxes, koans don't make sense to the logical mind. You have to go inside them, spiral around them, experience the solution on a higher and deeper level. That's often difficult for a culture like yours that values the straight line over the circle."

I sip my tea, recollecting. "To the extent that what I learned can be expressed, it was the Self as a microcosm of the Whole, the 'I am' as a reflection of the 'I AM.' Unfortunately, after each revelation my rational mind would exclaim, 'Got it!' and I would lose what I thought I had. Then I'd try again, catch it again, lose it again, find it again. Yet for minutes at a time I felt infused with the never-to-be-forgotten bliss of truth, beauty, ultimate belonging and perfect love."

"Sages don't need drugs for that," chides Moonji. "They can, if they choose, live every day on a mountain-top of bliss."

"Maybe so, but my experience at least gave me a hint of the possibilities—a mark to aim for."

Moonji tucks our cups and saucers under his cloak till it bulges around him like a Brown Betty teapot. "Here's another puzzle: what distance between two points is shorter than a straight line?" Placing the tea cozy on his head, he adds, "You may want the answer before you get home." He disappears in a puff of laughter.

I hike down a long hill toward a cluster of houses. Half-way there I'm overtaken by a boy on a bike who waits for me at the crossroads. Before he can ask the question every Indian child feels honourbound to ask, I beat him to the draw. "Do you have a pen?"

He bursts into giggles.

"I've forgotten mine. I'll pay you 30 rupees."

A ballpoint emerges smartly from his school case.

"Which way to Munnar?"

Since he points in a direction opposite to what I'm expecting, I repeat my question to three men sitting on a porch. They all indicate the same direction as the boy. Hailing an auto-rickshaw, I negotiate what I assume to be a fair fee based on the distance I believe I've travelled. He wheels around a corner, the equivalent of a block, then stops. At my hotel. I have hiked—as Moonji hinted—in a circle, and while I still don't know the answer to his question, I realize that the two points might be contained inside each other, or exist as spots on an imaginary leopard, or as thoughts, or in different dimensions, or with one in the past and one in the future or . . . *other?*

"Suburban" Munnar consists of two blocks of tin-and-clapboard shops and restaurants known as the Old Bazaar. Clustered on either side are workers' bungalows, a playing field and a school. Nailed to poles are signs bearing slogans like "Don't be a Hitler. Be a Mahatma." Cars with loudspeakers patrol the strip, exhorting the workers to common action—the sort of activity to be expected in a town with one employer in a state with a Communist history.

Behind Munnar's "shopping mall" is a broad river traversed by a suspension bridge with a sign warning "Maximum of 15." As boisterous children jump, hop and skip, turning it into a trampoline, I seem to be the only one who's counting.

Once released from its urban duties, this river becomes a natural wonder banked by meadows with *real* cows that graze in herds and give milk, not those city fellows who double as sacred icons and garbage converters. Flame trees bow their scarlet heads to the river's reedy shore, where waterfowl paddle amid white, purple and yellow blooms visited by hummingbirds and bumblebees. No sadhus take ritual baths here, and no women are washing clothes. Like most secular Indian rivers, this seems underutilized both for commerce and sport, though a one-man, government-run tourist office does offer two rowboats for hire.

Rowboats are objects of nostalgia to me, both the rented ones in which my sister and I fished Lake Scugog for perch and sunfish and the large all-purpose dinghy my husband and I launched when it was too rough on Lake Erie for canoe or sailboat. The tourist officer appears sceptical when I inquire about renting one. Though he's too polite to ask, I convey through the right sort of non-chalance that boats are second nature to me, and it's only because of a fleeting lapse that I sit facing the bow so that my first heave lands me back on shore.

This rowboat is a large one: if they'd had it on the *Titanic* they could have saved another fifty lives. The oars are leaden and lack functioning oarlocks, yet pride keeps me at my station while the perplexed tourist officer stares after me, arms folded, as if trying to memorize my face in case of police inquiries. By the time I've rounded the river's first bend, I seem to be getting the hang of it: a little tug here, a bit of a back-paddle there. Though I'm travelling downstream, these placid, silty waters are just like the rivers in those British jigsaw puzzles with thatched cottages that I mastered as a child. A painted river.

I pass under a footbridge from which a group of schoolboys stare goggled-eyed. As I spin, switching from oar to oar, one laughs, shattering their collective politeness like a baseball through glass. Between bouts of hilarity, they rain down questions. "What's your name?"

This isn't my fault. It's the river that's wriggling like a hopped-up snake. "Eileen."

"Where are you from?"

Why bring disgrace on my own country? "Detroit."

"What's your age?"

"One hundred and seven."

Breaking free of my whirlpool, I escape around the next bend. Now three house builders stop to watch. Though I know it's innocent—the inane questions, the prolonged laughter, the indiscreet stares—I'm growing resentful of the attention I attract all over India. Refocusing on the river's pastoral beauty, I slide around one bend, then another, till I come to an island of tall trees and pasturing bulls that squeezes the water into a narrow channel. Just ahead, smoke from someone doing something unfriendly to the environment chokes off my view. I turn the boat, or try to. The downstream current—like the riptide at Kovalam—has been deceptive. Under the best of circumstances, the upstream trip would be taxing. With the oars sliding out of their broken locks at every stroke, I'm not so much rowing as hacking the water. While I zigzag back, all the same people stare, though with tempered glee. Once beyond the footbridge, I'm in striking distance of the jetty, but before me stretches the broadest, swiftest part of the river. Exhausted, I head for a patch of solid shoreline, resigned to securing the boat and walking back.

No sooner have I touched land than a lively young woman with a confident stride and bouncy, shoulder-length hair materializes. "Let me row you."

I protest unconvincingly as she climbs aboard. "This is a terrible boat," she reassures me. "People are always abandoning it. I've lived on this river all my life, so I know how difficult it can be." She jiggles the oars rhythmically, never stroking or lifting them from the water. "How close did you get to the dam?"

The dam? I add that to *the casement window, the riptide, the train that crashed,* feeling like one of those silent comedians who absent-mindedly steps off scaffolding after scaffolding as plank after plank fortuitously materializes underfoot. "I appreciate your helping me."

"Anyone else would have been pleased to do the same if they knew you wanted help. In India you are never alone."

And that is true: my foreignness is like a cyclist's fluorescent vest on a dark highway. Here and everywhere else, even those who pestered me with services I didn't want were frogs ready to turn into princes at the hint of a crisis. As usual, I've spent the afternoon trying to assert my independence, only to discover that I have none.

Next day I hire an auto-rickshaw for a climb through clinging tea fields to the upper slopes of what, at 2,695 metres, is south India's highest mountain. With its bald head and weathered grey hide rearing out of the mists, it looks like its name—Anamudi, or Elephant Peak. At road's end I sign up with government gatekeepers for the upward hike into Eravikulam National Park. With the sweep of a ghostly hand, the brilliant, green-blue day is erased, leaving only the paved path under my feet and signs proclaiming this to be a plastic-free zone, threatening three months' imprisonment for carrying plastic into the park. Belatedly I uncover a wad of contraband in my purse, guiltily consider hiding it under a rock before returning to the checkpoint, then decide that is hardly the intention of the warning. After another few hundred metres, the same giant who green-carpeted the valleys unzips the clouds. Out tumbles blue sky and sun, allowing me to discover my toes just steps from a boulderslide down to fields glowing in cemetery green. Across a rocky divide I see a herd of crinkle-horned Nilgiri tahr mountain goats scattered vertically up a cliff. Hunted by the British to near-extinction, they've reestablished a stronghold here, even regained their trusting nature.

The fog rolls in, reducing the visible world to a slippery puddle around my feet, so that I'm groping rather than hiking. Just as I've decided to turn back, my head pokes through another hole, with blue sky sparkling overhead in a stained-glass dome.

As I perch on a ledge overlooking the valley, a voice close to my ear asks, "Why not use this height for more than just sightseeing?"

Moonji is levitating, cross-legged, about half a metre off the rock. "This isn't so difficult up here," he assures me matter-of-factly. "The thinner air on a mountain creates the same special effects and epiphanies as intense meditation. In fact, climb high enough, and the body undergoes the same physiological changes that produce near-death experiences. That's why prophets like Moses and Mohammad and Jesus went up into them. It's why shrines are built on them, why holy men live on them, and why lost climbers sometimes speak of mysterious figures who guided them through their darkest hours."

"When Charles Lindbergh soloed across the Atlantic, he said he saw spirits flying his plane during the hours when he dozed off."

"A plane fittingly called the *Spirit of St. Louis*!" retorts Moonji before inquiring, "With all this inspiration, isn't it time you tried your mantra?"

"I don't have one."

"What about the one you got with the $25 banana?"

"*Om*?"

"Of course! It's the cosmic egg that gave birth to the universe. Just as white contains all colours, so *Om* contains all spoken sounds, from the full-throated *O* to the tight-lipped *mm*. The reason Indian mathematicians were first to understand the profundity of zero is that they knew the principle of the one in the many and the many in the one. They knew Infinity."

When I make a face, Moonji chants:

"*Om*, the imperishable sound,
is the seed of all that exists.
The past, the present, the future—

all are but the unfolding of *Om*.
And whatever transcends the three realms of time,
That indeed is the flower of *Om*."

"Don't be afraid of your own voice," he continues to urge me. "Repetition of a sound sets up vibrations that dissolve rational meaning, creating a bridge to the unconscious as well as building energy. Think of the power of a single note to shatter glass, of soldiers in lock step to collapse a bridge, of the trumpets that brought down the walls of Jericho."

I try a gentle "*OOmm*." Once unleashed, it's not an easy sound to constrain and soon enough I'm resonating it. Unexpectedly, the mists part to reveal the heads of three Indian hikers. Before I have time to decide to be embarrassed, they let out a high-spirited whoop, then join me, taking on the other three directions, filling the valley with sound enough to melt mountains.

drunk on god

"Children, knowledge without devotion
is like eating stones"

I THOUGHT I'd experienced all the beauties and terrors that Kerala's bus jockeys had to offer, but I was wrong. The eight-hour rip-tear from Munnar toward Mata Amritanandamayi's ashram back on the west coast proves more gorgeous and more lethal than anything so far, delivered at ear-popping, roller-coaster speed as we swerve past signs warning "Dead Slow Single Lane," separated from a dizzying drop by one crumbling, knee-high brick wall. After leaving Munnar forty-five minutes late, we arrive at the town of Alleppey an hour early.

Built around a few narrow canals, Alleppey is sometimes called the Venice of India, which is like comparing a garden hose to Niagara Falls. Nonetheless, it has an engaging bustle based upon its main function—processing tourists for the backwater boat trip south to Quilon and the Amritanandamayi ashram. After running the gauntlet of touts offering cut-rate tickets on half-sunken rogue crafts, I'm cheerfully sold, for reasons unknown, a discounted fare on a government tour boat marked "For Children Twelve and Under."

In India, Divine incarnations are of three kinds: *avesa* avatars like Baba Brahma, whose bodies are used as temporary vehicles, *amsa* avatars, empowered for a particular purpose, and *purna* avatars, defined as full manifestations of the Divine in human form, as devotees of both Karunamayi and Amritanandamayi declare their leaders to be. Whereas Karunamayi was born into a prosperous family, identified early as an embodiment of Devi the archetypal mother, then prepared for her role, Amritanandamayi was an outcast who boldly anointed herself. During her twice-weekly *darshans* over the past twenty years, she has hugged an estimated twenty million people, sometimes fifteen thousand in a single session. No one is ever turned away, including a leper with putrid flesh dangling in strips like caterpillars, whom, according to many eyewitnesses, Amritanandamayi embraced and kissed before licking his oozing sores.

In contrast to Kerala's mountainous interior, these coastal canals, rivers and lakes are so tranquil that they mirror the shore for most of the journey—upside-down date palms, huts balanced on their thatched roofs, long-legged bamboo fishing rigs like coupling praying mantises. Egrets resembling white question marks punctuate paddy fields, cashew farms and mango orchards. High-prowed cargo boats, handmade without nails, carry everything from concrete blocks to the mail, while palatial, peak-roofed houseboats-for-hire bob amid flotillas of ducks. In contrast to this apparent serenity, the sky is alive with beaks and talons: grey-headed fishing eagles, the fearsome osprey, fluorescent blue kingfishers and the majestic, copper-coloured brahminy kite. Almost as predatory are the packs of boys who run alongside narrow channels shouting, "Pens! Pens!"

In the deck chair beside me is a minister from California, also returning to India after some twenty years. A scholarly man with compelling blue eyes, he tells me of an intriguing event that happened during that first adventure. "I was in my twenties and very unsure about what I would do with my life. After a long hike through the mountains of northern India, I came to a Buddhist temple. While I was still quite a distance away, a monk in saffron robes came running toward me. Embracing me, he exclaimed, 'You've no idea how long I've waited for you!' Imagine how I felt—I was this naive kid who'd never been among monks before. I studied for a year at that temple, with that monk as my mentor."

I prod, "Did he ever explain his odd greeting?"

The minister is silent so long that I'm afraid he isn't going to answer. "The subject never came up again, and because he was such a highly developed soul I was too shy to ask. I think if I had, he would have just laughed. It was he who encouraged me to follow a Christian rather than a Buddhist path. I had a feeling we were supposed to be connected through that during a past life."

"Did you ever see him again?"

The minister releases his folded hands like a pair of white doves. "I'm not sure. He died before I could return to India, but years later I was told his disciples went searching for, and found, his incarnation. I visited that lad a few weeks ago at that same temple where he is now studying. Certain mannerisms—the way he used his hands and his laughter—seemed familiar, and since I knew more about my teacher's past than anyone now at the temple, he was certainly interested in talking with me. It was a fascinating experience. I felt many things, but I just couldn't be sure."

The Mata Amritanandamayi Ashram rises pinkly from a coconut-palm forest between intercoastal waterways and the Arabian Sea. About one-third of our boat's passengers debark here, including the minister and his family. Figuring out where to register is complicated by the fact that the ashram has become a construction site for the high-rise residences needed to accommodate the twenty-five thousand pilgrims expected for the September celebration of Amritanandamayi's forty-sixth birthday. I'm assigned a fourth-floor room with bath in a new seven-storey complex, to be shared with an Israeli student who has been studying Buddhism at the Dalai Lama's headquarters in Dharamsala and a German woman who came to India solely to be with Ammachi (Dearest Mother). Each of us has been given a mat in the empty room, for which the fee is 125 rupees a night, with our passports as collateral. Though modest meals are included, most foreigners prefer the Western buffet featuring shorter line-ups and more choice, or the Western Café with items like omelettes, French fries and veggie burgers. We're also urged to sign up for two hours a day of karma yoga—voluntary tasks such as helping in the office or kitchen or even cleaning latrines. I elect to roll chapatis.

The six-storey temple is a blue-trimmed pink confection with all the naive Disneyland exuberance I've come to expect of Hindu shrines: ornate copulas, canopied balconies, pillared porches and a bevy of gods and goddesses. The path pursued by Ammachi's devotees is that of *bhakti*, or "devotion," manifesting itself in a personality cult focused on her as the Divine Mother. At five each morning, worship begins with the chanting of Ammachi's 108 names, followed by Devi's 1,000 names. Though classes in Indian scripture, Sanskrit, yoga and meditation are available for long-term students, the heart and soul of this ashram is devotional singing led by Ammachi, followed by her hugging darshans.

On the Friday evening of my arrival, I wait for several hours packed along the wrought-iron railing of a narrow balcony running in a horseshoe around the temple, painted in pink, blue, green and yellow pastels. Two storeys below, a thousand devotees squat on mats, men to the left and women to the right, clapping and chanting to a small but exuberant percussion band. Attention is riveted on the stage, also decorated in pastels like a little girl's birthday cake. Just as at a rock concert, anticipation builds during the carefully orchestrated waiting, with wave upon wave of adulation sweeping toward the stage as more and more devotees crowd into the hall.

A young woman in yellow robes, using her hands like grappling hooks, pries my body from the one ahead to squeeze between us just as curtains are drawn to reveal Ammachi on an upholstered throne—a short, compact, dark-skinned figure in white robes, who rises with upthrust arms to greet her followers. Her hair is slicked back from a round face, and the naturalness of her flashing smile is enhanced by the slight unevenness of her teeth. Her manner is robust as she flings her powerful arms to the rafters, torso swaying, eyes closed, face blissful, shouting the names of the Divine Mother with her microphone-enhanced voice soaring over the rest. She easily takes possession of her audience—a charismatic and ecstatic figure exuding energy and goodwill.

At a temple shop I purchase her biography, *Mata Amritanandamayi*, written by devotee Swami Amritaswarupananda. Though miracles are, by definition, part of the life of an avatar, Ammachi's story is one long incredible unfolding.

Sudhamani, meaning Ambrosial Jewel, was born to devout fisher folk in a thatch hut on this sandy peninsula on September 27, 1953. The fourth of thirteen children, she was said to have emerged from the womb with a beaming smile and in the lotus position. Her parents were light-skinned but she was blue-black—a colour associated with both Krishna and Kali. Though Sudhamani's mother had dreamed during pregnancy that she was given a golden idol of Krishna, she made no connection between this and her newborn, an unwanted girl.

At six months Sudhamani began walking, running and chanting the names of the Divine; at two she was composing songs to Krishna. Because of her mother's fierce prejudice against her dark skin, Sudhamani was obliged to leave school at age ten to serve her family full-time. She also took care of village elders who were neglected or ill-treated, sometimes even stealing her family's food for them.

Despite workdays that began at three in the morning and lasted till eleven at night, Sudhamani always found time for devotions focusing on Lord Krishna. When she entered puberty, her ecstatic moods, in which she fell into a deep trance or danced in God-intoxication, intensified. As she later explained, "I used to look at Nature and see everything as Krishna. . . . When the breeze touched my body, I felt that it was Krishna caressing me. I was afraid to walk because I thought, 'Oh, I am stepping on Krishna.'" When her parents attempted to marry her off to a local youth, Sudhamani chased him away with a pestle.

By age twenty-one, Sudhamani openly identified herself as Krishna. "I was able to know everything concerning

everyone. I was fully conscious that I myself was Krishna."
When taunted by villagers to prove herself, she agreed
to perform one miracle. Before a crowd of more than a
thousand she asked one of her tormentors to bring her a
pitcher of water. After sprinkling it on those around her,
she told him to look at what remained. The pitcher contained milk. When another sceptic insisted on dipping
in his fingers, he discovered banana pudding. Even after
the pudding was distributed to the crowd, the pitcher
remained full. On another occasion, when some villagers
were terrified of a cobra, Sudhamani neutralized it by
touching its flickering tongue with her own. When she
danced in bliss on the beach, fish clustered at the shore
where they could easily be netted.

During the one ecstatic trance that would define her
future mission, Sudhamani beheld a globe of brilliant
light from which the goddess Devi emerged "dazzling
like a million suns," sweeping her "in a tidal wave of
unspeakable Love and Bliss." Overpowered by this experience, she switched her devotions from Krishna to Devi.
"Each and every pore of my body was wide open with
yearning, each atom of my body was vibrating with the
sacred mantra, my entire being was rushing toward the
Divine Mother in a torrential stream. . . . Smiling, the
Divine Mother became a mass of effulgence and merged
in me. My mind blossomed and was bathed in the many-
hued light of Divinity. . . . Thenceforth, I saw nothing as
apart from my own self." She attributed this apparent

change in her devotions to the knowledge that "all forms of God are manifestation of the One." And again: "The entire universe exists as a tiny bubble within myself."

By now Sudhamani's darshans, in which she manifested as Krishna and later as Devi, were attracting devotees from outside her village. Powerful opposition emerged from the Committee to Remove Blind Belief also known as the Rationalist Movement. Sudhamani's parents, humiliated by the controversy, cast out their daughter, leaving her to fend for herself in the jungle, where "the sky became her roof, the earth her bed, the moon her lamp and the sea breeze her fan." Sudhamani would bury herself or roll in the sand in fits of laughter and tortured weeping. Sometimes her body would become extremely hot or light, sometimes it would grow stiff and hard. She would eat garbage and excrement, unable to distinguish it from healthful food.

Though Sudhamani had little human contact during this period of Divine madness, the animals of the village and of the forest were said to have tended her. A cow regularly offered her its udder to suck, refusing to feed its own calf until she was satisfied. When she became dangerously overwrought, a large snake glided over her, flicking her with its tongue till she returned to ordinary consciousness. A black-and-white dog, her constant attendant, also licked her to revive her. When a dog catcher attempted to separate the two, both she and the dog shed such a torrent of tears that the unsettled man released the dog. When Sudhamani danced, her devotees were enchanted to see pigeons spread their wings to hop with her. After she'd saved two fledgling eagles from children throwing stones, an adult eagle brought her raw fish to eat. "Human beings are not the only ones with the capacity for speech. Animals, birds and plants have this power, but we do not have the capability to understand. One who has had the vision of the Self knows all these things."

In May of 1981, twenty-seven-year-old Sudhamani founded an open-air ashram on a plot donated by her relenting father. She also adopted a new name—Amritanandamayi, meaning Mother of Immortal Bliss. Though the Rationalist Movement continued its opposition, the poisoned milk they gave her did not kill her, nor did the poisoned thorns strewn where she danced. When a cousin drew his knife to stab her in the bosom, he doubled over with agonizing chest pains and later died, vomiting blood. After she scolded her elder brother, who was one of her most bitter foes, for bullying a devotee, he hanged himself. A hired assassin dropped to his knees with his knife in his hands to beg forgiveness and then became a disciple. "Just as human beings have intense love for Mother, there are numerous subtle beings who love her as well. If somebody attempts to harm Mother, Mother will not react. . . . But these subtle beings will get angry and take revenge."

Today Amritanandamayi is head of a multi-milliondollar charitable trust with branches throughout India and fifteen other countries and with assets that include an orphanage, housing for the poor, a vocational centre for women, a cultural centre for traditional art and music, institutes for management and computer technology, a pharmaceutical college, a hospital, a cancer hospice and a medical research centre.

At ten-thirty on Saturday morning, I squat between Doric columns on the marble floor of the temple with several dozen other Westerners to await my hug. Though I can't accept Ammachi's biography as literal truth, I'm willing to believe that Enlightened teachers can transmit energy, like recharging another person's batteries. Given the weekend crowds, everyone must have a token to see Ammachi. Mine is number 4. Since she is already receiving a line of Indian devotees, I expect to be through within half an hour. Three hours later I'm still waiting. Until recently Westerners—proportionally few in number— were hustled through a side door. Now this unfairness has been replaced by an opposite one. It's two before the first Westerners are even allowed to line up and another half hour before we inch our way to the platform. We receive a flurry of instructions. "Remove all jewellery or purses that might hurt Ammachi. Let yourself be hugged rather than clinging or clutching."

Though by now I've watched hundreds of Indians tearfully and joyfully prostrate themselves, the long wait has wilted rather than whetted my enthusiasm. Awkwardly, I kneel before the woman whom millions of followers worldwide believe to be the Generator, Organizer and Destroyer of the Universe (G.O.D.). With an infectious smile she extends her powerful arms and enfolds me in a very earthy, maternal embrace. I feel . . . a pleasant glow followed by a wave of relief that I can now escape the humid, stuffy temple having been spiritually processed.

That night I have trouble sleeping. Sometime after midnight I awaken drenched in sweat. My body feels unsettled by a tension that it is unable to absorb, shake off or express. A jerking motion that I identify as the rising of kundalini starts in my midriff, at first with a flutter, then gaining force. Not wishing to disturb my roommates, I press my back against the wall, then seize control of my body through deep breathing.

In the morning I discover that my roommates are also experiencing physical disturbances. One has a debilitating outbreak of allergies, the other a severe migraine. Are our bodies reacting to a sudden influx of darshan energy that they must struggle to absorb?

This ashram is run by one thousand residential volunteers, including one hundred Westerners. Those who've been with Ammachi twenty years wear orange; those deeply involved for eight years wear yellow; the students here to attend school wear white.

I meet Prabha, whose name means the Glow of the Divine Light, in one of the temple's second-floor offices. Tall and elegant with refined features and a gentle demeanour, she migrated to this ashram from Switzerland nine years ago. "I was about ten years on my spiritual path when I heard about Amma," she explains. "I didn't think I would go to India because I was working from the Bible with a Catholic priest, and I liked that very much. By then I had had many teachers, but after some time each became my friend and could not take me further. Two of them said, 'You should have a guru,' and when I met Amma I was so in love with this person who touched my heart as only a Divine being like Jesus can do that I thought, 'If only I could be with her!' She was the one I was always looking for and everything after that was fated."

"Was it difficult to leave your family and friends?"

"I was divorced ten years and my daughters, who were eighteen and nineteen, knew me. They were with me when I started meditating and changing. They knew my search. They were also happy for themselves because they planned to stay in our house, and my leaving gave them more freedom."

Over our conversation, I hear the sounds of the construction machines that are converting this ashram into a small city. "Has life here changed much over the past nine years?"

"Oh, very, very much. When I arrived, this temple was not finished, and the heart of the ashram was Mother's hut, where everyone gathered, and we were only seventeen Western residents. We all felt very privileged, very close to Amma, and in the evening we worked with Amma carrying bricks and filling bags with sand. Now it is different, and we have to grow to a different place."

"Did Amma actually work on the construction of the ashram?"

"Oh, yes, the main person at the ashram is always Amma! All the big decisions and the small are hers, with advice from the people who know a special matter, like those who know the hospital. Even to choose the photographs of her that are sold—that is Amma too."

"Do you think you've changed much after nine years?"

"The real change is inside, on a very subtle level. If you have a different reaction and not the same attachment to a situation, and you're no longer impatient, that is very important."

"How has Amma changed?"

"Amma?" Prabha laughs. "She has not! We are always going further and acquiring this or that skill, but Amma always seems to have everything to begin with. She doesn't have these bad habits like us. She is always fully alive. You can look at her and see her greatness, but you can also see how simple she is. Nothing is artificial, each movement is coming from the same person, yet like an iceberg you can only see what is out of the water."

Early Sunday morning chartered buses begin to arrive at the ashram for one of Ammachi's twice-weekly hugging marathons. Though I landed here only Friday evening, I've already begun to feel like one of the regulars watching an invasion. Instead of lining up for a token allowing me to line up yet again for evening darshan, I decide to enjoy the ashram on my own terms until my boat leaves on Monday afternoon.

The hugging begins at ten in the morning, then continues till three. By the time the chanting starts at five-thirty, I've counted more than fifty buses in the beach parking lot. The floor of the gigantic dining pavilion is littered with sleeping mats. Pilgrims throng the stalls in the temple courtyard buying Ammachi dolls, key chains, paperweights, children's colouring books, comics written by her and even framed pictures of her feet.

Since this ashram borders the Divine Mother's birth village of Parayakaduva on the Arabian Sea, I had looked forward to swimming, but an ashram pamphlet called "Code of Conduct" warns, "Due to local traditions, swimming is not encouraged. However, if you wish to swim, please inquire at the Foreigners' Office. Nudity and Western swimwear is inappropriate. If you go to the tea shops, please refrain from socializing and 'hanging out' for a long time. This can attract a lot of attention and gossiping from the local people." Whatever allure the palm-fringed,

black-and-beige beach with its rolling surf might still
have is wiped out by the piles of excrement deposited
along the shoreline by the villagers for the tide to wash
away. A communal toilet that is flushed only twice every
twenty-four hours is not an attractive swimming pool or
even a salubrious place to meditate. Over 80 per cent of
Indians still defecate out-of-doors, in public latrines or
into buckets, so that it's common, while riding a morning
train, to pass field after field asquat with men relieving
themselves. Since Indian women have the same needs
and still manage to be both private and discreet, I can't
help regarding these smelly cobras, coiled at regular
intervals along the beach, as acts of aggression—the result
of males marking their territory.

Returning to the ashram, I sit with my back against a
tree, listening to devotional songs from the temple while
spared its claustrophobic heat. After about twenty minutes, I burst into a drenching sweat despite a pleasant
breeze. Though I've noticed no tell-tale variation in the
singing, I am certain that Ammachi has just entered the
temple, and a few seconds later I hear her distinctive voice
sail over the rest.

Despite my earlier decision, I find myself drawn to the
temple as if pulled by a silken cord. Though its broad,
two-storey staircase is packed with a standing-room-only
crowd, by now I know enough about its passageways to
infiltrate backstage behind Ammachi's throne, where a
few others have congregated. Grandly dressed in saffron

robes garlanded with marigolds and wearing a golden Wonder Woman crown, she has actively assumed the persona of Devi the Divine Mother. For the next hour she alternately holds her hands in prayer, then flings them skyward, shaking her body and rolling her eyes as devotees clap and sing with single-minded zeal, soaking up her energy while feeding her their own.

A statuesque woman in diaphanous yellow robes attempts to squeeze between me and the wall. As I'm trying to figure out how she'll manage, she gestures toward the dancers with an arm festooned in golden bangles. "In the East we call this the vertical path to Enlightenment." I notice with surprise that she speaks without moving her lips and that her palms are without lines: *Moonji* dressed as a woman!

Though flustered, I respond casually, "I suppose you're referring to the path of the shaman."

Moonji leans into the wall, which dissolves like a cloud behind him. "Muslims have their whirling dervishes, Hindus their tantric rites, South American natives their hallucinogenic plants, North American natives their sweat lodges, Africans their drumming. Time and again, though separated by ages and continents, societies have independently developed rites for inducing altered states as a way of initiating spiritual journeys. Time and again, those journeys have involved travelling through a universe consisting of three planes—the Underworld, the Earthworld and the Skyworld."

"I guess that's the journey Ammachi took during her years of Divine madness," I reply. "First, she buried herself in the earth, then she emerged to dance and sing and to transform herself through visions of Devi descending from heaven."

"It's also the journey enacted by the ancient Greeks in their Mystery cults when they disappeared into secret caves, only to emerge several days later, impassioned and empowered. It's the path of Orpheus and Persephone, and of Jesus Christ, who descended from the Cross into the Valley of Death, then returned to Earth on the third day before ascending to heaven."

While still trying to get used to Moonji as a woman, I comment, "Carl Jung thought alcoholics were mimicking the shaman's journey when they seemed to need to hit bottom before they could rise up out of their boozy hells." Gesturing toward Ammachi's dancing devotees, I add, "Maybe it's also the shamanic ritual that teenagers act out in their raves through wild dancing, loud music and drugs like Ecstasy."

"Yes, Western addiction to drugs and alcohol is a perverted form of spiritual quest—bottled spirits replacing Spirit!" agrees Moonji. "Your society has an obsessive craving for altered states, but because you have no sense of their spiritual purpose, you don't know what to do with them once you've achieved them. You use them as an entertainment, with no grasp of their role in healing, wisdom and Enlightenment. Where spirituality is concerned, Western society is metaphorically caught up in frenzied fore-play without having yet figured out how to perform the sex act, let alone produce a baby."

"How do you suppose this sorry state of affairs came about?"

Moonji makes an impatient gesture, causing his bangles to rattle like the tail of a rattlesnake. "It's that wearisome battle between science and religion that's hung you up for three hundred years! Tell a Western doctor that you're having visions or hearing voices, and he'll diagnose epilepsy or schizophrenia and give you drugs to get rid of them. Tell a shaman or a priest in any other culture the same thing, and he sees a potential prophet. The Western world wasn't always so close-minded. Hippocrates, the founder of Western medicine, called epilepsy 'the sacred disease,' and the Oracles of Delphi used convulsions both real and induced to forecast the future. St. Paul 'saw the light' after being struck down by lightning, which was likely some form of brain seizure. It was during convulsions that St. Catherine of Siena radiated light and fragrance. St. Joseph of Copertino, a simple-minded monk of the early seventeenth century, had fits of such intense bliss that—according to crowds of eyewitnesses—he flew. Your laboratory-trained scientists prefer to dismiss all these things as manifestations of disease because they can't stand unpredictability. Here in India Ammachi is a revered spiritual leader and the CEO of an international trust with multi-million-dollar assets, but if she'd been born in Toronto or Chicago, she'd have been drugged, institutionalized, perhaps given shock treatments and even lobotomized. That fine line between genius and madness drives your scientists crazy."

By now some of the Western women have also begun to dance, most self-consciously but a few with an apparent determination to shed their inhibitions. Rising to his feet, Moonji offers me his hand, which I surprise myself by refusing. Though I had hoped to participate freely in the life of the ashram, I find that all the waiting and the prostrating has set up a countercurrent in my spirit as wilful and strong as the one that swept me away from Kovalam. "Bhakti is too far from who I am," I protest. "I would feel too slavish and phoney pretending to be part of this. In Rishikesh you advised me to go through the door that's easiest. Since my driving force is curiosity—the desire to know—that makes *jnana*, the path of wisdom, the right one for me."

"Ammachi says you Westerners should practise devotion because you already think too much!" replies Moonji. "Intellectualization is part of the Western shadow."

"Maybe so, but at present all of India is, for me, an altered state. Western embassies are always having to rescue lost souls who've abandoned their own identities without having a clue about the demands and limitations of the exotic new ones they're trying to assume. Perhaps Ammachi is Divine, and perhaps she isn't—you've taught me it isn't my business to judge—but I'm not looking for anyone who's more exalted than an inspired teacher, and I don't want to play-act at being an Indian when I have *you* to do that for me!"

Moonji laughs out loud. "Fair enough, but remember that it's wise to keep every door open against a time when you might see things quite differently. Seekers are, eventually, supposed to find. To taste the fruit. To drink the wine." With a graceful leap, he joins the dancers, spinning himself into a buttery glow before dissolving.

Around six-thirty, the evening hug-fest begins for the five thousand pilgrims willing to wait several hours for their few seconds with Ammachi. I decide that if I awaken during the night, and if the crowds have dissipated, and if Ammachi is still in a hugging mood, I'll join the line.

As it happens, I awaken at 5:00 a.m. I join the persistent stream of devotees and I arrive at the stage an hour later. One woman is cradling an Ammachi doll, others are weeping. Though Ammachi has been hugging for over twelve hours, she's still generous in her responses, laughing easily, stopping to chat, even embracing some people twice. During that same period I've eaten dinner, spoken with friends, strolled the beach and had a night's sleep. Divine or not, she seems to have tapped into an energy source that is supernatural.

I'm one of those who receives two hugs, and while I feel no astonishing upsurge of emotion, it's a mellow experience full of grace.

Bhyanamripa Chaidanya, whose name means the Nectar of Meditation, is a commanding presence at the ashram, both because of his height and his dynamism. Against a sound curtain of chanting from the temple, he describes his first meeting with Ammachi in 1985, when he was a college student: "The information I got about Amma before meeting her was all negative—'She's just black magic. She captures youngsters'—but I happened to read her small book, *Selected 100 Quotations from Amma*, and I heard of her mystical experiences described through a song she had written, and that song was so inspiring to me. It was not possible for a fourth-grade village girl to write all this highest spiritual truth. What Amma was saying was so appealing that when she came to my town, I wanted to meet this person and then I fell in love with her. I had been searching for a master who could help me on my spiritual path, and I had come across many who were doing good work, but to make spiritual progress I was needing someone who could really hold my hand and lift me up, and I was praying to God himself, 'You must come in the form of a master and help me.' When I met Amma, that was the prayer in my heart, but I didn't tell Amma.

Before I could take her as my master I started testing her over the next two years to see if she knew everything that was happening with me even when I was away from her, and I did come to feel that she knew even what was happening in my thoughts, so I went to Amma and I asked, 'Will you accept me as a disciple?' She said yes, so I just prostrated myself at her feet and it was finished."

"Do your family and friends understand your decision?"

"They understand, but they don't agree with it. I'm only sad that even at the age of eighteen it came so late. Now when I meet my college friends after twelve years they come with two children, one on the left and one on the right, and their wives are pregnant, and I wonder how they can do it, really. They've grown up so much! I don't feel that I'm grown up. I feel I'm a little boy here because of the presence of Amma and her love. When I met Amma I thought she was my mother, not that I didn't have my biological mother—she too was still loving me so much, feeding me and if I didn't take food she would cry. She would wash my clothes and she would cook for me first, but I never felt that was love. Then when I met Amma, I felt this was love because there was some sweetness in this, some fragrance, some soothing effect to my heart."

"Everyone speaks about Amma's love and compassion, but can she be stern?"

He bursts out laughing. "Of course! When you want to progress and you don't do your practice properly, the master comes and shakes you. You have to be wakeful to elevate your heart, so if a child is not studying in the house, the mother who loves that child will be very watchful and scold and even beat the child. The child is not always aware of the goal, and if he loses the time he will spoil his life, so the mother will show a different face, but that anger is from love also."

"How have you dealt with the changes coming from the success of the ashram?"

"We don't notice them because our focus is on Amma. Thousands are coming and thousands are going, and we don't really see the change unless we go out for some time and then come back. It's just something that is happening along with us, a part of life like a river, and we just flow with that river where love is flowing and we forget about the time. We immerse ourselves and just let go."

I come upon it on Sunday afternoon huddled in the shade of coconut palms—a baby crow, puffy with speckled feathers, its mouth open, waiting to be fed. It looks parched, a little wilted, as if suspecting something has gone wrong, yet still hopeful, remembering other times when its mother swept down from the skies after a torturing absence to pop a tasty grub into its mouth. I try to drizzle a bit of bottled water down its throat, not sure whether I've succeeded or just frightened it. Then I search for a perch out of reach of predators. The coconut palms with their towering spear-like trunks and feathery heads are of no use, and I can find nothing else in the vicinity— no stump, no fence, no hut. A couple of metres away I see what is likely to be this crow's future: its sibling crushed under the wheel of a bus—maybe already the lucky one.

I try to forget the crow, but I can't: perhaps it's symbolic to me of all the needy and hopeful souls streaming to this ashram in search of their mothers. Perhaps it's easier to deal with one lost and dying crow than anything else I've encountered in India.

Before catching my afternoon ferry, I return to the beach, even though I vowed I wouldn't. The crow isn't where I last saw it. As I'm growing hopeful, I spot its inanimate body. At my approach, eight adult crows, high in the palms, create an indignant ruckus. They continue until I withdraw.

I don't know why these two nestlings fell, or how this one died, since its body is unmarked. I don't know where the adults were yesterday, but I'm glad they're here now and that they protest when I approach the tiny corpse. I'm glad they're standing sentinel and that this little death matters to them as I find it matters to me.

Aboard the ferry, I tell the minister from California about the crow, and I'm pleased when his words precisely echo my thoughts: "Attention has been paid."

the buddha

"Change yourself
and you change everything"

ALL I SEE of Christmas 1998 is one plastic Santa Claus and some electrified cardboard stars winking through coconut palms on my overnight northbound train to my Buddhist retreat outside Bangalore. Since the vipassana schedule fell into my hands a month ago in Delhi, my desire to attend this course has become the North Star by which I've charted the rest of my journey. Though I've been meditating in half-hour gulps since Rishikesh, the challenge of this eleven-hour, ten-day meditation marathon remains as formidable as ever. Yet I'm drawn to it the way climbers set their scopes on Everest, as a test of commitment, focus and their personal best.

This determination is independent of Buddha's promise to reward my efforts with liberation leading to Enlightenment in the here and now. Though that's a hefty warranty, I'm pleased—after weeks of exposure to competing patents on godliness—that he himself didn't claim to be Divine or even divinely inspired. His main credo, like that of Socrates, was "Know Thyself," and his task, as he defined it, was to apply his human powers to the diagnosis and cure of human suffering. His technique—

described in the vipassana literature as "radical surgery on the psyche"—is pragmatic, body based and experiential because, according to the Buddha, no teachings should be taken on authority or on faith, including his own. The only valid test is, Do they work?

As darkness descends and the miles clatter by, I read about Siddhartha Gautama, the man who became the Great Buddha, born more than twenty-five hundred years ago in the same extraordinary century that produced Pythagoras in Greece, and Confucius and Lao-tzu in China. Though evidence for the life of Jesus Christ is elusive, the Buddha's biography is well rooted in history. The only son of a prosperous king, Siddhartha was born in 563 B.C. at Lumbini in northern India, a place now marked by an inscribed pillar erected a couple of centuries later by the powerful Buddhist emperor Ashoka and unearthed by British archeologists in 1898. Because the king was disturbed by an astrological prediction that his son might become a great spiritual leader instead of his royal heir, he vowed, "I shall use all my power to see that he shall grow to love power, to seek it and lust for more power."

Despite the father's attempts to seclude and spoil Siddhartha, he developed into a highly intelligent, well-disciplined young man with a brooding temperament. When he insisted on touring his father's kingdom, he was horrified to encounter a decrepit old man—his first glimpse of the ravages of age. Soon after that, he came upon a man riddled with disease, and then a corpse being readied for cremation. "Does this happen to everyone?" he asked in bewilderment. Later, in a crowded market, surrounded by scenes of lust, chaos and suffering, the distraught prince discovered a meditating monk, serene and dispassionate. "That is what I wish to be!" he declared. To his father he announced, "Until I conquer old age, disease and death, I shall see you no more."

After six years in a forest, during which he studied the Vedas and fasted for long periods, Siddhartha found himself lying by a stream near starvation. Out of pity, a young woman poured milk into his mouth. When he had sufficiently recovered, he announced, "I have been a fool. Punishing the body does not purify the mind. There is no hope in asceticism alone, but there is hope in human kindness." After sitting under a mucalinda tree in the lotus position, Siddhartha had a vision in which he came to know thousands of his past lives. When Mara, the master of deception, sent a host of demons to frighten him, the young man saw they were just apparitions. When Mara sent his three beautiful daughters to seduce Siddhartha, he banished them as yet another illusion. When Mara personally tried to persuade Siddhartha to enter Nirvana on the basis of his own perfection, Siddhartha exclaimed, "Not until I can bring release to all of humanity!" He touched the ground as a covenant. "Let the Earth be my witness."

As Siddhartha rose from the mucalinda tree, a light radiated from him. He was now the Buddha, the Enlightened one, and the tree where he acquired wisdom became known as the *bhodi* tree, the tree of Enlightenment. In his first sermon, entitled "Setting in Motion the Wheel of Truth," Buddha preached, "There are two extremes, O monks, which a man ought not to follow—the habitual practice, on the one hand, of self-indulgence, which is unworthy, vain and fit only for the worldly minded, and the habitual practice, on the other hand, of self-mortification, which is painful, useless and unprofitable. To satisfy the necessities of life is not evil. To keep the body in good health is a duty, for otherwise we shall not be able to trim the lamp of wisdom and keep our mind strong and clear."

To this the Buddha added his four Noble Truths. The first Noble Truth is that existence is painful because "all things arise and pass away." Through meditation he determined that the physical world as experienced through the senses is not ultimate Reality but an illusion created out of subatomic particles that continuously spring into existence only to vanish again. This includes the physical body, which is just a flow of particles with no more permanence than an eddy in a river, and the mind, which is merely a process of events in a constant state of becoming. Though we can give ourselves a name, that doesn't bestow identity any more than naming a river alters its impermanence.

The second Noble Truth is that unhappiness is caused by selfish cravings and aversions, along with our ignorance of the law of karma, guaranteeing that every cause gives rise to an effect and every action a reaction. Buddha defined raw sensory data as having six sources: the five senses recognized by Western science and the mind, which he described as a mental sense organ existing throughout the body and not just in the brain. Craving arises when we label sensory data as pleasant and try to prolong and intensify it, while aversion develops when we define it as unpleasant and seek to terminate or avoid it. Since the results of karma are instantaneous and ongoing, each of us creates our own heaven and hell in the here and now through our own thoughts and actions.

Attachment often takes the form of craving sensual gratification, which leads to suffering since such pleasures are always impermanent. Sex has a proper place in everyday life when tied to commitment to a single partner. Even then passion dies, to be replaced by natural celibacy, bringing greater harmony and joy. Meat eating is not an evil in itself, but in partaking of the flesh of a beast without consciousness, one takes on its cravings and aversions. Material possessions are acceptable as long as one has no attachment to them. Attachment can also take the form of pride in one's self-image or personal beliefs under the false concepts of "I" and "mine."

The third Noble Truth is that the end of pain comes with the end of desire. By detaching ourselves from craving and aversion we dissolve our ego on the deepest level, liberating ourselves from the Wheel of Suffering and entering a permanent state of bliss or nirvana.

The fourth Noble Truth is that desire can be conquered by following the Noble Eightfold Path, consisting of right understanding, right intention, right speech, right action, right livelihood, right effort, right awareness and right concentration. A beneficial or right action is one that helps another. A harmful action is one that hurts or disturbs the peace and harmony of another. This doesn't mean we should allow others to wrong us. Stopping a harmful act creates good karma if we do it with compassion rather than from anger or hatred since it is the intent of an action that decides its karmic result. Unlike in a court of law, the thought is more powerful than its vocal or physical expression; therefore, merely refraining from harmful word or deed does not protect us from karmic consequences. Similarly, while we are not held karmically responsible for unintentionally harming another, that does not give us licence to be careless.

Buddha died in 483 B.C. at age eighty. His final words were "All created things are subject to decay. Practise diligently to realize this truth." Because he left no heir and taught through dialogue, it wasn't for another four hundred years that his wisdom was committed to writing.

Though he didn't invent the concepts of karma, nirvana and reincarnation, he forged them into a wise, consistent and practical moral code. When Emperor Ashoka, who unified India, converted to Buddhism in 262 B.C., he declared his kingdom to be Buddhist and was active in establishing schools and monuments. Nevertheless, while this discipline spread north and east to Tibet, China and Japan, by the thirteenth century it had almost died out in India, as a result of Muslim invasion and a revitalized Hinduism. By the twentieth century it was thought that many of Buddha's earliest teachings had been lost; however, an upsurge of interest in both India and the West led to the discovery that they had been preserved by the monks of Burma.

In 1971, Burma-born S.N. Goenka founded the Vipassana International Academy outside of Bombay, which now introduces some fifty thousand students a year to Buddha's guidelines. While amassing a fortune as an industrialist, Goenka had been afflicted by migraines, which could be eased only by morphine. Fearing addiction, he had travelled to Europe and America in search of a cure. As he later stated, "I was treated by the best doctors of these countries. And I am very fortunate that all of them failed. I returned home worse than I had left."

In 1955 Goenka consulted Sayagyi U Ba Khin, a Burmese civil servant who taught Buddhist meditation. U Ba Khin advised, "The disease of yours is really a very minor part of your suffering. It will pass away, but only as a by-product in the process of mental purification. . . . Come not for physical cures but to liberate the mind."

Though a Hindu, Goenka applied himself with such vigour that he transformed his life while simultaneously achieving freedom from pain. When he founded the Vipassana International Academy, he was fulfilling an old Burmese prophecy that Buddhism would return to India twenty-five hundred years after the Buddha's death. As the late U Ba Khin used to remind Goenka, "Twenty-five centuries are over. The clock has struck!"

On the afternoon of December 24, I arrive at Ganga Farm, outside Bangalore, where I am to undertake my ten-day vipassana retreat. Scattered amid coconut palms and banana trees are what look like concrete bunkers with corrugated metal roofs. An Indian woman, who communicates with gestures so as not to break her silence, escorts me to the women's dorm, consisting of two high-ceilinged rooms unadorned except for windows. As I make my bed on the assigned mattress, I am joined by twelve other students mostly in their thirties and forties. The only other foreigner is Olga, a sixty-year-old linguist from Moscow.

That evening—Christmas Eve—we fill out forms guaranteeing we will stay for ten days and securing this promise with our valuables, including all foreign passports, cameras, tape recorders, radios, books and medications that have not been preapproved. We review the rules: no smoking, no drinking, no drugs, no meat eating, no lying, no killing, no stealing, no sex, no "high and luxurious beds," no bodily decoration, no talking, no reading, no writing, no music or singing, no telephones, no incense, no mantras, no beads, no praying, no fasting and no yoga.

Vipassana has begun.

At the 4:00 a.m. gong, the seven of us who share this room stumble out of the intricate web of blue plastic mosquito netting imprisoning us. Someone switches on our dangling overhead lights, and the rush begins for the latrines and wash stalls outside our window, at first with a show of diffidence and then gaining in competitive edge. It's dark, dewy, chilly and smoky, thanks to the fumes from our wood-burning water heater. Because our vow of Noble Silence means no communication of any kind, we move as automatons, averting our eyes, refraining from smiling, reduced to the barest of courtesies.

At four-thirty, a second gong summons us to the meditation hall, another high-ceilinged concrete room open to the elements, with rows of straw mats and cushions facing the teacher's elevated perch. Each of us is assigned a permanent place, women to the right and men to the left. Because of strict sexual segregation, meditation is the only time we will see the men, who outnumber us two to one, with four foreigners. The pillows on which we will be sitting for more than 150 hours are state of the art—of decent size, firm enough for support, yet soft enough to mould. This is no small matter since sitting cross-legged is one of the yoga positions I find most difficult, with my knees poking up like shark fins instead of lying flat. Because our instructions read "assume a comfortable, upright position," I'm technically free to sit with legs outstretched, but the space between rows isn't deep enough, and besides I'm determined to master the Buddha position because I understand that it's best for generating and maintaining an energy circuit.

As soon as our teacher is seated on her dais, she turns on an audiotape, on which the gravelly voiced S. N. Goenka informs us that according to Buddhist techniques, the most effective way to concentrate the mind is by focusing on the breath. This is because the breath is a necessity of life available to all; it's both voluntary and involuntary, thus linking the conscious and the unconscious; it connects us to the present with its variations reflecting our current physical and mental condition. In *anapana*, the technique leading to vipassana, we focus on our breath as it enters and leaves the nostrils, not to control or change it but merely to observe it: is it heavy or light, long or short, regular or uneven, shallow or deep? Meditation must not be confused with daydreaming, self-hypnosis or trance. Nor are we to use a mantra or any visualization technique that would distract us from our breath. While the body needs to be fed only at intervals, the uncontrolled mind is voracious for sensation every second of the day. When it drifts off to the past or the present in search of stimulation, we must patiently refocus it without self-judgment or sense of failure. We are to do this for the next two hours, eyes closed and without changing position till breakfast at six-thirty.

Within fifteen minutes, my legs have begun to cramp. From the cracking of joints, the rustle of shawls and the tinkle of bangles, I know that many of the Indian women who've grown up using the cross-legged position are also having difficulty. Though such petty reassurances are out of sync with Buddhism's equanimous goals, they're in line with the process, which is to float negativity to the surface, like scum on a pond, to be observed without reaction as a way of washing it away.

Though six-thirty breakfast has been billed as "simple vegetarian fare," it consists of several delicious, delicately flavoured dishes. Again, while sitting on straw mats on the concrete floor, I struggle to keep my legs tucked under me because Indians consider pointing the feet at someone to be rude.

Our second meditation lasts three hours, from eight till eleven with five-minute hourly breaks. Though my leg cramps are a distraction, the pain at least keeps my mind rooted in the present. Every once in a while I remember this is Christmas and wonder what I'd be doing if I were home. Then I remind myself it isn't Christmas yet in Toronto because of the time lag. I recall having two Christmases in 1977 when I crossed the International Date Line—one in the air and one in Hawaii—before jerking my focus back to my breath.

During our two-hour lunch break, I explore the campus, segregated into men's and women's sections. Ganga Farm is an anomalous place with a ponderous air of past grandeur and present decay. A broad staircase leads up to the ruins of a deep circular swimming pool designed as if for a Roman villa. Other banks of stairs plunge down into the earth, leading from nowhere to nowhere. A concrete disc seems to await the touchdown of a flying saucer. Obelisks arise amid scraggly plantings of marigolds, banana trees and coconut palms. We move among these concrete ghosts, eyes downcast, with measured steps like inmates doing time.

By our afternoon meditation—from one to five with five-minute hourly breaks—the hall is uncomfortably warm. Though it has fans, these are not turned on for fear the breeze against our skins will distract us. I can hear traffic from the nearby highway, along with the yelping of the dog pack in permanent residence here. Hostility centres on the mother dog who is attempting to wean a litter of five hefty pups, with her past failure reflected in the presence of two unweaned teenagers. The outrage on both sides is loud, fierce and continuous. I try not to label any of these sounds as pleasant or unpleasant. Objectively, some of the dog and bird cries are sharp and intrusive while the traffic is low-pitched and rather energetic. I temper my joy at the occasional breeze against my sweaty cheek by reminding myself that if I were around a log fire at a ski resort I'd probably consider this temperature cozy. Having assured myself that all is relative, I refocus on my breath.

During this never-ending session, the teacher summons us in threes and fours to discuss any problems with the technique—the only few minutes when we can speak, and not to be used for philosophical debate. To hear the sound of my own voice, I mention that the wood smoke combined with highway exhaust fumes is making me ill. I already know the response: "Simply observe your reaction."

From five to six we break for supper. For first-time students this means fruit and a cup of savoury dry cereal. For the students who've taken the course before, it means only water with lemon. Since food is so plentiful at our other two meals, I'm seldom hungry. This snack is more something to do than something to eat.

During our six-to-seven meditation, I'm so relieved to have almost made it through the day that I apply extra effort, manage to hold my focus, and feel hopeful about the possibilities. Afterwards we watch an hour-long video in which S. N. Goenka—plump, rumpled and greyhaired—assures us in the rambling, anecdotal style of a favourite uncle that the ultimate aim of the course is not withdrawal from society but more effective, more aware living within it. Though this may be the goal, it's now clear that vipassana itself is about flattening the landscape of one's life to the smoothness of a well-made hospital bed; its technique is as inspirational as reading a book of knitting instructions, and its practice as relentless as a day spent doing push-ups.

This Zen Buddhist dialogue sums up my first day:

> A monk says, "Please teach me."
> His teacher replies, "Have you eaten your rice porridge?"
> The monk answers, "I have eaten."
> The teacher says, "Then you had better wash your bowl."

I sleep in exhaustion: *from what?* Washing my bowl.

As we assemble at four-thirty for our second day, we prepare our sitting stations with the diligence of operating-room nurses setting up for surgery. First we establish the exact position for our pillows between students to front, back and sides. Some like me use a second cushion to relieve leg pressure through greater lift off. Others support their knees with pillows—a trick I fail to appreciate until after I return home. Once a station has been prepared, a few pummel it like a cat kneading its bed before committing. Then blankets must be adjusted for the expected range of temperatures and a decision taken re socks: *off or on?* In this room of boredom, torture, peace and bliss, such details are our signatures—islands of identity and control in a rising tide of anonymity.

Instead of building on yesterday's modest progress, my mind flits like a tipsy flea. Discouraged, I challenge myself to focus for the entire hour on counting my breaths. When I report my success to the teacher during our afternoon review, she rebukes me: "Your task is to observe the breath, not to change it. This is not an exercise in breath control." Nonetheless, that false victory gives me the confidence to apply myself more diligently.

By day three, our meditative focus has been extended from our nostrils to our upper lip—an area we are to patrol for sensations for the purpose of observing them till they disappear. According to the Buddha, every thought, emotion and action leaves a biological trace. The most fleeting are like lines written in water, but the more often we repeat them the more they become like lines inscribed in the sand or carved in stone, destined to be passed from incarnation to incarnation until we gain enough insight to eradicate them.

In the flatline state in which we are now living, our surfacing sensations are likely to be from the past, the way a dieter burns off stored fat. Because Buddha identified the unconscious mind more than two thousand years before Freud, he taught that repressing these conditioned responses, called *sankharas*, only pushes them deeper. True detachment can be achieved by allowing them to surface and then observing them, without labelling them until they are weakened and dissolved. Unlike psychoanalysis, this practice does not require tracing the sensations to their source as aversions or cravings, just as it isn't necessary to know the source of dirt to clean it from a garment. The process itself does the job. Similarly, we don't have to replay each sensation separately since this technique floats out chunks at the same time—not like soap but like detergent.

I observe my breath at my nostrils, like a cat crouched patiently at twin mouseholes, waiting for something to happen so as *not* to pounce. Given our state of sensory deprivation, an itch, a twitch or a trickle of sweat becomes a big event, the way an extreme close-up turns a pimple into a mountain.

On the morning of day four, we are told that we will switch this afternoon from anapana to vipassana, as yet unexplained. All morning I strive to perfect the present breathing technique. My posture has improved—head straight on spine, shoulders firm but relaxed, knees closer to the floor—as I rest calmly, if not yet blissfully, in the "now." Though we've been warned not to label such impermanent sensations as pleasant, or to form an attachment to them, I can't resist feeling pleased with myself.

I arrive back from lunch eager to learn this thing called vipassana. When the teacher repeats the Goenka instruction tape we heard the day before, followed by one of his long chants, I grow disappointed, then annoyed, then angry and finally enraged. I struggle to observe the changes in my breath as a reflection of my emotional state—its quickening pace, its dryness and its roughness—without reacting; however, as the chant drones on, three days of suppressed boredom and frustration coalesce into rampant fury so that I visualize hurling my pillow at the audio machine, as I stamp, screaming, from the room. By the time the new tape is played, it's too late to rid my system of its self-created poison. I listen numbly, in shock, as we are guided through a brief ritual in which we ask the teacher to share vipassana knowledge. Apparently meditation has stripped me not only to a deeper level of anger but also to a place where I have no defence against that anger. I remind myself that this is the point of the process: to encourage negative conditioning to coalesce in a nasty boil for the purpose of lancing it. Meanwhile, every cell in my body is in pain, providing proof, if I still need it, that the first victim of my own aggression is me.

I start this new day—my fifth—full of contrition and good intentions. Instead of confining us to the moustache area, vipassana lets us systematically scan the whole body, from crown to toe, for sensations. It's unbelievable freedom, like receiving the keys to a city after four days spent locked in its jailhouse. Where we encounter blocks in the form of gross sensations we're instructed to spend a minute observing this part of the body in smaller and smaller portions until we have dissolved down to the underlying layer of subtle energy, felt as mild vibrations. We are to do the same in areas where we feel no sensations until we experience the whole body as a single energy field with every cell vibrating.

After scanning my face half a dozen times without picking up any sensations, I find that my right side feels so different from my left that each is cancelling out the other. I also discover that I breathe only through the nostril that corresponds to the side of the brain that I'm using: for example, when I'm focused on my breath, I'm using my right brain and left nostril, but when I'm analyzing the process this is reversed. I also discover that I can ease the cramps in my leg simply by shifting my breathing nostril.

When I try to report this insight to the teacher as an exciting new method of pain management, she cuts me off: "What you are doing—all that evaluating—is *not* vipassana. Stop it and get back to observation."

That night I fall asleep reciting a Buddhist precept: "Before Enlightenment, chop wood and carry water. After Enlightenment, chop wood and carry water."

Having run out of past and future thoughts, I'm spending most of my meditative time in the present, by default. Quite often I do experience myself as a single hum of energy, like the purr of a cat, but by now I know this good stuff can't last, and it doesn't. The pain that has been gumming my right leg suddenly acquires teeth, and nothing I do—observation, shifting breathing nostrils, altering position—helps for long. I ask myself the question I should have asked a couple of days ago: since I have an unusually high pain threshold, why am I suffering so much from just sitting still?

An answer flashes to mind: because I feel victimized.

Victimized? That makes no sense, yet I suspect this insight is true. Something here—perhaps the authority structure, perhaps just the process itself—makes me feel like a victimized child, not because I am, but because I once was, and now I'm replaying that old record with its accompaniment of infantile outrage. Since this is irrational, my conscious mind represses that emotion, resulting in stress felt as pain, thus arousing more anger. A vicious circle.

Though I'm pleased with this insight, it also depresses me. Victimization is a very old story in my life and one I thought I resolved decades ago. Now apparently vipassana is cutting deeper into this complex to perform radical surgery on the cellular level, as promised. I think of the times during this trip alone that I've overreacted to minor annoyances, such as my fury at the guy who put down his window shade. Why didn't I just ask him to raise it, if it bothered me so much? The truth is, I preferred to fume because it helped to drain the reservoir of repressed anger that meditation is now releasing. Though this insight isn't entirely new, the experiential level supporting it is. However, by now I know better than to report any of this to my teacher. She and the other instructors are protecting the technique from foreign additives, which I respect, but I can't excise a lifetime of alternative learning, and I wouldn't if I could.

Having decoded the message of my cramped legs, I find my posture adjusts subtlely and automatically to ease the pain, as if my body knew how to correct the problem once I freed it from carrying unconscious messages. However, I find I still want to shift my position every fifteen minutes out of boredom. The phrase "change for change's sake" flashes to my mind, flooding me with memories of times

I disrupted my life, sometimes paying a serious penalty, because of addiction to change.

Though we're seven days into the course, our vow of silence means that I know my roommates only by their superficial habits: who is first to turn on the lights in the morning and who turns them off; who unfastens the mosquito nets and who ties them up. While I'm glad our silence allows me to focus inwardly without feeling either rude or as if I'm missing something, I find averting the eyes and refraining from smiling a disagreeable way to behave. Without such minimal acts of friendliness, stereotypes of ethnicity, age and sex remain unchallenged. Significantly, the only people with whom I feel any closeness are the two I spoke to before our vow, particularly Olga. It's also with Olga that I break my silence. Since I know she has a miserable head cold, I pass a new Vicks inhaler to her under her mosquito netting. Minutes later I hear a hoarse and plaintive "What is this for?"

I mime sticking the tube up a nostril, then hunker back down into my bedroll.

Another tug at my netting. Olga signals in bewilderment, the inhaler dangling from her nostril.

Laughing, I whisper, "You have to take the top off first."

As I'm falling asleep, I remember this is New Year's Eve and imagine what I'd be doing if I were home. Then I remind myself that it's only about 10:30 a.m. in Toronto.

Suddenly the whole concept of time as fixed seems absurd. I consider the process by which Westerners came to both measure and hoard it: first by observing the sun's apparent journey across the sky, then by following a shadow around a circle, then by designing machinery to duplicate that movement, then by eliminating the circle in favour of digitized numbers—an abstraction of an abstraction of an abstraction of an illusion. How much more rational to think of time as moments co-existing like droplets in an ocean into which we dive, float, paddle, swim and eventually drown. How easy, when seeped in the lessons of inner space, also to regard the material world as an illusion.

In last evening's video, Goenka urged us to practise sensuous awareness, especially during the next twenty-four hours, but without judging any sensation as either pleasant or unpleasant. Now as I start my day, I pay attention to the changes of texture underfoot—from straw matting to concrete to grass to gravel and back again; to the flavour of toothpaste, water and porridge; to colour shifts in the sky from midnight black to lemony lime to mid-morning blue; to changes in the air from dewy to humid to crisp to chilly; to mutations of scent from loamy to antiseptic to smoky; to the blast of predawn music from someone still celebrating New Year's and the yips of the mother dog still attempting to teach her pups Buddhist detachment.

Fittingly, during this ten-day period in which we are cleansing our psyches, washing clothes emerges as our only off-duty recreation. The Indian women fill the lines with vibrant saris, blouses, shawls, skirts, petticoats and salwar kameezes. *Slap, slap, slap*—they whack their clothes against the sloping granite slab outside my window with the vigour of peasants along the Ganges, making me suspect that generations of Indian women have received as much therapeutic release working the sides of sacred rivers as their husbands bathing in them. Though I get no satisfaction from beating up my clothes, I enjoy hanging and turning them to catch the moving sun, remembering how my mother held court with the neighbours each Monday morning as she pegged sheets and shirts to her roller line, or reeled them in with the smell of the sun trapped inside, or spotted with rain, or frozen board-stiff, or finely coated in cinders from the Hamilton Steel Company.

Toward nightfall I sit on the edge of the ruined swimming pool, watching black-and-white butterflies soar up into the palms for what may be their only day of life, contemplating impermanence. Zen poem: "Sitting quietly doing nothing./Spring comes and the grass grows by itself."

Most days I've eaten well, slept well and dreamed vividly, but tonight I have trouble nodding off. As the minutes tick by, I grow anxious, knowing how soon 4:00

a.m. will come and how deadly it will be trying to meditate while exhausted. A little fiend taunts me: "Just turn over one more time and I'm sure you'll drift off. . . . Swat that mosquito and that should do it." And then, more insidiously: "If you look in your medicine kit, you'll find the sleeping pills you forgot to hand in. Why not take one? a half? a quarter?" As I fight temptation, I hear Goenka's voice firmly in my ear, instructing me to detach myself from the craving for sleep and to observe myself without reaction. Resolutely I follow this advice, falling asleep around two, and awakening at four feeling refreshed.

In the evening's video, Goenka provides the same instruction, adding that our minds and bodies don't need more rest than meditation provides and leaving me to wonder if I had somehow tuned in to today's lecture.

Our last full day of vipassana. By now I'm spending a significant part of each hour in a subtle vibrational state. In fact, it's more often the pleasant feelings that cause me to break a position as if too much success is to be avoided like too much chocolate mousse. Is this another destructive habit—cutting off good consequences because of some hidden negative agenda?

In the evening lecture, Goenka explains that Buddhist detachment doesn't mean indifference to the pain of others, but "holy indifference," which extends compassion equally and unconditionally to all people; therefore, whenever we encounter someone victimizing another, our task is to protect the weaker from the stronger and the stronger from himself or herself, without judgment. Similarly, we should not distinguish between those who wish us well and those who wish to injure us. Even love for another individual should be avoided as just another form of self-love: a reflection of our own self-image, or what we want from that person, or who we want that person to be for us.

Given the West's Hallmark ideals of romantic love, family values, personal friendship and individual self-worth, this is heretical thinking. As Christians we are told that Jesus died on the Cross out of love for each one of us so that we have only to repent of our sins and to love him in order to receive life everlasting. In Buddhism, everyone must save himself because no one else will—not Buddha or Jesus or Krishna or Devi or God, who, if he exists, is irrelevant since the laws of karma are self-sustaining. Adam and Eve were forbidden fruit from the Tree of Knowledge, but Buddha urges us to avail ourselves of knowledge, symbolized by the Bodhi Tree of Enlightenment. There is no Day of Judgment; instead, by practising the Four Noble Truths, each of us creates heaven and hell here on earth during many lifetimes until we merge into the collective bliss of Oneness that is "unborn, unbecome, uncreated, unconditioned." When Buddha's followers asked what part of the Self continued from incarnation to incarnation, he refused to answer on the grounds that he was a pragmatist and not a metaphysician—not why, or even what, but only how.

At noon on our ninth day we end our vow of Noble Silence, and suddenly everyone is comparing notes. Not surprisingly, I discover that under the traditional saris, bindis and bangles, the Indian women with whom I've been sharing mat space are strong personalities with firm views and considerable professional training of all kinds.

During our afternoon meditation, Goenka urges us by audiotape to beam compassionate love to the world. I'm expecting a silent meditation; instead, he chants at length in what I've come to regard as a theatrical voice. Throughout the course I've suppressed a dislike for these chants, which I find an impediment to meditation rather than an aid, and now this negative suppression is making itself known through a fiercely throbbing leg.

When the gong rings, I escape to the ruined swimming pool in an attempt to resolve my feelings, unwilling to end the retreat on such a sour note. It's an ironic task, using Goenka's imparted wisdom to combat the frustration I'm experiencing toward him, like trying to filter the good from the bad one inherits from one's parents. At the same time, I recognize that what I'm undergoing is just a predictable inner revolt: my ego, already tasting freedom, is attempting to regain control of my psyche by debunking my teachers.

When I return to the meditation hall for the day's final session, my psyche is in order and I experience the best meditation yet. As I'm leaving, an Indian woman falls into step beside me. "I wish I could translate Goenka's words for you. They're often so lovely. His chant this morning for compassionate love was so moving that it sent goosebumps up my arms."

As happens so often in India, I receive exactly the message I need when I need it: chance, coincidence, telepathy or something more mysterious?

The instant the 4:00 a.m. gong sounds, we're all up washing, packing, returning mattresses, blankets and mosquito netting.

In Goenka's final lecture, we're urged to spend two hours a day meditating for the rest of our lives. He assures us—as did the dadis of the Brahma Kumaris—that meditation breeds time by focusing our minds for other tasks. In fact, vipassana and BK philosophies are similar: both teach karma, reincarnation, the illusionary quality of the material world, living in the here and now, the importance of thought over speech and action, renunciation of sensory pleasures, celibacy, indifference to miracles, selfless service and universal compassion. Their basic difference

lies in the source of their inspiration—Buddha or Baba—
and their approach: whereas the BKs attempt to bypass
the body on the road to Enlightenment, Buddhism uses it
as a vehicle; whereas the BKs inspire through example,
Buddhism teaches self-empowerment through knowledge.

In our day-to-day practice, Goenka reminds us not to
become attached to specific goals or to one state of consciousness over another. When gross sensations break
through after a period of equanimity, this is not a reversal
but another opportunity for progress, allowing us to eradicate conditioning at a deeper level. Outside of meditation,
we should give our undivided attention to any important
task, and if a problem arises, take a few seconds to become
aware of the breath and any sensations. We should not
dwell on frustrations from the past, for when we review an
injury or a defeat ten times, we convert a single wound
into ten wounds, and one discouragement into ten.

Vipassana is only valuable if it leads to changes in our
lives, and that will only happen if we practise it on a daily
basis. How will we know that it has taken hold? The space
between our present aversions and cravings will grow
longer while our recovery time grows shorter. We will
experience gratitude, along with a desire to give selfless
service, and one way to do this is to share the knowledge
we have acquired at this retreat.

As I say goodbye to the other participants, gratitude is
already in place. I know that I've made a genuine commitment to something that will affect the rest of my life,

perhaps radically, and while my Four Horses of the Apoc-
alypse—impatience, anger, wilfulness and pride—are as
yet untamed, I've managed to throw a saddle over a couple of them.

I sit on my bag along the highway outside Ganga Farm
with a dozen locals awaiting a bus to Bangalore, psyche
freshly scrubbed, soul squeaky clean, excited to be back
in the "real" world. After ten days of sensory impoverish-
ment, I've decided to head north for the beaches of Goa
before flying to India's holiest city, Varanasi, on the Ganges,
which will be my final destination. Most buses career past,
with arms and legs waving from windows and doors like
some half-metal, half-mammal creature from *Star Wars*.
Occasionally one does stop, allowing a few locals to
squeeze on. Hobbled by luggage, I don't have a chance,
and phoning for a cab isn't an option. More people pile
up at the stop, including a dozen men from the vipassana
workshop. As one hour stretches into two, I struggle to
hold on to my freshly minted equanimity.

A pickup truck stops a few metres up the road.

"Bangalore?" I shout. Dragging my bags up the gravel
shoulder, I offer its driver 100 rupees to take me to the
train station. As I climb into the front seat, everyone else
at the stop jumps in back. Though disconcerted, the driver concludes, correctly, that he can't do much about it, so

pulls away with his load. I offer him an extra 100 rupees for the gang behind, while deciding privately to top that with another at the station. I feel exhilarated: this small opportunity to give service seems exactly the way to begin my life post-vipassana.

Unfortunately, my prototype good deed starts to lose lustre like the shiny big fish Hemingway's Old Man tried to smuggle past the sharks. Reneging on his agreement, my driver deposits us on the outskirts of Bangalore; not content with a free ride to town, the locals aggressively swarm me demanding rupees; neglecting to say a simple thank-you, vipassana students jam my auto-rickshaw, now assuming a free ride to the station. While I chide myself for becoming attached to my Good Deed, I don't yet realize that this is as pleasant as the day is going to be, and that I'm standing on a slippery slope, about to begin an ignominious downward slide. The details of this—the hours spent standing in lines, dealing with cheats, misunderstandings and cancellations—are too tedious to relate, but by evening I have sufficiently sorted out my plans to at least be boarding a luxury sleeper bus for Panaji, the capital of Goa. For the other passengers travelling in couples, *luxury sleeper* means an upper or lower double bed in its own private compartment. For me—a single traveller—it translates into a narrow metal bunk on the aisle leading into the driver's cockpit, where the bus personnel smoke, where gas fumes collect, where oncoming headlights beam and where the driver keeps his thumb glued to the horn.

Forget Buddhist detachment—by now, I certainly have. Early in the day I gave birth to a tiny devil of animosity that has fed voraciously on each inconvenience. Now I watch helpless and bewildered as this creature wearing my identity devours me. For the record, my bunk is better than I expected since I'm at least fully reclined, but it's not as good as others have, so I can't stop bitching—to myself since there's no one else to listen.

Though I sleep only fitfully, as we climb the rugged green coastal hills at daybreak, I do lighten up. Goa, the hub of Portugal's Eastern empire from 1510 to 1961, is an Indian state like no other. Its towns are distinctive for their quaint whitewashed Roman Catholic churches and tile-roofed houses with overhanging balconies, mouldering balustrades and graceful staircases. Panaji, reached over a narrow causeway lying on water like a floating carpet, is a town of old bungalows and stately trees nestled between the Mandovi and Ourem Rivers. However, I won't be staying here. In yesterday's frenzy of bookings, cancellations and rebookings, I reserved a room at Anjuna Beach, ten kilometres up the coast. As I emerge, blinking, at the bus depot, I gird myself for the usual battle with local transport providers—in this case, taxi drivers, since Panaji has no auto-rickshaws. Happily, the first one I approach offers to drive me for what I know to be a fair price. As we meander north along the coastal highway from one resort to the next, my sense of well-being seems to have returned; however, the beast once aroused is not so easily appeased. As the countryside grows flatter and drier, I begin to grouse to myself that I've chosen the wrong beach, and when we arrive at Anjuna, which seems to consist of far-flung rundown buildings plunked in grassy yellow fields, I'm convinced of it.

I perk up when I see the Red Cab Inn, rambling and eccentric like Snow White's cottage. Unfortunately, it's overbooked and I'm offered only overflow accommodation at a beach guest house with a boy to carry my luggage.

What I'm told is "a ten-minute stroll" turns out to be a hot, arduous haul through a scattering of bungalows and ruins that would have seemed intriguing if I weren't so disgruntled. Our destination—Rose Garden Cottages— is built motel-style around a parched courtyard: no cottages, no garden and certainly no roses. Inside each concrete box is a bed, a light, a table, a fan and an attached bathing stall without hot water, offered at a price that usually includes a colour TV. For ten minutes I pace the courtyard, spewing complaints to a sun-drenched and peaceable young man painting an abstract on his porch, feeling embarrassed for myself but unable to stop. I want to return to one of the more stylish beaches closer to Panaji, but the only available taxi driver has tripled his price, and besides, I don't want to sail off into another collection of uncertainties. Feeling boxed in, I decide with bad grace to stay the night.

Though Rose Garden Cottages is only a few metres from the beach, the first thing I notice is that the cove isn't as impressive as the one at Kovalam and that it has no surf. It does possess something else of interest: a windswept heath rearing up from the honey-coloured sand with its rocky white and black arms striving to recapture the retreating sea. Though I set out to explore the exposed shoreline, I find myself climbing the heath, sometimes by path, sometimes by footholds. It's the back way but not too steep and only occasionally thorny. This isn't a casual climb. I feel driven. Red and black boulders heave from the heath's grassy shoulders. Sudden rock clefts provide V-shaped slices of sea, sand and palms. Sudden gashes in the iron-rich earth seem to gush blood. On the first plateau, I encounter a Christian shrine like a shrouded white nun looking out to sea, along with a glorious view, but I'm only briefly distracted by piety or beauty. Again I begin to pace through the heath's yellow hair, clothes plastered to my body by a driving wind, thinking with despair of all the fury and ill will I've generated for myself and everyone else during the past thirty-six hours. Plunking down on a pocked and red-veined rock bearing the cindery scars of inner upheaval, I begin to cry—almost to howl—unable to stand being locked inside the bitter she-devil that has emerged from the rusty sediment of ancient wounds and wrongdoings. Seizing control of my breathing, I put myself into a meditative trance in which I review, step by step, my journey from Ganga Farm, observing the birth and flounderings of that tortured creature and dissolving the chains that bind me to her. It's exhausting work, a holdover from all that was begun at Ganga Farm, but when I'm through, peace settles over me in a downy white cloud: the ego fortress in which I was entrapped was not made of bricks and mortar as I thought but of scar tissue many decades old.

A serpentine path leads up through yellow grass turned orange by the red earth. I climb it, accompanied by a couple of tail-wagging dogs, to a tableland ribbed with the stony remains of houses and animal pens, along with an ancient orchard now reclaimed by birds. I identify spotted doves, swifts with backswept wings, split-tailed drongos, handsome white-and-black shrikes, mynahs with orange eye rings, even a golden oriole with yellow breast and helmet. Those I can't see, I hear cooing and twittering as they nest for the night.

When I descend the heath, the coconut groves cast long, cool shadows across the beach, and my path is an easy one now that I've left the thorny side of the cliff to the snakes and the scorpions.

I swim in the cove. Though it has reefs that must be negotiated, they merely offer challenge while supplying character, so that by the time I emerge from the ocean I've fallen in love. I'm grateful to be living on the beach in Anjuna with all shortcomings easily overwhelmed by the beauty of the setting: *Change yourself and everything changes.*

I have dinner at one of the inviting palm-frond restaurants strung along the shore. It seems that every place in India catering to tourists has its speciality: fresh-caught fish or massages or pineapples served on sticks like popsicles. In Anjuna it's ear cleaning. I've barely seated myself when I'm approached by a man bearing a fifteen-centimetre reed he wishes to stick in my ear at a cost of several hundred rupees. He even carries a book of testimonials from other tourists who've had their ears prodded with this thing and, perhaps like Aesop's fox who lost its tail, are willing to rave about it.

Anjuna's other signature attraction is its Wednesday flea market. At dawn, Goan vendors set up several acres of booths heaped with handwoven blankets, sandalwood, lacquerwork, carvings, incense and spices, while the remnants of Anjuna's hippie colony, which once turned these magnificent coves into havens for crime, sex and drugs, now sell gemstones, crystals, jewellery and paintings.

When the last catamaran taxis have left the beach, I assemble with the locals to watch the sun set and the moon rise. Hawkers with portable cooking stalls make omelettes for the hungry crowd or sell pop from tubs of ice. As I search for satellites and shooting stars, I remember that summer night when I, age seven, slept in my backyard with my best friend in a tent improvised by draping canvas over the iron frame of an old porch swing. This was the night of the Perseids, when meteors ripped like a swarm of angry fire bees from a radiant north of the constellation Perseus. With our heads poking out the door, we watched awestruck as the formerly immutable stars firewebbed the sky, thinking that this must happen every night.

By the time I go to bed at eleven, the rave is just getting started. When I leave Goa at sunrise, headed northeast for Varanasi, partygoers are strewn across the beach like shipwrecked sailors. I pick my way among them, suspecting that if I turned them over, one by one, I'd find my own discarded corpse washed down from the heath.

death
and
reincarnation

"Being born twice
is no more remarkable
than being born once"

MY MEMORY of Varanasi on the Ganges from twenty-two years ago is of being perpetually lost in a labyrinth of vaporous laneways steeped in the scent of incense, camphor and spices. Around me are pyramids of brilliantly coloured face powders and stacks of brass posts. In front is a corridor of maimed and filthy beggars who claw at me as I descend to the river. In the Varanasi of my dreams, it's always twilight—a surreal world of undulating shadows, ghostly shapes and tolling bells owing something to the fact that I was feverishly ill all the time I was there. Founded about three thousand years ago on the west bank of India's holiest river, Varanasi (also known as Benares, Benaras and Kashi) has a claim to being the world's oldest living city; ironically, its business is death, as demonstrated by its annual cremation of thirty-five thousand corpses.

I arrive at Varanasi after an overnight bus trip from Goa to Bombay, followed by an early-morning flight via Delhi. Now, on this overcast January day, the ghostly memories of my first visit inform my feelings as I travel from the airport by bus, then by auto-rickshaw, pedal-rickshaw and finally on foot, struggling to keep up with my porter as he pads through lanes that darken and narrow to tunnels, trying to memorize twists and turns before giving up. Twice we pass funeral processions, the first with a saffron-wrapped body lashed to the roof of a car, followed by a phalanx of chanting mourners, the second with a white-shrouded corpse bound to a bamboo stretcher carried on the shoulders of four silent men.

My destination is a guest house on the west bank of the Ganges, directly overlooking Scindia Ghat where bodies are cremated. Breaking from our corridors of darkness, we arrive at the man-made limestone shores of the Ganges. Before my eyes can adjust, we're climbing a rough, hard-packed cliff, about a hundred steps in all. The hotel's spotless lobby—just large enough for a desk and two chairs with knees touching—is occupied by a husky man with a Middle Eastern face and a thin moustache. I book his most expensive room, up a couple more steep flights, because it has a balcony offering a sweeping view of the Ganges—boats, stupas, pavilions, temples—all wrapped in smoke from the funeral pyres next door. As I stand on my wrought-iron balcony, the diffuse light of the sun churns sky, land and water to the same yellowish grey hue, one-dimensional without shadow, sound or motion. I think of the word *tirtha*, meaning a crossing place where heaven and earth meet, like the finger of God stretching across the abyss to man, nearly touching.

After descending the cliff to the limestone bulwark, I continue down another staircase to the water. About a hundred of these ghats line the western shore, curved and continuous like an amphitheatre, yet each with a different name, a different history and even a different owner: one is for the Muslims, one for the Jains, one for Bengalis; one is dedicated to a famous Hindi poet and one to a princess; one has the sculpture of a pink stone cow, one a Brahman saint's footprint and one a temple to Shitala, goddess of smallpox; one was built by the maharaja of Varanasi, one by the maharaja of Jaipur and one by a gambler with the winnings of a single night. However, Varanasi has only one real landlord: Shiva, the destroyer. Two thousand of its temples are dedicated to him, along with a hundred thousand lingams.

I wade into the Ganges, the colour and texture of mercury, remembering my first dip nearly three months ago at Rishikesh, with the green water bubbling around my legs, fresh and clear, eager for its journey. Since the river's Himalayan birth, it has lost its innocence, grown slow and opaque with its burden of experience.

Dwelling in the matted locks of Shiva . . .
Resembling the autumn moon . . .
Destroying the poison of illusion . . .
Flowing through the three worlds . . .

Though I'm not yet up to my knees, my feet have disappeared as if amputated—one more set of body parts to find their way southeast to the Bay of Bengal.

Protector of the sick and suffering who take refuge
  in you . . .
Giving complete emancipation . . .
Destroyer of sin . . .
Flowing in a staircase to heaven.

I look back at this city of nearly a million and a half, a towering cliff of temples and palaces and mosques, layer upon layer, curved in both directions like the golden horns of a bull with tips buried in the mist. On the eastern bank is nothing but mud flats . . . tirtha.

I walk south along the shore past a five-storey white-and-gold spire constructed of cloth and plywood, where thousands of pilgrims are chanting under a red canopy. As I approach the burning ghat, the sweet-smelling smoke—a blend of sandalwood and human flesh—catches in my throat. Everything here is the colour of mud and ashes relieved by garlands of marigolds and shrouds of saffron and gold. On the far side of a pyramid of wood and a giant weigh scale, I stand upon a mud-caked staircase from which I can see a platform with a couple of dozen pyres. Some are freshly stacked, while others have been reduced to bone and ash. Six burn like golden lotuses around their white-shrouded corpses.

According to five-thousand-year-old Hindu teachings, the physical body is connected to six increasingly more subtle energy bodies: the etheric that gives it its form, the astral, the emotional, the intellectual, the spiritual and the Divine. In death, the soul ascends through these higher planes, growing ever finer in texture; in rebirth, it descends till it materializes in flesh and bone. The greater the soul, the higher the chakra from which it departs, with holy persons exiting through the crown. Just as birth is completed by the cutting of the umbilical cord, so death is finalized by the severing of what ancient texts, including the Bible, refer to as the silver cord connecting soul to body.

Awakening at dawn, I drift out onto my balcony, wrapped in blankets against the morning's chill. The indignant squabble, as little brown figures dart in every direction, alerts me to the fact that what I thought to be a pleasant place to have coffee is actually a monkey latrine. Like a one-eyed god, the sun rises through layers of smoke and mist, creating a golden pathway over the water, lumpy with its unnatural burden of body parts. Again sky and river are churned to the same shades of slate, copper and bronze, divided only by that thin line of mud flats lying like a corpse on the eastern horizon. By the time I descend to the river, the all-night chanting at the cloth temple has ceased but not the activity at the burning ghat. As I walk into smoke and ashes, I know that with each inhalation I'm taking in particles of flesh and bone from last night's funerals—not just second-hand smoke but second-hand souls.

A couple of saffron-and-gold shawls float in the sooty water, along with discarded strings of marigolds, like the tinsel and popcorn trimmings from a Christmas tree that has burned, consuming an entire family. A bull munches on marigolds. A cow kneels in a still-warm puddle of ash while a mongrel feeds her pups in another: the cycle of life.

Once again I stare at the burning pyres inside their wood corral, each topped with its own smoky question mark, conscious of being the only foreign spectator. A smiling Indian in jeans and leather jacket with mirror sunglasses materializes at my elbow. Pointing to a derelict tower overlooking the burning ghat, he informs me, "You can get a better view from there. Come, I'll take you." Though he represents himself as a public-spirited friend eager to help me to understand Varanasi, I know that I'm entering a negotiation. With shawl held over my nose and mouth to filter the smoke, I allow myself to be escorted up two flights of stairs, past cows, sleeping men and squatting women. Directly below I count eleven bodies, several with half-burned faces or limbs poking through their bindings, a scene both awesome and banal.

My guide points toward a newly arrived body being dipped into the Ganges. "That is its last bath before the burning."

At another pyre not yet set aflame, a man with shaved head walks counterclockwise around the corpse. "That's the oldest son. He must go around five times." After the corpse's gold covering is removed, sticks are placed across the chest by the son and other mourners. "Now they will add ghee to make it burn and sandalwood paste to make for the good smell. Then the son will light the fire. After it burns for about three hours, he must toss a pot of Ganga water over his shoulder to put it out, then walk away without looking back."

"What happens to the body parts that are left?"

"The bones are thrown into the river. By then the soul is gone. It leaves when the son cracks open the skull. That also stops the skull from exploding when the brains cook. The corpses of children are put into Ganga without burning. They are just flowers and you do not burn flowers. They are too delicate. You don't burn pregnant women either, and you don't burn holy men—they don't need to be purified. Lepers are not burned because the disease makes such a bad smell that people don't like it, so you just put them into the water."

A grey-hooded figure looking like Father Time pokes at the logs with a long pole. Others pile on more wood or carry off ashes. "Those are Untouchables. No one else will do those things because it is unclean."

Though Gandhi reclassified outcastes as Harijans, meaning Children of God, and a government quota system now gives them access to education and jobs, clearly prejudice lives on. "Why do you say this work is unclean?"

"When touching the body they cannot protect themselves from its bad karma. Neither can the son who also must be cleansed."

I point to a foot protruding from the flames. "Why are its soles painted red?"

"That is a Bengali. I know by the way the body burns, how the wood caves, that it is a woman. Men are strong through the chest, women through the hips."

"I don't see any women mourners standing around the corpses."

"Only men can be with the body while it is burning."

"Is that because women are of lower status?"

My guide gravely shakes his head. "That is so they do not decide to become sati or are forced to do it. Death should not be a sad time. That brings bad luck. Death is a time of happiness, when the soul of the dead person is set free from the sorrows of this Earth." He smiles at me expectantly, then adds, "There is a question you haven't asked." With a broad sweep of both arms, he continues, "You haven't asked how much this making of a funeral costs."

"Do all foreigners ask that?"

"All Americans. You are American?"

"Canadian."

He laughs too jovially. "Ahh, then maybe that is it." Again, an expansive gesture. "A funeral is a very expensive thing. For one dead man it takes eight hundred pounds of wood, sometimes more, depending on what a family can afford. Even for wood that is little more than sawdust, it costs 600 rupees, and then it is only a half-burned body that goes into the water. For a man of more means it could cost 10,000 rupees. This matter is a serious one for a family. Sometimes a son must work for a year just to pay for the death of his father, and it is worse when a man is without family. I myself am a social worker. I work at a hospice where people are dying. They worry because they do not have money for wood to burn their bodies after they die. That is all they think about, even when they should be preparing for death. It is a terrible thing not to have the wood. Do you understand what I am saying?" An eloquent pause, during which I stare at myself in his mirror glasses waiting for the sucker punch. "I have a friend who needs 500 rupees to buy wood so he can die in peace. He is tortured by this."

I am blunt. "I don't believe you are a social worker, and I don't believe you are collecting for a hospice, but I appreciate the information you've given to me and I'll pay you well as a guide. You can donate your fee for wood if you choose."

Without protest, he accepts the money and hustles off.

I continue along the broad stone walkway to a place where men with thick hoses flush impacted mud down to the river. During the monsoons the water in the Ganges increases twenty-five times, raising it an astonishing twelve metres, covering this path, all the ghats, the shore temples, even the first storeys of palaces, hostels and restaurants. What I'm seeing here today are Varanasi's exposed bones.

The sun has risen high enough to burn away some of the mist. Single helmsmen in their dinghies, silhouetted against the sky and Xeroxed in the water, beckon to me like Charon while their agents ply the shore. "You want a boat? One hundred rupees." Though as many as ten million pilgrims visit Varanasi each year, the few now occupying the ghats approach the water like brave members of the polar bear club. Death may not take a holiday, but apparently pilgrims do: given a choice between the Ganges in January or in June, most opt for spring.

I watch an emaciated old man break away from his two assistants. Scooping water, he holds his cupped hands toward the sun before ecstatically pouring the liquid over himself. Others dunk five times, then rinse their mouths. I think of the remains of the thirty-five thousand corpses dumped in here each year and the unburned bodies of lepers, along with the ninety million litres of raw sewage flushed each day from Varanasi's fifteen main sewers. In a much-quoted study, a well-known French physician, D. Herelle, reported that Ganges water was not only without harmful bacteria but that it actually destroyed disease cultures. Though his findings could never be replicated and government figures place the fecal coliform count at many times maximum allowable levels, Hindus take the purity of Ganga Mata on faith: one dip in her waters and all bad karma floats away like the sankharas I struggled to scrub out at Ganga Farm.

Farther along the shore, I come upon a dog gnawing on what looks like a thigh bone. A couple of ghats have been taken over by women washing clothes. One young women, looking as beautiful and as lost as a Scott Fitzgerald heroine, stands waist-high in a black silk slip with pink toiletries spread over a rock, meticulously washing her long black hair in the filthy water. When I try to engage her in conversation, she shrugs or shakes her head, either bored with me or uncomprehending or perhaps spaced out on drugs.

At each step I'm dogged by boatmen and their agents with prices that fall as the sun rises: "Fifty rupees. . .30. . . 20. . ." Many dinghies have been painted with red-and-white Coca-Cola logos, now faded to pink and grey, yet another layer of foreign imperialism being absorbed into Indian culture. One boatload of surgically masked Japanese can't pull away from shore because of four smaller craft clinging like crabs while their oarsmen try to sell trinkets.

At Dasaswamedh Ghat, where the main street of Old City intersects with the waterfront, the mood is more like Brighton Beach in high season than River Styx. Hawkers sell kites and balloons along with shrouds and marigolds. Instead of children filling pails with sand, pilgrims scoop Ganges water. Chai-sellers offer newspapers rolled on sticks as in a British private club. While masseurs rub down their customers, barbers shave heads, ritually committing the hair—like everything else in Varanasi—into the Ganges. On platforms under rotting bamboo umbrellas, *pandits*, wise in the scriptures, chant Sanskrit verses and offer blessings marked by smears of white sandalwood paste or red *kum-kum*, while astrologers acquaint their clients with the whims and ways of the stars.

A few boys in both Eastern and Western dress play cricket. One chubby-cheeked kid rushes toward me, right hand extended, the other rubbing his stomach. Unfortunately for the case he's trying to make, he's wearing Nikes. When I turn away, he changes his pitch to "Pen! Pen!" Though I'm chilly and would like some chai, I remind myself that Varanasi is the fatal disease capital of India. As I vacillate, the vendor casually dips a used glass into a pail of Ganges water for recycling, reminding me of the AIDS warning freely translated: *Drink from this glass and you've drunk with all the corpses ever dunked in the Ganges.*

Someone calls my name. An Australian couple, whom I met at the Amritanandamayi ashram, sit beside some cows on the ghats, drinking Cokes. "I can't get over this place!" exclaims Matt. "It feels like a summer resort. Everyone's so bloody cheerful."

"It's like we're on the riviera," adds Amanda.

"The riviera of death."

"Are you going to go in?"

"I already have. In my shower. It's the same water, isn't it?"

I join them on the ghat, stained red with betel juice, under Shitala Temple, dedicated to the goddess of small-pox. We listen to the Song of Varanasi—a laughing, shouting, mooing, barking, bell-ringing, chanting, twittering, splashing celebration of death.

I stroll back along the walkway to my hotel, snapping pictures of the fantastical blue, orange, yellow, green and red layer cake of buildings with their frescoes and idols, their balconies and stupas. A cube-shaped man—square body, square face, square jaw—steps in front of me with hand raised like a traffic cop: "Stop! Don't you know this is a holy place?"

Glancing over my shoulder I see that I'm nearing Scindia, a burning ghat where photos are forbidden. "Sorry. I didn't realize I was so close."

My honest apology is rejected. "How dare you! I will call the police. You are not fit to be here. I will see you are run out of India!"

His rage builds. "I will take that camera from you. I will smash it against your head! Give it to me."

Another Indian intervenes. "I am afraid you will have a bad time here. This man is one who is easily angered. He will follow you everywhere you go." Drawing me aside, he adds, "I think I know a way to help. I am a social worker. If you donate 500 rupees to the hospice where I work . . ."

Pulling away, I confront the first man. "Call the police. I want to tell them how you are trying to get money from me." Still puffed with indignation, he strides off. Though I know I've been caught in the Eastern version of bad con, good con, I also sense that the rage directed against me as a foreigner is real. It's not the first time some moral arbiter has used a minor infraction, real or anticipated, to dump a truckload of secular fury on me. It's the shadow side of Indian fervour, and one reason that I have lost my taste for visiting shrines, too often finding them the least holy of places.

By seven of a January evening, it's pitch-black in Varanasi. Though I generally avoid going out at night, a rumbling stomach is an insistent thing. I would like to have dinner at the cliffside Ganpati Guest House a couple of blocks down the ghats, but the waterfront isn't illuminated and I'd have to pass the muddy hillock where bulls congregate. My only alternative is Varanasi's poorly lit inner labyrinth. I've seldom found my way by daylight, and now the shops are closed, making the lanes interchangeable, like trying to follow one thread in a tangled black skein. My flashlight illuminates a sign, "Ganpati Guest House Restaurant," accompanied by a directional arrow. Gratefully I follow it to a second arrow and a third, like blazes through a forest. I halt. Three bulls and a calf gaze at me from under a moist and breathy cloud. No matter how tightly I'm swaddled in shawls, I don't fool the locals, and I most certainly don't fool the bulls, who smell me for the steak eater I once was. As the lead minotaur lowers his horns, I retreat back to the last arrow and the one before that. I turn a corner. The same three bulls and calf confront me. The calf is a foot from the wall. Reciting my *om shantis*, I slither along the slimy limestone, shove its rump between me and the bulls, then squeeze by. I'm elated, until I find myself in a square with many lanes and no arrows. After shining my light down each, I become so confused that I no longer remember which leads back to the bulls. A male voice issues from the darkness: "Turn left down the steps, turn left and climb." Though I flash my light, I can't see anyone. For all I know, it's the voice of God. Speaking a heartfelt "thank you" into the void, I do as instructed. The first left takes me onto the ghats, the second to a staircase leading up to Ganpati Guest House, silhouetted in the light of a last-quarter moon.

I choose a corner table high above the Ganges, and sometime during the evening I meet Swami Madavananda Giri, the Ganpati's resident guru from Long Beach, California. With a curly auburn beard and his hair in a topknot, he joins me at my table, wearing saffron robes and carrying a Coke. "The owner complains I'm turning his place into an ashram!" he jokes. "Just today I finished a little group with a Hungarian, two Israelis, two Japanese and an American."

"How long did you work with them?"

"Two weeks. I was teaching them to awaken kundalini through meditation, and they all got it except for this one Israeli guy. He said, 'This is a load. I'll meditate the way you say but I don't believe it.' So last night I went inside him with some of my own energy, and this morning he was almost in tears, 'My heart is about to stop! I don't know what to do, Swamiji.' I helped him through that, which was a very profound experience for him."

"Is meditation your basic method of teaching?"

"That and knowledge, and of course it's important to live as good a life as possible or"—a hearty laugh—"if you can't be good, be careful!" Swamiji looks with approval at my meal of *mattar paneer* (peas and cheese). "A vegetarian diet also helps. I don't believe the body is a cemetery. It's best to take as little other life as possible to sustain one's own."

"How did you get to Varanasi from California?"

"Soul surfing. Sometimes after surfers have been at it a long time, they experience a deep awakening, the same as through yoga and meditation. I began every morning with a mantra, then went to sleep repeating the same mantra. After about nine months I awoke hearing the mantra. It was so beautiful when this happened that I cried and cried, and once you have a taste of the Self you don't have to chase after it. It will chase after you."

"Do you miss being a California beach boy?"

"The meditation I experience is so beneficial that I'm willing to give up all the pleasures in the world for it. There's nothing magical about the process. If you lie on a railway track in front of a train, it doesn't take any faith to know that train will hit you—that's a fact and it doesn't matter if the driver is a Muslim or a Christian or a computer. It's the same with my meditation. It's real and true, no doubt at all, and it's part of a very natural process."

I ask the question that comes easily in Varanasi. "But what do you think all this is for?"

"The purpose of life?" Pausing to finish his Coke, Swamiji replies, "My understanding is that by experiencing things on the physical level, we're instrumental in allowing the universe to experience its own Self because we *are* the universe. A swami told me that I'm very close to the outer edge of consciousness, and this is the conclusion of many other swamis about me. He also told me that only three things are holding me back, 'Impatience, anger and doubt.' Being from California, of course I replied, 'Swamiji, I doubt if I'll ever have the patience not to get angry,' but he didn't think that was funny."

"Are you part of a community here in Varanasi?"

"Very much. I'm the only Western swami, and for a couple of years they gossiped about me and they thought I was a cheater because 99 per cent of the people who wear orange do it only so they'll have food and a place to live. But then they found I'm celibate and I don't do drugs and I don't drink and I give as much as possible to help in any way I can. Now when I wander off to sit somewhere and meditate for hours and hours and get lost in that, someone will bring me back to this ashram where they have much love for me. I like to take toffees with me to feed people, especially the children, but I also take a walking stick to whack at someone for being naughty, like smoking after they've told me they quit."

"Is it important for you to be in Varanasi?"

"No one has to come to this place or any ashram to become enlightened, but several times a week I go to the burning ghats because it reminds me that time is of the essence and tomorrow won't do. All the same things can happen in a hotel room in any city and you don't even have to lead a particular life. Meditation is everyone's heritage—our birthright that's too often kept from us."

I lie in my unheated room under a mound of blankets beside a dead air conditioner as large as a walk-in freezer. The rectangle of stars framed by my window, along with the smell of smoke from the burning ghat, conjure up the coal-heated attic bedroom I once shared with my sister, surrounded by cubbyholes we were convinced contained the ghosts of our ancestors. Now all the people who shared my natal home are dead—my grandmother, mother, father, sister—so many deaths, each surrounded by its own psychic aura. . . . *That wintry April day when I was eight, afraid to come home from school for lunch because I'd already envisioned what I would see when I turned the corner— the shiny black windowless car that bore away my grandmother who had died of a heart attack while I was at school. I knew the instant my father died, though I was thousands of kilometres away . . . wakened by an unearthly shriek that I later identified as the whistle of a train through the mountains, weirdly amplified; looking at my bedside clock and saying the words, "My father could be dying right now and I wouldn't even know it"; later discovering that was exactly when he did die, confirmed by my mother who had checked her watch at that moment. . . . On the day that would bring my mother's death, I awoke with my mind steeped in ghostly images that caused me to cancel a lunch date to wander through a cemetery. . . . At a time when my sister's cancer was supposed to be in remission, my dreams told a more sinister story. Yet my eeriest date with death occurred that July day when I wrote my former husband's name on a piece of paper followed by "January 6, 1987"—the day on which he died six months later.* Now as the last of my line, I am the keeper of the memories. Nothing of my intimate past exists except as I remember it, and when I die, all that will dissolve for want of witnesses. Even as I lie here I begin to wonder, did I have a cat called Smoky and a stuffed bear called Teddy Umcline? Did my sister and I read *The Star Weekly* comics on the veranda steps and play Monopoly on the living room floor? Did my grandmother twist rag rugs from dead clothes, did my father play Solitaire, did my mother sift ashes for lumps of coal? What are events but words and images written on water? History itself is less real than the books written about it, which at least exist as artifacts.

"There's another way of looking at these things."

I smell his sandalwood beads before I see him, squatted on my air-conditioner wrapped in a saffron and gold winding cloth. Gesturing eloquently, he continues, "Think of your life as a garden for all seasons. Everything in it exists at one and the same time, just as the fragrance of the carnation exists simultaneously with the velvet texture of its petals. It's only when you create a path through the garden that you notice that the crocuses seem to bloom before the roses and the roses before the chrysanthemums."

As I sit up in bed, I'm startled to see how grey Moonji's hair looks in the starlight, how wrinkled his skin, once as smooth as the shell of a pecan, now more like the nut inside. "You're reminding me that time doesn't pass. Only our journey makes it appear to do so."

"And either all that's been experienced still exists—including the path and the traveller—or none of it ever did. Just as you can't separate two sides of a sheet of paper, so you can't separate the present from the past. Time is just another dimension of space, and what appear as shifts in time are really just shifts in perspective—different facets of a diamond turned to catch the light of the Eternal Now."

Moonji's skin seems as luminous as a ghost's, adding urgency to my words as I tell him, "From my life, and from the lives of those close to me, I see patterns emerge that are too meaningful to be anything but purposeful. I'm especially touched by how much some people learn on their deathbeds, despite the pain and the drugs and the operations. To learn from dying has no evolutionary value unless this is a moral world where the soul continues in some way."

I can see by Moonji's smile that he's pleased with my comments. "I think that your Californian guru had it nearly right when he said our purpose is to aid in universal evolution. Through strife on the physical plane, we humans ascend to ever-higher Self-consciousness, allowing the Supreme to fully realize itself through us." He draws a book from his lungi—the *Tibetan Book of the Dead*—and, opening it, reads with quiet dignity: "My consciousness, luminous and pure, inseparable part of the Great Radiating Body, knows neither birth nor death. It is the unrelenting light."

Placing the book on my bedside table, he dissolves in a shroud of radiance.

It's a heavenly day, the air crisp, the sun warm, the sky pale blue, despite the fourteen flaming bodies on the burning ghat. I buy six tiny leaf boats, each bearing a couple of spoonfuls of wax set with a wick, then hire a helmsman with a boat. As we push from shore, I see all of Varanasi at once, like slipping through a keyhole into a panoramic world.

It seems appropriate that in this place where they burn a lot of bodies, they also fly a lot of kites—small squares in primary colours that swoop and glide with the agility of birds. Children fly them from the ghats, young men from the rooftops. For days I've tripped over a mesh of invisible lines, raising cries of distress from small boys. "Oh, madame, please!" Offering an apology, I would disengage one foot or another while the kite flyer refocused on his sky-entry, trolling the clouds as if for souls, eyes shining, body as taut as his string.

Now leaning back against the stern of my boat, I watch dozens of kites soar up through Varanasi's perpetual shroud of smoke like a flock of phoenixes, collectively sweeping and sailing with the verve and subtlety of Shiva, the cosmic dancer. *"He rises from his rapture, and dancing sends through inert matter pulsing waves of awakening sound, and lo! matter also dances, appearing as a glory round about him."*

A sudden shift of the wind, and one after another loses its updraft to begin its dizzy descent while its owner struggles to pull in the slack, discovering that he wasn't in control of his kite's destiny as he'd thought: it was flying on the unseen wings of the gods.

Somewhere near the middle of the river I ask my boatman to stop. I light my leaf candles, one by one, giving each a name, then launch my little flotilla. None lasts long, just time enough for me to say goodbye before it sputters and sinks.

In my pocket I have the stone I brought from Rishikesh. Warming it between my palms, I hurl it high to
release, in a glory of white wings, the bird trapped inside.

*I am following my porter from my guest house back through the
twisted lanes of Old City. Finding ourselves in threatened collision with a corpse on its way to the burning ghats, we squeeze
into a doorway to let it pass. Though the four bearers are almost
upon us, I hear no sound—not their footsteps, or my porter's
breathing, or my own. The sparrow overhead seems to have
stopped in mid-flight. The only thing moving is the funeral
procession, in slow motion, the knees of the four bearers rising
and falling as they negotiate the narrow lane. When the corpse
draws near, I catch my breath, sealing my nostrils against the
anticipated smell, sweet or sour, decaying flesh or sandalwood, it
makes no difference, both unwelcome, the scent of death. As I
stare eye level at the lump that is the corpse, its shiny saffron-
and-gold winding sheet stirs, then lifts. Moonji stares at me, his
hair white, his gaunt face mournful yet smiling. Mesmerized,
I watch as his features subtly melt and shift until I am looking
at an ancient version of myself.*

The funeral procession passes.

The sparrow lands.

My porter steps from the doorway.

I follow, leaving Varanasi behind.

fool's gold

"We keep what we have
by giving it away"

MY TRAIN TRIP to Delhi—
the final one—is slow, cold and murderous, through dense
fog with many unscheduled stops. From the windows on
either side I see swamps of dead trees, their lower limbs
mounted with birds of prey, carnivorous beaks silhouetted in the half light, forced by a low ceiling to draw closer
to their watery dinner plates.

Delhi is experiencing a cold snap: instead of a high of
sixteen Celsius and a low of nine, that low is as high as
it gets. I have only light clothes; my Canadian blood has
thinned, and my Paharganj hotel doesn't have central heat-
ing; however, my long, narrow room like a private train
car is newly furnished with a plush settee, colour TV, even
a tea wagon like one my mother used as a limbo for anything doomed never to be completed—unread magazine
articles, unmended socks, untried recipes for duck *à
l'orange*, jigsaws with missing pieces. Wrapped in blankets and noshing on veggie burgers courtesy of room service, I feel snug and content as I eavesdrop through my
blacked-out street-level window on conversations I can't
understand orchestrated with bells and whistles and horns,
conscious of the plane ticket sitting on my bed table and

feeling happy to be going home because I know I'll be coming back.

Now that the summer crowds have thinned, the Paharganj reminds me of the woods in late fall when the undergrowth has died, laying bare the contours of the land. I feel mellow as I poke from stall to stall buying souvenirs for friends, finishing my last roll of film and already feeling nostalgic. Everywhere I go beggars thrust amputated stumps into my face, display their boils and soulfully dramatize needs that don't require exaggeration. By the time I return to my hotel, I'm feeling tattered and depressed. During the past three months, I've searched in vain for some reasonable and consistent way of responding to them—giving a certain sum each day, giving my change till it runs out, giving selectively to the handicapped and infirm, giving out of gratitude when good luck comes my way, giving as a reward for a song or some other small offering, giving to rid myself of their nuisance or not giving at all. Delhi's beggars are not the able-bodied sadhus of Rishikesh trading on their orange robes or schoolkids cadging pens. They're more likely to be limbless torsos or mothers with undernourished babies. When I meditate on my feelings of panic, pity, helplessness, horror, compassion, guilt, fear, impatience and resentment, I see that my problem begins with my inability to separate the tug of one hand on my sleeve from the tug of ten thousand of them, or to distinguish the needs of the one person standing before me from the needs of all of India. Taking twenty 100 rupee notes, I wander the Paharganj, distributing them as discreetly as I can, looking past physical damage into the faces of the recipients: some smile or laugh or fold their hands in prayer; a couple hurry off in case there's been a mistake; one kisses the money; another couple seem indifferent. No one person's needs are bottomless and the only consistent response is my own—a burgeoning sense of gratitude for all that India has given to me.

I relax in the most peaceful place in the Paharganj, perhaps in all of Delhi—the Indian Christian Cemetery behind a busy market reached through a cream-coloured arch mounted with a cross. Most graves are aboveground—whitewashed concrete mounds or marble rectangles. Some are caged in wrought iron; many bear crosses and English inscriptions charmingly misspelled in perpetuity: "May the sun chine on him" "Eracted by . . ." "Loove Never Falls." After Varanasi with its mass-produced cremations, this grassy nook seems a quaint and stubbornly personal requiem, yet the message of life's impermanence is the same.

I sit down under a tree—my bodhi tree—to count my Indian blessings, beginning with the wise folk of Mount Abu; my Indian family at Pushkar, especially my hosts; my Indian and Canadian wedding hosts and their welcoming guests; Ishak in the Thar desert and the porter at Jodhpur; the Sikh family and Lakshmi on the train from Amritsar; the Sikh who helped the injured child in Delhi and Abdul the refugee from Srinagar; the Christian minister on the train down the west coast of Kerala and the lifeguards of Kovalam; the Little Sister of Jesus and Kamini on the bus to Periyar; the young woman who rowed my boat at Munnar; the diligent and inspired souls of Ganga Farm and the beggars who kept tugging at my sleeve until I paid attention.

I think of the wisdom offered to me: lessons about giving and receiving, listening and being, trusting and surrender; of the five-thousand-year-old spiritual tradition to which I've been granted unlimited access; to the moral codes, the insights and the confirmations of Mystery. I am certain that meditation, with its gift of equanimity, joy and wholeness, will remain a permanent part of my life. I know I've rid myself of the barbed-wire hair shirt that initiated my trip, even though I suspect I'll find another a few layers deeper. I've become acutely aware that thought crimes aren't victimless, and I've learned to accept the transcendental power of the law of karma—not just the part where I'm the first victim of my own negativity but the part where the universe repays in kind. I'm also willing to believe that kundalini, as described in ancient Indian texts, is a biological force opening consciousness to higher dimensions governed by principles that supersede those of the physical world, with or without the existence of a God.

When I board my plane, I'll be taking with me a hum of contentment much less affected by external events and a hunger to hear good music: after opening my inner ear in the Golden Temple, in the forests of Periyar and the mountains of Munnar, I've developed an ardent desire to fill my head with the sounds of flutes and violins and harpsichords and pianos. I've come to believe that music is our primary art, beyond the beauty and importance of words and images, bringing each moment into greater harmony with the next and turning linear events and individual transactions into collective waves that wash against the shore of consciousness, recede, build, overlap, wash, recede and build again.

Although it will take several months for me to catch up with the profundity of what happened at Kovalam, when I do, the part that will surprise me most is the strength of my denial: how loath I was to recognize something miraculous might have happened, how shaken I was by the prospects of perhaps having been its cause, and how unprepared I was to allow the transcendental into my life, even though I thought myself to be in search of it.

Where did the rope come from? If, indeed, I wasn't "supposed to" die, why didn't I just experience a super-charge of adrenaline, allowing me to swim to shore so as to preserve the laws of physics? I have no answer, except one that presupposes that the point of the experience was to teach me a lesson: if I had reached safety under what appeared to be my own efforts, I might have thought I was the person in charge, a superhero, reinforcing the ego I went to India to lose. Alternatively, if I did hallucinate the rope out of a desperate need to prop up my confidence while I swam to shore, what of the rope that struck me twice before I knew I needed rescue? I wasn't desperate then, and when I scoured the cove, which was in easy view, I found no source.

A friend not given to solutions that invoke the mysterious surprised me by suggesting that perhaps I'd been in trouble with the currents well before I realized it, and that I was offered two chances to save myself before I seized on the third. I can provide no better explanation. The truth is that I—the conscious I writing this book—don't know what happened at Kovalam. The stubbornly pragmatic part of me still prefers to believe that the rope was just an ordinary rope attached to an ordinary fishing net that I was extraordinarily lucky to have found when I stuck my hand down into the ocean. That seems miracle enough.

I remember a story from my Grade 2 reader about a boy who lived on the west side of a deep valley. Each evening he gazed with yearning toward the house on the opposite hill, its windows radiant with gold, vowing that one day he would visit this house whose owner was so wealthy that he could afford golden windows. When that day arrived, the lad set out at first light, emerging in darkness on the eastern cliff and arising next morning with the sun. What he discovered was an attractive house much like his own, with ordinary windows. In disappointment, he looked across the valley, over the difficult route he had travelled: the windows of his own house were shining like gold.

Metaphorically, I began with a house that seemed in reasonably good condition, then set about to expose its weaknesses for the purpose of renovation—the garbage in the basement, the dry rot in the cupboards, the secret passages, the clutter of outdated ideas in the attic. While the lure of golden windows may fuel our youthful journeys, the motivation and the energy for those marking life's second half are more likely to come from converting our own dark matter—the neglected gifts, forgotten dreams, blind spots, blocks and prejudices, which, like the dark matter in the universe, may contain a powerhouse of unrealized potential. This alchemy is the task of the bold and hardy innocent fool also lying dormant in each of us. And the reward? Another paradox: fool's gold.

As I arise from under my bhodi tree, a flock of jade green parakeets takes off from its branches. For a few seconds they hang like a stained-glass window against the blue sky before breaking into shards and flying up into the sun.

notes

Meditation

page

4. Details of city populations and distances here and in other chapters are primarily from *India*, 2d ed. (Hawthorn, Australia: Lonely Planet Publications, 1997).

9. Biographical reference to Maharishi Mahesh Yogi from *Quantum Healing* by Deepak Chopra (New York: Bantam Books, 1989).

15. Reference to Philemon from *Memories, Dreams, Reflections* by C. G. Jung (New York: Vintage Books, 1989).

16. The 108 names of Mother Ganges quoted from *Slowly Down the Ganges* by Eric Newby (London: Macmillan Publishers Ltd., 1983).

20. Some of the dialogue about Superstrings suggested by Chopra, *Quantum Healing*.

22. Reference to the yogi on Mount Arunachala, the nine-year-old devotee at Varanasi and the Naga Babas from *Travels Through Sacred India* by Roger Housden (London: HarperCollins Publishers, 1996).

22. Reference to the sadhu at Varanasi with fingernails grown through his palm from *Empire of the Soul* by Paul William Roberts (Toronto: Stoddart Publishing Co. Ltd., 1994).

Om Shanti

37. Biographic material on Baba Brahma from *Adi Dev* by Jagdish Chander (Brahma Kumaris World Spiritual University, 1981).
65. Seventeenth-century philosopher Blaise Pascal's wager is from his *Pensées*.

Brahma's Moon

81. References to Sufism and the Chishti Orders based on material from *Travels Through Sacred India* by Housden.

Chakras

91. Historical details re Maharaja Roa Jodha from *Rajasthan, Land of Kings*, photographed by Roloff Beny, text by Sylvia A. Matheson (Toronto: McClelland & Stewart Ltd., 1984).
92. Information on sati, Roop Kanwar and dowry deaths primarily from *May You Be the Mother of a Hundred Sons* by Elisabeth Bumiller (New York: Ballantine Books, 1991).
96. Reference to Ramakrishna from *Travels Through Sacred India* by Housden.
96. Pineal gland research based on information in John Bleibreu, *The Parable of the Beast* (New York: Collier Books, 1969), and *Where Science and Magic Meet* by Serena Roney-Dougal (Dorset: Element Books, rev. 1993).
98. Gopi Krishna quotations from *Kundalini* (London: Vincent Stuart & John M. Watkins, Ltd., 1970).
101. Historical research on Jaisalmer sati from *Rajasthan, Land of Kings*.

Karma

131. Reference to the chakras as a musical scale from *Sound Health* by Steven Halpern (San Francisco: Harper & Row, 1985).
139. William Cox research from *Through the Time Barrier* by Danah Zohar (London: Heinemann, 1982).

Miracles

159. "Miracles do not happen in contradiction to nature, but only in contradiction to what we know of nature."—St. Augustine.
162. Great Mother research from *The Chalice and the Blade* by Riane Eisler (New York: Harper & Row, 1987).
164. Population density research from *Snakes and Ladders* by Gita Mehta (London: Minerva Paperbacks, 1997).
169. Biographical research on Karunamayi from *Sri Karunamayi* by Murugan (India: SMVA TRUST, 1992).
176. For more on the theories of David Bohm, see his *Wholeness and the Implicate Order* (London: Ark Paperbacks, 1983).
177. Pygmies anecdote from *Where Science and Magic Meet* by Roney-Dougal.
177. Captain Cook anecdote from *The Eagle's Quest* by Fred Alan Wolf (New York: Touchstone, 1992).

The Sound of Silence

189. "Each atom is constantly singing a song." – Lama Anagarika Govinda.

199. Report of the Lucknow incidents from *The Indian Times*, 29 November 1998.

206. Research on sound from *The World Is Sound* by Joachim-Ernst Berendt (Rochester, Vermont: Destiny Books, 1991).

220. OM poem quoted from *Travels Through Sacred India* by Housden.

Drunk on God

223. "Children, knowledge without devotion is like eating stones." – Mata Amritanandamayi.

230. Biographical material on Amritanandamayi from *Mata Amritanandamayi* by Swami Amritaswarupananda (India: Mata Amritanandamayi Mission Trust, 1988).

242. Carl Jung's views on the connection between alcoholism and spirituality as stated in a 1961 letter to Bill Wilson, co-founder of Alcoholics Anonymous.

The Buddha

254. Biographical information on the Buddha primarily from *The Quest for Serenity* by George N. Marshall (Boston: Beacon Press, 1978).

259. Information on S. N. Goenka, Vipassana and Buddhist teachings from *The Art of Living by William Hart* (New York: Harper & Row, 1987).

Death and Reincarnation

289. "Being born twice is no more remarkable than being born once." – Voltaire.

300. Dr. Herelle's findings on Ganges water from *Mother Ganges* by Sri Swami Shivananda.
300. Reference to the annual cremation of thirty-five thousand corpses and to the pollution of the Ganges from *A Walk Along the Ganges* by Dennison Berwick (London: Hutchinson, 1986).
312. Description of Shiva dancing from *The Dance of Shiva* by A. K. Coomaraswami (New York: Noonday Press, 1969).

glossary

amma, ammachi   mother, dearest mother
Amritanandamayi   Mother of Immortal Bliss
anapana   breathing technique used in meditation
*ashram*s   spiritual retreat formed around a *guru*
avatar   god incarnation in human form
baba   father, term of respect
Baba Brahma   founder of Brahma Kumaris, born 1876
Bhagavad Gita   Song of the Lord, sacred epic poem about
    Krishna setting forth principles of Hinduism
bhajan   devotional singing
bhakti   path of devotion
bindi   decorative forehead mark worn by Hindu women
bodhi tree   tree of Enlightenment associated with Buddha
Brahma   Absolute Truth behind all manifestations, Creator of
    the Universe
Brahma Kumaris, BKs   daughters of Brahma, a sect
brahmin   member of highest priestly caste
Buddha   the Awakened One, Siddhartha Gautama, founder of
    Buddhism, born 563 B.C.
caste   hereditary status tied to occupation

chai   spicy Indian tea

chakra   energy wheel or centre in human body

chapati   unleavened Indian bread

dadis   senior sisters

darshan   sighting of holy person or diety

Devi, also Mahadevi   Great Goddess or Earth Mother

dharma   Divine law or way of righteousness

dhoti   male sarong drawn up through legs

dhurrie   Indian rug

Durga   dark form of Devi, temptress and slayer of demons

Ganesh   elephant-headed god of new beginnings, son of Shiva
   and Parvati

Ganga Mata   Mother Ganges, a personification

ghat   steps or landing on a river, also a hilly range

ghee   clarified butter

Grantha Sahib   sacred Sikh scriptures

guru   one who leads from darkness (*gu*) to light (*ru*)

Guru Nanak   founder of Sikhism five hundred years ago

harijans   Children of God, name given Untouchables by
   Gandhi

Hanuman   monkey-headed loyal servant of Rama

haveli   stately home, especially in Rajasthan

Indra   Vedic god of rain, storms and war

ji   honorific used as a suffix

jnana   path of wisdom

K's, five   symbolic items of Sikh dress: kancha, kangha, kara,
   kesh and kirpan

Kali   Black Goddess, fiercest form of Durga

Kaliyuga   the age of Kali

karma   action, law of cause and effect

Karunamayi   Compassionate One

Khalsa   Sikh brotherhood or Pure Order

kohl   black eye cosmetic used by Indian women

Krishna, Lord   incarnation of Vishnu, central to Bhagavad Gita

kundalini   life energy stored at base of spine

lingam   phallus, symbolic of Shiva

lungi   Indian male garment

mantra   sacred sound

Mahadevi, also Devi   Great Goddess or Earth Mother

maharaja   king

maharishi   great sage

Mara   Buddhist god of evil

math   monastery

maya   illusionary material world

Moghul, also Mughal   Muslim dynasty of Indian emperors

mullah   Muslim scholar or priest

Murli   the Flute, a BK ritual

nada Brahma   "the Universe is sound"

nirvana   bliss culminating cycle of reincarnation, Buddhist

Om   universal sound from which all others are created

Om shanti   "I am a peaceful soul"

paan   mild stimulant of spices and betel nut

pandit   scriptural scholar

Parvati   form of Devi, consort of Shiva

puja   rite of worship

qawwali   ecstatic sufi music

raja yoga   a form of meditation

Rajasthan   Land of Kings

Rajput   Hindu warrior caste

Rama, Lord   incarnation of Vishnu, hero of epic Ramayana

rishi   wise man

sadhu   wandering ascetic

salwar kameez   trousers and tunic worn by Indian women

samadhi   blissful union with the Divine, Hindu

sanskara   imprint of an experience, conditioning

Sanatana Dharma   Eternal Way, Hinduism

sanskrit   ancient language of India

Saraswati   consort and daughter of Brahma

sari   dress created by draping single piece of cloth

sati   a widow's immolation on her husband's pyre

Sati   wife of Shiva

sati mata   wife who martyrs herself on husband's pyre

satsang   gathering where a guru teaches

Shiva, Lord   Hindu god of destruction and rebirth

Sikh   a disciple of Sikhism

Sikhism   a mystical religion combining elements of Hinduism and Islam

Sita   consort of Rama

sri   honorific used as prefix

stupa   Buddhist dome

sufi   Muslim mystic

Sufism   mystical branch of Islam

swami   Hindu monk, "he who knows himself"

tirtha   crossing place of heaven and earth, life and death

Untouchable   without caste, outcast

Upanishads   part of Vedas devoted to metaphysical inquiry

Vedas   four earliest Indo-European texts c. 1200–1000 B.C.

vipassana   Buddhist insight meditation

Vishnu, Lord   Preserver of the Universe

yoga   to yoke or unite with the Divine, also physical exercises used to achieve union

yogi   one who practises yoga

bibliography

Amritaswarupananda, Swami. *Mata Amritanandamayi*. Mata Amritanandamayi Mission Trust, India, 1988.

Beny, Roloff, and Sylvia A. Matheson. *Rajasthan, Land of Kings*. Toronto: McClelland & Stewart Ltd., 1984.

Berendt, Joachim-Ernst. *The World Is Sound*. Rochester, Vermont: Destiny Books, 1991.

Berwick, Dennison. *A Walk Along the Ganges*. London: Hutchinson, 1986.

Bumiller, Elisabeth. *May You Be the Mother of a Hundred Sons*. New York: Ballantine Books, 1991.

Chander, Jagdish. *Adi Dev*. Brahma Kumaris World Spiritual University, 1981.

Chopra, Deepak, *Quantum Healing: Exploring the Frontiers of Mind/Body Medicine*. New York: Bantam Books, 1989.

Cushman, Anne, and Jerry Jones. *From Here to Nirvana*. New York: Penguin Putnam Inc., 1998.

Hart, William. *The Art of Living*. New York: Harper & Row, 1987.

Housden, Roger. *Travels Through Sacred India*. London: Harper-Collins Publishers, 1996.

Krishna, Gopi. *Kundalini*. London: Vincent Stuart & John M. Watkins, 1970.

——. *The Biological Basis of Religion and Genius*. Toronto: Fitzhenry & Whiteside Ltd., 1972.

LeShan, Lawrence. *How to Meditate*. New York: Bantam Books, 1975.

Lonely Planet Publications. *India*. Hawthorn, Australia, 1997.

Marshall, George N. *The Quest for Serenity*. Boston: Beacon Press, 1978.

Mehta, Gita. *Snakes and Ladders*. London: Minerva Paperbacks, 1997.

Murugan. *Sri Karunamayi*. India: SMVA TRUST, 1992.

Newby, Eric. *Slowly Down the Ganges*. London: Macmillan Publishers Ltd., 1983.

Paz, Octavio. *In Light of India*. New York: Harcourt Brace & Co., 1997.

Roberts, Paul William. *Empire of the Soul*. Toronto: Stoddart Publishing Co. Ltd., 1994.

Roney-Dougal, Serena. *Where Science and Magic Meet*. Dorset, England: Element Books Ltd., 1993.

Ward, Tim, *Arousing the Goddess*. Toronto: Somerville House, 1996.